Values, Curriculum, and the Elementary School

Values, Curriculum, and the Elementary School

Alexander Frazier

Professor of Early and Middle Childhood Education Emeritus
The Ohio State University

Houghton Mifflin Company   Boston

Dallas • Geneva, Illinois • Hopewell, New Jersey
Palo Alto • London

Library of Congress Catalog Card Number: 79-87862

ISBN: 0-395-26739-0

Printed in the U.S.A.

Contents

v

The Cultural Heritage

List of Exhibits

Foreword

Learning to value has much to do with learning how to live. Setting priorities, choosing between or among competing goods, weighing one kind of behavior against another — these are things each person does at least a dozen times a day. Valuing and learning and living are all part of the same process, for people build their lives on what they learn to value.

It is this book's contention that helping children learn to value is what school is — or ought to be — all about. School offers children a chance to become aware of new sources of satisfaction and to experience, and thus learn to value, the many ways of being and behaving that are vital to both individual fulfillment and social effectiveness.

Today there are many parents and other adults who are eager to help teachers make sure that children learn to value. As a result, in many schools and school systems, familiar content is being recast and unfamiliar content added to create a new, value-oriented curriculum for children.

This book is a report on this new curriculum. Part I begins with an analysis of the current state of knowledge about valuing (Chapter 1). A key chapter (Chapter 2) then describes the values (or value axes, as we term them) that we believe to be most important in the education of children. In Part II a pair of chapters is devoted to each of three major areas in the education of children: the world of everyday living (or basic skills), the cultural heritage, and the moral-ethical-political realm. Chapter by chapter, we report on what is going on and try to predict future developments. Finally, Part III deals with some of the problems involved in bringing a value-centered curriculum for children into existence.

As is evident throughout the book, we ourselves are strongly committed to furthering the role of schools in the teaching of values. Specifically:

We believe that schools must work for a liberating mastery of basic skills by every child — and also for the skills of critical thinking that can free persons, young and old, from undue dependence on things as they are or have been.

We believe that schools must work for the skills and understandings that provide access to an arts heritage that should be the birthright of every child — and for the competencies needed to behave creatively so that our heritage will renew itself to the advantage of us all.

We believe that schools must work as hard as they can to provide every American child with an understanding of what a government like ours means, how it came to be, and why it deserves our allegiance — and to develop a comprehension of the ways our government and society can be changed that go beyond the past to a humanistic vision of a better way of life for all of us.

Finally, we believe that the new learning-to-value curriculum for children can help in the realization of these goals and will enable more of our children to grow up equipped to enjoy the riches of our present society and to create in their turn a society that may prove even more rewarding.

We would like to thank all those who have been so helpful in preparing this volume, especially Professor Dorothy Huenecke of Georgia State University and Professor David Myrow of SUNY at Buffalo for their thoughtful comments on the work in progress.

A. F.

*Values, Curriculum, and
the Elementary School*

Part I

Learning to Value

Chapter 1

How Values Develop

Doing more to help children learn to value is much on the minds of educators and parents today. They seem to be newly agreed that the young deserve all the help they can get in learning to make wise choices between or among competing ways of being and behaving. In the past, parents and teachers certainly did not ignore value development. But a new sense of urgency about maximizing the value dimensions of children's experience has come into existence.

Why this greater concern? Partly it is a result of knowing more about how values develop and how children can be aided in this process. And partly it is a result of changes in society, which have made learning to value increasingly complex, arduous — and necessary.

VALUE DEVELOPMENT IN A CHANGING SOCIETY

Children pick up many of their ideas of what is good, better, and best from what they see and hear about them. Through television and the other mass media, children today are being exposed more frequently and at an earlier age than ever before to a rapidly changing and troubled world, and to a repertoire of ways of being and behaving of almost unbelievable scope. The electronic media have made participants of us all. Never before in human history have the young — and the old, too — been given so much to think about and to sort out.

A Troubled World

Every evening television projects into viewers' households events that even adults have difficulty making sense of. How, then, are they perceived by children? Films of rioters and bloody confrontations offer graphic evidence of how conflicts based on religious, racial, or political differences are resolved throughout the world. Torture, kidnapping, bribery, and blackmail have become familiar practices in world politics, and incidents involving hijacking, terrorism, and even mass suicide are no longer unknown.

On the national scene in recent years have come revelations of top-level political chicanery, news of political assassinations, and disclosures about a nearly catastrophic accident at a nuclear power plant. Locally, crime statistics continue to mount, and detailed accounts of murder, rape, arson, and child abuse are common in the news.

Discussion of troubling subject matter is not confined to the evening news hour, however. Weekly entertainment series and movies shown on television often dramatize these subjects and in addition deal with a variety of other sensitive topics. Violence, of course, has long been a staple of television fare.

Changes in Standards

Changing standards of behavior in a good many areas of daily living are another potential source of confusion to children. Divorce rates are on the rise, and as a result many children are being reared in other than traditional family arrangements. The growing number of single-parent families, joint custody arrangements, and families containing stepchildren and half brothers and sisters has left some children bewildered and perplexed by the varieties of family life. "I have two mothers," boasts a child whose father has just remarried. "Why don't you have any children of your own?" another child asks a parent with visiting privileges.

Children may also be affected by a greater frankness in society. Pictures and books that seem to degrade or at least exploit human sexuality can be found in many places, including some homes with children in them. The young are sometimes privy to discussions of topics — such as homosexuality, abortion, and cancer — that once were seldom dealt with openly. We all seem to know more about more things, children as well as adults.

Pluralism as a Way of Life

Pride of membership in a racial, ethnic, religious, regional, or some other well-defined subculture can contribute to the self-esteem of a person and to the richness of the common culture.

But children may need help in reconciling certain kinds of cultural differences. ("They don't look like us." "Josh goes to church on Saturday." "Why does Maria have so many brothers and sisters?") They also may need help in bringing the values of their own subculture into consonance with those of the larger mix. ("Mrs. Tullberg expects us to speak good English in school, but my folks would only laugh at me if I spoke that way at home.")

Toward Full Human Development

It may be difficult for children to understand the importance of values and valuing in their own lives. Many values are accepted or grown into without much awareness of what they may signify when translated into behavior. Thus, some working-class children may develop negative attitudes toward school because in their neighborhoods they gain more praise for evidence of physical and social maturity than for signs of intellectual precocity. Similarly, some middle-class children who enjoy working with their hands may decide to become lawyers or accountants because in their neighborhoods physical labor is looked down upon. What is at stake, then, in making children more conscious of valuing is nothing less than their ability to achieve full human development.

The Role of Teachers

We as teachers have good reason to be concerned about the role of values in the lives of children — and about the role of teachers as well. In our classrooms we are called upon to meet head-on the issues raised by shifting standards, cultural pluralism, and a confusing and troubled world. And we are sensitive in a way we may never have been before to the impact of values on human fulfillment. Indeed, many of us see valuing as integral to almost every act of learning both in school as well as out. Ours is an age of dramatic challenge and change, and children, along with their teachers, are right in the middle of it.

Children need our help to make sense of their world, to find their way through the new profusion of choices toward greater personal fulfillment and the creation of a more rewarding common culture. But to help children develop values requires knowledge of how values develop. In the rest of this chapter three basic approaches to value development are examined: the value development theories of Piaget and Kohlberg, the values clarification methods of Raths and Simon, and the efforts of the anti-environmentalists who seek to bring about specific value changes in the current moral environment.

STAGES OF VALUE DEVELOPMENT

How do values develop? Attempts to answer this question have taken a number of directions. But predictably one of the first and most profitably pursued has been finding out about how values come into being as children grow up. For, in whatever subject we wish to instruct children, readiness for learning is where we always hope to start.

Many studies of value development as an aspect of maturation have been conducted. But there are two contemporary investigators of moral judgment whose work forms a whole of great significance to everyone concerned with helping children toward informed choice making in valuing. Our reference, of course, is to the pioneering work of Jean Piaget and the subsequent studies of Lawrence Kohlberg.

Piaget: From Constraint to Cooperation

Children are born into a world of rules and regulations. Adults interpret and enforce these laws, with varying success. To the young child, laws seem to come from outside the individual. They have an existence of their own that has to be respected, even if the reason for doing so is a bit mystifying.

By the age of six or seven, although they often cannot "remember" to behave properly, children are true believers in retribution for wrongdoing. A broken cup, an inkstain, and a lie are all acts deserving of punishment. But six- and seven-year-olds have their own ways of reasoning. Whether cups are broken or ink spilled through clumsiness or as a result of mischief is not at issue. Punishment fits the size of the crime. The more cups that are broken or the more outlandish the lie, the greater the punishment should be.

What lying is and why it is bad is particularly confusing to children of this age. Untruths and bad words are both "lies" — that is, forbidden language. "We don't say things like that," children are told in both cases. As for making up stories, children may believe that if what they invent could have happened, then talking about it as if it did happen is not too bad. In fact, at this age *could have* and *did* are hard to tell apart.

As they grow older, of course, children begin to make more sense out of the constraints under which they live. By the age of nine or thereabouts, rules begin to be perceived by the child as having their uses. People tell the truth so they can depend on one another and do things together that they want to do. People learn to follow the rules of a game so that winning or losing will be due to something more than chance. (See Exhibit 1–1 for levels through which children move in learning to play games by the rules.) In time, when they reach eleven or twelve, children see that people can change rules if they agree to do so. Through cooperation with others, a rule becomes a "free product of mutual agreement and an autonomous conscience." In this final stage of moral development, "obedience withdraws in favor of the idea of justice and of mutual service, now the source of

Exhibit 1-1

Learning Rules of the Game: Stages of Development (After Piaget)

Stage	Characteristics
1. Motor (or manipulative) behavior (age 5 or under)	Uses marbles, jacks, or other game pieces as playthings; individual random manipulation, without much if any concern for rules
2. Egocentric behavior (ages 6–8)	Imitates older players; sees rules as coming from outside; each player has own version of rules to make winning more likely
3. Cooperative behavior (ages 9–12)	Understands and follows rules; realizes that rules can be changed by mutual agreement; accepts that there can be only one winner; all players agree on same rules

Source: Jean Piaget, *The Moral Judgment of the Child,* trans. Marjorie Gabain (London: Routledge and Kegan Paul, 1932; New York: Collier Books, 1962); copyright © 1962 by Macmillan Publishing Company, cited by permission of the publisher.

all the obligations which till then had been imposed as incomprehensible commands."[1]

This in short is the message to be derived from Piaget's inquiries. Questioned in detail about their responses to numerous little incidents dealing with mishaps and misdeeds, his Swiss subjects, aged six to thirteen, showed an uneven but eventual evolution from a morality of constraint to one of cooperation. An example of this gradual evolution is provided by the increasing percentage of children in one study who saw paying for a broken toy to be a more just punishment than having one's own toys taken away. Of the six- to seven-year-olds, 28 percent chose restitution as against deprivation; of the eight- to ten-year-olds, 49 percent; and of the eleven- to twelve-year-olds, 82 percent. These figures serve, too, to make clear that levels overlap within age groups. Indeed, the moralities of constraint and cooperation are mingled in each of us. "There is an adult in every child and a child in every adult."[2]

According to Piaget, the drive for self-direction is inherent in children. But situations that call for cooperation can help the drive emerge. Toward this end, games and creative play experiences are engaged in by children on their own. With many opportunities to work and play together in school and out, children can be expected to move from a morality of constraint to one based on cooperation and the twin values of justice (or fair play) and equality under the law — the great moral guidelines that must be adhered to if mutuality, or shared commitment, is to have meaning. Movement in this direction can be generally taken for granted, Piaget contends, especially with the emphasis in today's schools on small group activity as a way of learning.

But teachers need not stand by as merely neutral observers of the moral process. Based on an understanding of the stages through which children progress, teachers can actively encourage the process of moral development. The support needed is similar to that which teachers must provide for intellectual development. Both kinds of development call for an environment that invites active exploration by and interaction among children. Validation of what is right is very much the same process as validation of what is real. Both require that

[1] Jean Piaget, *The Moral Judgment of the Child*, trans. Marjorie Gabain (London: Routledge and Kegan Paul, 1932; New York: Collier Books, 1962), pp. 28, 404; copyright © 1962 by Macmillan Publishing Company, quoted by permission of the publisher.

[2] *Ibid.*, pp. 209, 85.

a consensus, to be meaningful to a child, come from consciousness of options and freedom of choice.

Kohlberg: More than Just Growing Up

The work of Lawrence Kohlberg on moral reasoning begins with and supports the findings of Piaget but goes beyond them.[3] In Kohlberg's view, very young children are relatively lawless and live apart from any system of social constraints (this is analogous to Piaget's motor behavior phase in learning the rules of the game). Once they become aware of do's and don'ts, children enter the social arena at Stage One, in which prevails obedience through punishment enforced by adult power (Piaget's level of constraint morality). Stage Two is arrived at after more experience in living among and learning to get along with age mates. Its key ideas are fairness and give-and-take (Piaget's level of cooperation).

The remaining four stages identified by Kohlberg go beyond childhood and thus beyond the studies conducted by Piaget. Stage Three is an extension and enlargement of the idea of cooperation as a necessary way of life, with well-established rules of behavior. At Stage Four, persons are able to deal with the idea of maintaining the social order through responsible moral behavior. These two stages are considered part of the *conventional* level of value development because they involve learning to appreciate and live with things as they are and within the rules of the game as they are commonly known.

Stage Five is a big step up. At this point, persons have learned to handle moral principles that transcend present practice. The concepts of human rights, social welfare, and redress through the legislative and judicial processes are all understood and honored. Stage Six is reserved for those few persons (none under age thirty) able to rise above purely national interests to a concern for universal principles, especially "the principled sense of justice."[4] Stages Five and Six are

---

[3] Lawrence Kohlberg and Elliot Turiel, eds., *Recent Research in Moral Development* (New York: Holt, Rinehart, and Winston, 1971); and Lawrence Kohlberg, *Collected Papers on Moral Development and Moral Education*, 2 vols., rev. ed. (Cambridge, Mass.: Moral Education Research Foundation, Harvard University, 1976).

[4] Lawrence Kohlberg, "The Moral Atmosphere of the School," in *The Unstudied Curriculum: Its Impact on Children*, ed. Norman V. Overly (Washington, D.C.: Association for Supervision and Curriculum Development, 1970), p. 121.

sometimes labeled as belonging to the *principled* level. They are the stages of full moral maturity.

Although Stages Three to Six of the Kohlberg model are open to all, progress into and through them is not inevitable. Most persons will move into Stage Three of the conventional level and many into Stage Four. But in present-day society not more than one in ten persons will move into full maturity and the level of principled moral reasoning, and even they generally will not go beyond Stage Five. As things now stand, Stage Six seems beyond the reach of most of us.

Kohlberg's stages of moral reasoning are the product of many years of research. His main instrument for collecting data has been the dilemma story, an account of a moral predicament to which the subject is asked to respond. For example:

One of a pair of shoplifters is detained while her partner escapes. Should the one apprehended make things easier for herself by telling on her friend?

A poor man is desperate because his family needs food and medicine. He steals what he needs. Can his behavior be justified in any way?

Thoreau went to jail rather than pay a tax to support a war of which he disapproved. What do you think of his actions?

Originally, Kohlberg defined his stages from the responses to situations like these of fifty subjects of various ages, whose development he followed over a number of years. Since then, his findings have been verified by numerous other investigations, including studies conducted in nine different countries.

Research efforts have explored many specific dimensions of the Kohlberg model. Relationships between Kohlberg's early stages and the developmental stages defined by Piaget have been established. More men than women have been found at Kohlberg's later stages, which some might see as proof of the sexist nature of education in our society (and others might offer as evidence of the moral "superiority" of men). A greater number of mature moral thinkers have been identified in the United States, Great Britain, Israel, and Canada than in less well developed societies. It has also been discovered that a good many secondary school teachers have learned how to facilitate movement of their students toward the upper levels of moral reasoning.[5]

---

[5] See Ronald S. Brandt, "On Moral/Civic Education: An Interview with Edwin Fenton," *Educational Leadership*, 34 (April 1977), 487–494.

Kohlberg, like Piaget, has found that children move from one level to another in both moral judgment and moral reasoning as their experience broadens, but that beyond childhood or the early stages of moral reasoning, much help has to be given to keep the young moving toward full moral maturity.

A central concern of much of Kohlberg's research is the question: "What spurs progress from one stage to another and why do some individuals reach the principled stages while others do not?"[6] No doubt much remains to be discovered, but the following are three of the factors that Kohlberg has identified as critical to the process of learning to value (and to programs seeking to help children in this process):

Social interaction is the means by which moral development is furthered. Role taking, discussion, decision making, and direct social action all have a place in any balanced program.

The focus of moral development needs to be on moral conflict, both through posed situations and through the handling of real problems faced in "the social and moral functioning of the school" or in society itself.

The goal of moral development is the definition and use of the larger moral principles in the resolution of interpersonal issues. Only then will students become free to function on their own at a higher level.

In summary, both Piaget and Kohlberg urge that the process of value development be helped to happen. Waiting upon the child to grow up is not enough to ensure the entrance into consciousness of the "hidden curriculum"[7] that predisposes the young toward acceptance of things as they are. Freedom of choice depends upon knowledge of a variety of options. And that is surely where teachers come in.

[6] Lawrence Kohlberg and Richard H. Hersh, "Moral Development: A Review of the Theory," *Theory into Practice*, 16 (April 1977), 57 ff.; copyright © 1977; ideas summarized by permission of authors and editor. For other articles by Kohlberg that express these central ideas, see "The Child as a Moral Philosopher," *Psychology Today*, 1 (September 1968), 25–30; "Moral Development and the New Social Studies," *Social Education*, 37 (May 1973), 369–375; "The Claim to Moral Adequacy," *Journal of Philosophy*, 70 (October 1973), 630–646; "The Cognitive-Developmental Approach to Moral Education," *Phi Delta Kappan*, 56 (June 1975), 670–677; and "Moral Education for a Society in Moral Transition," *Educational Leadership*, 33 (October 1975), 46–54.

[7] Kohlberg in Overly, *The Unstudied Curriculum*, pp. 104–107.

TEACHERS AND THE PROCESS OF
VALUES CLARIFICATION

Unclear or confused though they may be, values of one kind or another operate in everyone's life. They serve as guidelines to our behavior. What we do with our time, our energy, our very existence is shaped by our ideas of what is most likely to be rewarding. How tempting it is then to offer our own set of values or guidelines to the young.

Yet we know that would not be truly helpful. Values are grown into as children experience more and more of life. Thus, the task of educators is to bring experience in learning to value under the auspices of the school and to add to it those elements that will make it more broadly based and more thoughtful. Children need to be given opportunities to choose among promising options and then to test out their choices. Providing children with experience in the process of learning to value is the essence of any meaningful approach to value development.

The Values Clarification Approach

Values develop, then, as children have opportunities to examine, choose, and test out alternatives. But what should be the role of the teacher while the process is being pursued? A provocative and also very practical answer has been provided by Louis E. Raths and associates.[8] Clarification is the goal, whether the teacher's contacts with students are casual or formal in nature, aimed at an individual or focused on the group. And in forwarding clarification, perhaps the two central functions of the teacher are listening and questioning.

If values are to be really tested and strengthened, key questions about choosing, "prizing," and acting must be asked and answered. (See Exhibit 1–2.) The teacher's task is to keep such questions before the young long enough for something to come of it all. Obviously, for example, alternatives have to be brought into consciousness before choice makes any sense. Yet it is at this stage that the young and old alike tend to short-circuit the valuing process. If this is allowed to

[8] Louis E. Raths, Merrill Harmin, and Sidney B. Simon, *Values and Teaching*, 2nd ed. (Columbus, Ohio: Charles E. Merrill Publishing Company, 1978).

Exhibit 1-2

Helping Children Clarify Values: Some Key Questions (Adapted from Raths)

Steps in process of valuing	Key questions to ask
Choosing	Did you consider any alternatives?
	Have you thought about possible consequences?
	Was this something you yourself chose to do?
Prizing	Is this something you really feel good about?
	Who have you told about this?
Acting	What have you done about this so far?
	What will come next?

Source: Louis E. Raths, Merrill Harmin, and Sidney B. Simon, *Values and Teaching*, 2nd ed. (Columbus, Ohio: Charles E. Merrill Publishing Company, 1978); based on analysis found on p. 28.

happen, the rest of the process — professing and performing — will not amount to much. Children will simply come out of the experience very much as they went in.

The most significant aspect of the values clarification approach is that it recognizes the process of valuing as open and continuous as well as active. Traditional approaches to value development — setting an example, persuading and convincing, trying to inspire acceptance of a given value, making much of trying to live by set rules and regulations, appealing to conscience, and the like — assume the task to be that of selling the young on what the adult mentor sees as the proper outlook or attitude. Not so the method presented by Raths and his colleagues: the young are to learn to value by becoming aware of a number of possibilities, choosing from among these the one that seems most promising, and then acting to test out the consequences as well as they can. Valuing so conceived truly does become a process of active learning very much in line with the positions taken by Piaget and Kohlberg.

Values Clarification in the Classroom

Once it is agreed that values develop through a process of choosing, prizing, and acting, then the challenge is to find ever more ways to bring the process into play in the school. Some teachers set aside a daily or weekly period for values clarification activities. Others try to build attention to valuing into their teaching of regular subject matter. In either or any case, help is needed in finding interesting and effective new procedures.

To provide students with many productive opportunities for developing values through clarification, teachers may want to prepare study materials that pose problems related to such value-laden topics as money, friendship, leisure, politics, religion, and morals. Role playing, making reports, being interviewed, and taking part in action projects are other useful activities for focusing attention on values.[9]

One widely welcomed source of values-related classroom projects is *Values Clarification: A Handbook of Practical Strategies for Teachers and Students* by Sidney B. Simon and others. The seventy-nine activities or "strategies" offered in the book are wide ranging and concrete, as can be seen from the following summarized examples:

[9] *Ibid*; see especially pp. 51–196.

Values voting: Teacher reads list of questions revealing a variety of opinions, usually on a particular topic, and asks students to choose among these. When tally has been completed, discussion follows.

"I wonder" statements: Students complete sentences beginning with phrases such as "I wonder about . . ." or "I wonder why. . . ." Then they are asked to share one of their statements with the rest of the class. The intention is to stimulate personal inquiry into areas where knowledge seems to be needed.

Removing barriers to action: Individual or small group chooses a desirable action and then lists barriers that may stand in the way of such action, with steps to be followed in disposing of them.

Values in action: Students list five changes they think should come about at school or elsewhere. Then they are invited to select one to act on. Things to do might include distributing leaflets, wearing a button, writing letters, and attending or organizing a meeting.

Diaries: Students keep a diary for a week on a common theme, such as how time was used, kinds of disagreements encountered, compliments given or received, male-female roles or behavior practiced, high or low points of each day. Diaries may be shared at end of week in small groups and a report made to larger group on new insights derived from the experience.[10]

These activities can be treated as a self-contained unit of study and need not be dependent on or related to the content of other subject fields. If organized into a sequence to highlight choice, affirmation, and action, the strategies could provide a content of their own, thus making it possible to add a separate values clarification strand to the regular curriculum. Indeed, the authors report that "in some schools, there are elective courses in values clarification, identified by many different titles."[11]

Other schools may prefer to integrate values clarification strategies with regular subject matter. Traditional courses can be reoriented to give students opportunities to deal with value-laden situations or topics.

The teaching of composition, for example, could be refocused along lines similar to those proposed by Sidney B. Simon and asso-

---

[10] From *Values Clarification: A Handbook of Practical Strategies for Teachers and Students* by Sidney B. Simon, Leland W. Howe, and Howard Kirschenbaum, copyright 1972 Hart Publishing Company, Inc., reprinted and summarized by permission.

[11] *Ibid.*, p. 21.

ciates. They note that "the act of composition engages the student in three growth-producing activities: reflection, clarification, and commitment," and then suggest specific composition activities to encourage growth in achieving personal identity. The sample activities may be grouped as follows:

Patterns and preferences: Reporting instances of one's own anger, to be shared and discussed with small group of other students; defining success in one's own terms, using worksheet with goals to be rated; listing and evaluating things one really loves to do.

Influences: Listing characteristics of persons found in magazine advertisements as a way of studying stereotyping; examining qualities admired in peers and adults; writing out what seem to be the "Ten Commandments" of various groups — peers, teachers, family — to compare with one's own list.

Competencies: Listing things one is good at and then classifying these in some way; listing and evaluating one's own achievements by age levels — early, middle, recent.

Body: Describing what one's own offspring will be like at age sixteen; listing changes one would like to make in one's own body.

General: Creating and describing one's own coat of arms; listing and ranking one's most satisfying recent experiences.[12]

Obviously these activities are intended for older students of middle school or secondary school age. It should also be noted that the written assignments in the proposed program are preceded by and based on oral composition or interaction. But despite the restrictions of this specific program, it should be plain enough that a composition program can be recast in terms of personal growth in the values realm.

Other segments of the regular curriculum might be similarly recast.[13] Many new approaches to teaching the process of valuing are currently being tested in classrooms across the country, perhaps more

[12] From *Composition for Personal Growth: Values Clarification Through Writing* by Sidney B. Simon, Robert C. Hawley, and David D. Britton, copyright 1973 Hart Publishing Company, Inc., pp. 75, 22–61. Summarized by permission. For books in a similar vein, see Sidney B. Simon and Jay Clark, *More Values Clarification* (San Diego: Pennant Press, 1975); and Sidney B. Simon and Sally W. Olds, *Helping Your Child Learn Right from Wrong: A Guide to Values Clarification* (New York: Simon and Schuster, 1976).

[13] See Merrill Harmin, Howard Kirschenbaum, and Sidney B. Simon, *Clarifying Values Through Subject Matter* (Minneapolis: Winston Press, 1973).

often at the secondary level. A textbook series for grades nine to twelve, for example, features as one component a dilemma discussion strand based on the Kohlberg model. In the area of social studies, a number of schools report that they are doing more with discussion of moral problems and issues.[14] In later chapters of this book, specific suggestions for reorienting course content are discussed at considerable length.

VALUES AND ENVIRONMENT

One other aspect of how values develop deserves to be highlighted — the impact of the total environment on value development. As indicated in the beginning of the chapter, it is their awareness of the undesirable educative impact of some aspects of the general culture that has led concerned educators and parents to declare themselves in favor of doing more about value development in the lives of children and youth.

The Environmental Influence

Sociologists and social psychologists have worked hard to analyze the interrelationship between child and community. Over forty years ago George H. Mead spelled out his findings in no uncertain terms. The individual self emerges from a process of learning through interaction with the immediate cultural context. The persons around the child (the "significant others" of early experience, mainly family members) indicate their approval or disapproval of successive acts of behavior in many ways and thus shape personal development. As time goes on, the child becomes a part of the group, acting in terms of values or guidelines to behavior that have been deeply internalized.[15] When we remark that a person possesses a certain value, we are recognizing, as Milton Rokeach notes, the presence of "an enduring prescriptive or proscriptive belief that a specific mode of be-

[14] See Edwin Fenton, ed., "Cognitive-Developmental Approach to Moral Education," *Social Education*, 40 (April 1976), 187–230.
[15] George H. Mead, *Mind, Self, and Society* (Chicago: University of Chicago Press, 1934).

havior or end-state of existence is preferred to an opposite mode of behavior or end-state"[16] — or perhaps preferred to any other that might be identifiable. The person has developed "a standard" that "guides and determines" behavior in many aspects of life.

In short, the child gains personal and social identity through accepting and acting within the values of those around him or her. With experience, the context becomes broader. The individual grows into what Kohlberg defines as the conventional level of shared values (Stages Three and Four) to be found in any given community or society. But sociologists like Mead might claim that the roots of identity remain deep in the home and neighborhood culture.

If the environment is so all-powerful, is it impervious to our will to change it? Must the values of a neighborhood or community culture invariably prevail or can we bring consciousness of alternatives, new competencies, and freedom of choice into the realm of value determination? These are the questions that puzzle us here — and also are of deep concern to society as a whole. In recent years there have been several forms of challenge to the idea that the cultural environment is all-powerful — that its impact is both inevitable and unalterable. By examining the efforts of these "anti-environmentalists" we may be able to find some answers to these troubling questions.

The Countercultural Challenge

In the sixties a good many young people, shocked by what they saw as the materialism and militarism of a mass society, withdrew from it in one way or another. Some took to the road, living as they could, to see what really went on in their country. Others took off for Greece or India or Japan to widen their search for meaningful values. A good number sought to set up new communities similar in intent to the New Harmonies and Brook Farms of a century and a half ago. Altogether, these dropouts from things as they were came to be perceived as members of a variety of countercultures. They seemed to be proposing new or competing values to those of the majority culture.

By the end of the decade, the points of greatest interest to the

[16] Milton Rokeach, *The Nature of Human Values* (New York: The Free Press, 1973), p. 25.

critical young had become well understood by much of the rest of society. Immediacy, austerity, authenticity, and the like — these were values or virtues that made increasing sense to old and young alike. (See Exhibit 1–3 for an effort to define the "new" values.) By the late seventies, the concerns of the earlier dissidents seemed to have been taken over by the larger community, or at least to have become identified with movements acceptable within a broadened appreciation of cultural pluralism — the conservationists, religionists of various faiths, potentialists (those devoted to meditation, interpersonal relations, creative behavior, and so on), consumer advocates, and political activists in many fields.

Consciousness Raising as Re-education

Another challenge to the notion of the unalterable impact of environment on value development comes from advocates of the kinds of activities now generally described as consciousness raising. They believe that most persons take too many ideas for granted. Thus, consciousness raising seeks to unsettle individuals by providing experiences that will cause them to re-examine their lives and thoughts from a fresh perspective.

Racism has been a major target of cultural re-education. Sit-ins, picketings, rallies, disruptions of meetings, and confrontations with government and institutional officials have helped to increase individual awareness of the extent and effects of racial discrimination. In the area of education, attention has been drawn to racial bias and imbalance in failure rates, special education and remedial class enrollments, and textbook treatment of minority contributions.[17]

Oppressed or impoverished ethnic groups, most notably Puerto Ricans and Mexican-Americans, have joined in the campaign for re-education. The problems of bilingualism and absence of respect in schools for other aspects of the Hispanic heritage have been highlighted.[18] Educators have also been challenged by both racial and ethnic groups for their well-meaning but obtuse handling of school

[17] For a classic report in this area, see Maurice R. Berube and Marilyn Gittell, eds., *Confrontation at Ocean Hill–Brownsville: The New York School Strikes of 1968* (New York: Frederick A. Praeger, 1969).

[18] See James A. Banks, ed., *Teaching Ethnic Studies: Concepts and Strategies* (Washington, D.C.: National Council for the Social Studies, 1973).

Exhibit 1-3

Countercultural Values: Points of Critical Concern

Point of concern	For	Against
1. *Immediacy* Concern for the quality of immediate experience; honoring now, the present; joy	Primacy of aesthetic experience Maximizing of intimate personal relations Physical functioning: sports, dance, out-of-doors Action now, not later Enjoyment of what is available	Preparation: for future, for life, etc. Work as an end in itself Mass media entertainment Realization of ideal some time hence Perfectionism, utopianism
2. *Austerity* Concern for spending time and money on first things; investing in what really matters; essentiality	Public monies devoted to social ends Better distribution of income Frugal living; earning money to live rather than as an end in itself More money spent on books, art, music Education as self-development	Consumer exploitation in a commercialized society Overconsumption Exploitation of sex Pollution of environment for gain Education geared chiefly toward getting a job

Exhibit 1-3 (cont.)

Countercultural Values: Points of Critical Concern (cont.)

Point of concern	For	Against
3. *Authenticity* Concern for truth, for revelation of facts and feelings; telling it like it is; honesty	Straight reporting of facts; absence of glamour Purposeful clarification of conflicts in feelings and values Frankness in language and expression of thought Congruence between inner and outer worlds Enlargement of processes for finding truth	Image building; public relations; managed news Repression of emotional reactions Channels of communication Good manners Truth as factual, final
4. *Openness* Concern for new possibilities in every area of human existence; valuing the new, the unfamiliar, the untried; risk taking	New family patterns, church practices, art forms Community-centered decision making Contributions from non-Western cultures Respect for and protection of the different or divergent Inventiveness, innovation	The so-called establishment in all forms: political economic educational religious musical dramatic graphic arts

Point of concern	For	Against
5. *Autonomy* Concern for universal emancipation from institutional, social, or political pressures; deciding for oneself; self-hood	Alternatives Questioning of accepted values and practices Trust in one's own "innards" Associations outside institutions as now existing Open choice making	Oversocialization into prevailing roles and values Acceptance of authority as fixed; adjusting to authority Popular culture as commercialized: television, best sellers, etc. Status seeking Bureaucracy
6. *Responsibility* Concern for living by values that transcend national boundaries, reach out to world; acting in terms of what one knows to be right; community	Dissent and protest against: military service and support lack of responsiveness to poor practices that contravene human values in politics, legislation, courts, international relations Sense of absolute personal responsibility for one's own behavior, free from majority pressure	Militarization of society Delay in meeting needs of poor, racially victimized, etc. Instances of injustice Capital punishment Lack of personal involvement and commitment

Exhibit 1-3 (cont.)

Countercultural Values: Points of Critical Concern (cont.)

Point of concern	For	Against
7. *Reverence* Concern for meaning in human experience; searching for the significant; worship	Worship as an act of community Eclecticism; drawing on many sources of inspiration Love of life: acceptance and trust Release rather than restriction Celebration	Sectarianism Formalism in religious worship Self-denial; constriction of instincts and feelings Censoriousness Fear of death: revulsion and anxiety

Source: Adapted from Alexander Frazier, "The Quality of Life and Society in the United States," in *A Man for Tomorrow's World,* ed. Robert R. Leeper (Washington, D.C.: Association for Supervision and Curriculum Development, 1970), pp. 62–78. Copyright © 1970; reprinted by permission of the publisher.

programs for the culturally "deprived" and "disadvantaged" — or different.[19]

Most recently sexism has come under attack in much the same way. Women as well as men have much to learn about the dimensions of cultural miseducation in gender roles. And schools are being asked to do still more to redress the unequal treatment of boys and girls, both in teaching materials and in the instructional program itself.[20]

Personal Awareness Training

A third challenge to the unthinking acceptance of our culture's values arises from a movement originating in the field of psychotherapy. The goal of this movement is the re-education of persons believed to have been left emotionally underdeveloped by a depersonalized society. Its proponents contend that too many adults seem to have been taught to conceal their feelings, hide their true thoughts, and deny their natural desires for attention and affection. Only as they are given new experiences can such persons function fully in humanistic terms.[21]

The movement has been identified with some of the most insightful psychologists or psychotherapists of our times, among them Gordon Allport, Abraham Maslow, and Carl Rogers. The names and forms of this kind of corrective education are many — emotional education or re-education, affective education, encounter therapy, expressive or self-awareness or sensitivity training. One recent addition is assertiveness training, in which persons plagued by shyness or undue deference toward authority are helped to become more expansive.[22]

[19] See Carl A. Grant, ed., *Multicultural Education: Commitments, Issues, and Applications* (Washington, D.C.: Association for Supervision and Curriculum Development, 1977).

[20] See Esther Zaret, "Women/Schooling/Society," in *Schools in Search of Meaning*, ed. James B. Macdonald and Esther Zaret (Washington, D.C.: Association for Supervision and Curriculum Development, 1975).

[21] See Donald A. Read and Sidney B. Simon, eds., *Humanistic Education Sourcebook* (Englewood Cliffs, N.J.: Prentice-Hall, 1975).

[22] See, for example, Robert E. Alberti, ed., *Assertiveness: Innovations, Applications, Issues* (San Luis Obispo, Calif.: Impact Publishers, 1977).

However labeled, the movement as a whole has weighed heavily against social overadjustment. With a goal of psychological wholeness before the learner, self-actualization becomes a matter of personal investment in undertakings perceived as worthwhile by the individual. Not everyone may reach a "self-transcendent state of rational altruism,"[23] but all may work toward making better use of their own resources. Maslow's steps to self-fulfillment[24] are not greatly different in tone from Kohlberg's stages leading to moral maturity. Both are defined as equally remote from realization; perhaps both serve chiefly as contemporary restatements of the enduring theme of human perfectibility.

A SUMMARY AND A LOOK AHEAD

Concern for values is back in the school picture — and for good reason. Everyone is concerned about the images and impressions that crowd in upon today's children. What a burden it imposes, this taking in and sorting out of reports from a world at odds with itself, from a society confused by changing standards, from a community trying to come to terms with cultural pluralism. Adding to this concern is a rising awareness of the part values play in full human development.

Yet if the situation is grave, our opportunities are many. We must do more about values — and we can. Never before have we known as much about how values develop or about how people can actively help in the process.

Some Approaches to Value Development

This chapter has looked at three approaches to value development.[25] First, it has examined the findings of Jean Piaget and Lawrence Kohl-

---

[23] Robert E. Valett, *Affective-Humanistic Education: Goals, Programs, and Learning Activities* (Belmont, Calif.: Lear Siegler/Fearon, 1974), p. 148.

[24] Abraham Maslow, *Motivation and Personality* (New York: Harper and Brothers, 1954).

[25] For a composite list of stages of value development drawn from many sources, see Elizabeth M. Drews and Leslie Lipson, *Values and Humanity* (New York: St. Martin's Press, 1971).

berg about stages of moral judgment and reasoning. Both agree on the characteristics of the early stages, when children are perceived as moving from a kind of playful anarchy into conformity under constraint. The next stage of childhood is, as Piaget prefers to call it, the level of cooperation on the basis of give-and-take. Although he attaches no age limits to his levels, Kohlberg identifies stages beyond childhood through which the valuer may move. Both investigators agree that adults can help children along. Indeed, they contend that they have an obligation to do so.

Second, the chapter has looked at the work done with the valuing process itself. In the model of values clarification proposed by Louis E. Raths, valuing focuses on choice, affirmation (or "prizing"), and action. Within this framework, many kinds of teaching activities — or strategies, to use Sidney B. Simon's term — have been found useful. More recently, Kohlberg's studies have given rise to a process of valuing based on dilemma discussions. Both the Raths and Kohlberg approaches can be taught within the context of regular subject fields or they can be treated as a separate content strand.

Third, the chapter has reviewed some of the ways in which critics of the cultural environment have tried to offset its impact. The counterculture of the sixties gave rise to a new or newly defined set of moral guidelines, many of which have achieved wider acceptance in the seventies. Consciousness-raising activities have helped many persons become aware of the personal and social effects of growing up unthinkingly. Emotional re-education in its many versions, although an older aspect of offset education with origins in psychotherapy, has won fresh acceptance as a way of bringing persons more closely in touch with their own values.

Clearly, there is a lot going on in values education, both in and out of school. What has been gained more than anything else is a broadened sense of what values are and how they function in our lives. Thus, we have something more to build on today than we had in the past.

What Comes Next?

As persons concerned with learning, we always welcome information about how children develop in any area of education. What may we expect? What conditions support — or impede — development? At the same time, we have learned to be cautious about a too great reliance on a developmental approach to learning or an undue dependence on the readiness concept. We are aware that if we are too complacent or passive in our approach, we can sometimes take too much for granted, wait too long, and miss opportunities that might have forwarded desired learning.

In the area of values, this means that teachers may welcome the findings on moral development without relinquishing their sense of responsibility for making sure that what can happen does happen. While we are grateful to Piaget and Kohlberg for charting moral growth in the early years, we also agree with them on the need for nurture.

Similarly, teachers can pay tribute to the insightfulness of the work done in values clarification without assuming that the procedures so far worked out necessarily provide an adequate framework for a total program. The process of valuing is something to which we agree we must attend. But where to base the exercise of the process remains open to our best thinking.

When we look at those concerned with affecting values by one kind of awareness education or another, we have similar misgivings. Consciousness raising can be equated with the first step in valuing. But what then? If values education were to be confined only to those aspects of existence in which oversight or ignorance prevail, would that lead to a balanced program?

Educators have made much progress along the road to an understanding of valuing. But they have far yet to go. The next task is to provide a broader and more balanced base in the curriculum for the exercise of valuing.

In Chapter 2, we lay out the dimensions within which learning to value needs to be considered. In our view, learning and valuing are very much of a piece in most of the major curriculum areas. Our purpose throughout this book is to indicate how current changes in curriculum bear on the prospect of helping children choose more wisely and rewardingly among the many goods open to them in today's world.

ACTIVITIES

1. Select several of Piaget's test stories (to be found in *The Moral Judgment of the Child*) and try them out with children of different ages. What do you find?

2. Which events or issues do you think are the hardest, in terms of values, for children to make sense of today? After viewing television shows that children are likely to watch — afterschool and Saturday-morning programs, evening news shows, early evening programs — identify seven or eight areas where children may become confused.
3. The investigation of moral valuing has been criticized on the grounds that it is all based on what people say and not on what they do. How might actual behavior be investigated? Propose a number of situations in which behavior might be observed and recorded.
4. What more can schools do to provide opportunities for children to experience the give-and-take of cooperation? Propose five or six learning activities in one subject field that would require two or more children to work together productively.
5. Study the values clarification activities and strategies cited from Raths and Simon. Develop eight or ten of your own that you feel would also be worth doing.
6. Select a content area of interest to you. Propose several activities within the area that you feel would forward children's knowledge of content and also provide experience in valuing.
7. Examine the list of critical concerns found in Exhibit 1–3. Which of these do you consider most important? Which if any would you drop? Are there others that you think should be added to the list today?
8. A good many books have been published recently that try to provide more varied gender roles for boys and girls. Locate eight or ten of these books to share with others.
9. What in your opinion are the strengths and weaknesses of the various approaches to value development described in this chapter? Which would you expect to be most influential in the long run? Why?

Chapter 2

A Framework for
Teaching Values

Educators generally agree on the importance of values in the education of children, but they are less likely to be of one mind when it comes to specifying which values deserve emphasis.

In Chapter 1's review of how values develop, the question "Which values?" was for the most part not at issue. The developmentalists as such equate moral maturity with commitment to fair play and justice, but they are not much interested in exploring the full range of values. Those engaged in the values clarification approach are quick to deny any interest in specific values as such; their concern is with process — with means, not ends. And the groups seeking to challenge and offset the impact of environment on personal-social development most often concentrate their energies on righting some particular source of moral wrong, such as racism, sexism, or emotional malfunctioning. None of these approaches, then, focuses on the first task of those seeking to teach valuing: deciding on the values to be investigated.

SOME CRITERIA FOR VALUE SELECTION

The failure to come to grips with the problem of identifying which values to be emphasized is no mere oversight. It is a difficult task at best. Yet in developing a values program, the choice of values need not be made mechanically or solely as a reflection of the teacher's own beliefs. Criteria exist for choosing values that can make the program richer and more meaningful for all its participants. To arrive at these criteria, we must first decide where we stand in relation to some conflicting trends in values education.

Talk Versus Action

It is a convenient — and not at all uncommon — practice for teachers to post lists of behavioral guidelines in their classrooms. For example:

In Mrs. Robinson's room, we:

1. take turns in talking
2. do not say mean things to other children
3. do our own work without bothering others

Being nice to others, not being afraid of something just because it's new, keeping at a project without having to have continuous attention and approval, telling the truth most of the time, and tattling as little as possible — these are behaviors we might hope to find developing in students as we study and work together during the year. Certainly, friendliness, fearlessness, self-direction, truthfulness, and less talebearing are all admirable moral guidelines, and discussions about them can help students understand them better. But talking about how to behave has its limits, as does posting lists of rules for group guidance and reference.

Children need to investigate, act out, and test values that are important to them, values that will make a difference in how well they live and work. Thus, the moral guidelines that we choose to emphasize must be more than just another list of things for children to talk about.

Morals Versus a Full Range of Values

We know teachers have to come to grips with maladaptive behavior such as cheating, lying, or stealing. But if such behavior becomes habitual, efforts at teaching morals are likely to give way to trained counseling and therapy. Clearly, then, we do not want a program of values education to operate from a base of morals defined strictly in terms of personal-social behavior.

The worthy virtues are many and varied, as witnessed by this selection from a list to be found in the front of a Gideons' *New Testament*: cleanliness, consecration, contentment, courage, diligence, duty, endurance, faith, forgiveness, freedom, fruitfulness, happiness, honesty, honor, hope, humility, joy, kindness, labor, love, obedience, overcoming, patience, peacefulness, perseverance, pure thinking, resolution, sincerity, steadfastness, temperance, trust, truth, watchfulness, and zeal. These could be categorized to cover a range of personal and social behavior that would be much broader than simply being honest and truthful, important as these attributes are.

But our concern is for an even more extensive range of values. A values program should explore guidelines for every aspect of living, not personal-social behavior only.

Private Versus Public Values

Whose values are we to honor in our program — yours, mine, or ours? In the late 1920s, W. W. Charters noted that of the then accepted ways of determining curriculum content, only individual opinion or consensus seemed appropriate for use in determining which ideals should be taught.[1] Identifying personal traits thought to be needed for performing well or analyzing qualities demonstrated in actual behavior, while useful in setting up a bookkeeping course, seemed inapplicable in the area of values.

[1] See W. W. Charters, *The Teaching of Ideals* (New York: The Macmillan Company, 1929), pp. 44–79.

Yet simple agreement may result in too narrow a values base. The values selected by parents in south Boston or proposed by boards of education in the strip-mining hilltowns of West Virginia or in the citrus-growing and truck-farming areas along the Rio Grande — or in many other towns or cities seemingly sequestered from the mainstream of American thought and feeling — might not withstand the test of a larger framework.

Today we are freshly aware that our chief challenge is to work for greater breadth and more alternatives in politics and in most other arenas of modern life. At their best, then, truly public values will serve us well, guarding us against the provincialism of our first and sometimes worst impulses.

The Ideal Versus the Real

The kinds of values proposed for study by children may appear to be too much for them to handle. Are children actually going to be able to tangle with concepts like equality, freedom, and justice? And ought teachers to try to do more with things as they really are — with, for example, poverty, or restrictions on educational and vocational opportunities, or inequities before the law?

The ideal may strike us as too abstract, the real as too tough and gritty. Thus, we may be tempted to confine our efforts to pledging allegiance to the flag, celebrating the birthdays of presidents, and making the most of what children can learn through the activities of the student council and the safety patrol.

What we have to do, of course, is to unite the ideal and the real. We must help children perceive ideals in Dewey's words, as a "collection of imagined possibilities"[2] that can inspire efforts to change conditions when they are found to be intolerable.

Good/Bad Versus Good/Better/Best

On his pilgrimage to the Celestial City, John Bunyan's hero found none of the roads easy. But few were as nerve-wracking as the

[2] John Dewey, *Reconstruction in Philosophy* (Boston: The Beacon Press, 1948 [first printing, 1920]), p. 118.

pathway through the Valley of the Shadow of Death, running narrowly as it did between "a very deep ditch" and "a very dangerous quag." For "when he sought in the dark to shun the ditch on the one hand, he was ready to tip over into the mire on the other; also when he sought to escape the mire, without great carefulness he would be ready to fall into the ditch." It was dark as the devil down there, and close by was the mouth of hell.

The heaven/hell orientation to values education is still on the scene, even though most of us are uncomfortable with it. We realize that when we try to use an either/or approach, we are likely to end up preaching rather than teaching. Yet detached though we may profess to be, the moral problems or dilemmas we pose for children to discuss often do have right and wrong answers or good and bad solutions.

Rather than treading in Christian's cautious footsteps, we might do well to view valuing as a choice among many competing ways of behaving and to echo what King David, before being gathered to his ancestors, had to say to his son Solomon: "Be strong, and show yourself a man." Or as we might phrase it today: "Live the good life and live it to the full. There are many goods to choose from, but only one life. So choose well and choose wisely."

Is it any wonder, then, that with such decisions before us, we are slow — or have been — to name the values or guidelines we want to put before children? We prefer action to talk, but we get mostly talk; we need both in any kind of balanced program. We don't want morals only, but they have to be part of the mix. We want values that are public in the best sense, enduring and universal in Kohlberg's terms rather than merely consensual. The ideal and the real are two sides of the same coin. Good/better/best may still not make sense to some persons unless bad/worse/worst is somewhere close at hand.

A NEW APPROACH TO LEARNING TO VALUE

The old framework of "this versus that" has already ceased to work for many of us in the education of children. Slowly but surely a new outlook has emerged that builds on and extends the three approaches reviewed in Chapter 1 and that embodies many dimensions of valuing. In this new approach the total curriculum is redeveloped for its values education potential and is reoriented toward making the most of every opportunity to help children learn to value.

Our new understanding of valuing as a learning process, sharpened by the contributions of Piaget, Kohlberg, Raths, and the others who have been working in the moral-ethical-political realm, has undoubtedly made us more responsive to demands upon the schools by the larger society: to help more children break through the restrictions that tend to impede free choice among more rewarding ways of being and behaving in all aspects of living. Too often in the past, schools may have written off some children as being victims of an unfriendly value system learned in a nonsupportive neighborhood. But what are schools for if not to help the young develop behavior guidelines of their own? Valuing one thing over another is a process that is learned — and thus can be taught. Consciousness of options, competence in their exercise, and comparison of competing goods are the steps involved in the process of learning to value. (See Exhibit 2–1.) Why shouldn't the process apply across the board to every aspect of life in which choices between the less and the more rewarding deserve to be made?

No doubt the content of the emerging curriculum for values education could be presented in many ways. In our analysis, however, we have chosen to focus attention on new developments in three areas of human experience: (1) the world of everyday living, (2) the cultural heritage, and (3) the moral-ethical-political realm.

Additionally, we have found it helpful to identify in each of these three areas a balance or *axis of emphasis*. The mastery of certain content remains essential for developing the kind of competence that makes freedom of choice possible. But beyond such *receptive* learning lies another challenge. Children also need experience in learning to value the *innovative*. Genuine emancipation from things as they are comes only when people are able to imagine things as they might be. To emphasize the dual nature of valuing, this book pairs chapters in each of the three areas of human experience. Each area is seen from both a receptive and an innovative point of view. Thus, the curriculum for learning to value in the world of everyday living is discussed first in terms of accommodation and then in terms of criticism. Similarly, appreciation and creation form the axis for the cultural heritage, and allegiance and reform for the moral-ethical-political realm. (See Exhibit 2–2 for a brief description of these axes.)

The next three sections of this chapter outline what this framework for a broadened approach to value development may be expected to look like. The chapter closes with reflections on some of the problems that can be anticipated as values education moves into the mainstream of curriculum making.

Exhibit 2-1

Valuing as a Learning Process: Its Three Phases

1. Becoming aware of differing values	Previous learning may have restricted awareness that other ways of being and behaving exist. As its first task, the school opens the eyes of young learners to new possibilities among which choices may or might be made.
2. Putting competing values to the test	Unless or until a learner is able to gain satisfaction from something new, no real challenge to present satisfactions can arise. Therefore, the school helps the child become competent in many new ways of being and behaving.
3. Comparing values and selecting those to live by	Although new learning enlarges the arena of choice among competing ways, the school needs to provide repeated experiences with the satisfactions to be derived from many ways of being and behaving. Only then can young valuers make fully informed choices between or among the less and the more rewarding.

Exhibit 2-2

Value Axes in Major Areas of Human Experience

Area of human experience	Receptive end of axis	Innovative end of axis
1. *Everyday living*	*Accommodation* Acceptance of or adjustment to established ways of living and working together; concord, harmony; gratification, satisfaction; affiliation, agreement, compliance, conformity, submission	*Criticism* Questioning of things as they are or have been; analysis, interrogation, antagonism, assertiveness, contention, correction; boldness, courage, dissent, doggedness, outspokenness, strong-mindedness
2. *Cultural heritage*	*Appreciation* Cultivation and assimilation of what has been accumulated in the arts and humanities; enjoyment, esteem, exaltation, wonder; possession, proficiency, virtuousity	*Creation* Creation or discovery of something not hitherto in existence; experimentation, exploration, inquiry, investigation, research, speculation, theorizing; novelty, originality, venturesomeness
3. *Moral-ethical-political realm*	*Allegiance* Devotion to rightfulness of legal authority in control or governance; homage, respect, tradition; constancy, fidelity, loyalty; cooperation, duty, responsibility, unity	*Reform* Rejection of reliance on authority, independence of judgment; deliverance, emancipation, freedom, liberation, release, separation; autonomy, openness, risk taking; change, development, revolution

THE WORLD OF EVERYDAY LIVING

Children need to learn all they can about how things are. Otherwise, they will be in no position to define different ways to use their time. If they do not learn to read, books and libraries and lifelong self-education will have little meaning for them. If they have to count on their fingers and toes, then they can forget about finishing high school, or even pumping gas or waiting on tables. If schooling doesn't take, the first step of entering into valuing as a conscious process cannot occur, for alternatives will never obtrude upon the more or less unconscious ways of life children learn simply by growing up.

What Must Be Learned

Our first objective is to help children master the fundamentals of knowledge. But the fundamentals need to be broadly defined. They must include skills of body management and social skills, as well as skills of book learning. Schools have long accepted the teaching of such basic skills as their first responsibility. And never have they been more eager to succeed than they are today, or more aware of the cruciality of teaching all, not just some, of the children what they need to learn.

In terms of values, then, teaching for skills mastery — or for accommodation to things as they are — is a major need of children and the starting point in the process of learning to value.

The Right Kinds of Questions

With accommodation is paired criticism as a second focus of values. You might think that insistence on being given good reasons for formal learning of any kind would come naturally to most children. But for a good many children, the demand for accommodation as defined by society may transcend their sense of personal interests or rights. Children can be socialized into holding their tongue or saying "Yes, ma'am" to the detriment of the free exercise of their critical intelligence. Rousseau assumed that the first task of the tutor or teacher is to enable each child to find a sensible answer to the question, "What will this be good for?" about everything taught. We must assume no less.

The questioner can be an eager learner. In truth, properly freed to ask and answer questions, children will cover more ground than teachers might expect or assign. A critical approach on the part of children toward learning whatever they have to learn also makes for the right kind of self-assertiveness. Moreover, questioning is an integral part of coming to terms with the world, at least in a society like ours. When children's questions and critical thought are focused on problem areas, the learning that results can have truly great social consequences.

We have tried to define one area of curriculum concern — everyday living — in such a way as to highlight a pair or axis of values that our society considers to be highly important in the lives of children. The exercise and development of these values is dependent, at least in part, on the school. Society demands that children be taught to be at home in the world of basic learning. The hope is for a balance between accommodation and criticism in what the school teaches so that children will be equipped to make the most of things as they are without being weighed down by them. We want increasingly competent children who can make their way in the real world with their eyes open to new possibilities. Toward this end, Chapters 3 and 4 propose ways to redevelop relevant portions of the curriculum for children. (See Exhibit 2–3 for a vocabulary of key terms used in this approach to helping children learn to value.)

THE CULTURAL HERITAGE

Another field of study deserving new emphasis is the arts and humanities. Learning to read is not the same as learning to love good books. Singing songs every morning may serve to open the school day but does not necessarily open the door to the world of great music. An easel or two near the sink and a folder of study prints on the window ledge do not guarantee automatic entry into the world of great art.

If children are to take advantage of their cultural heritage, they have to learn a good deal. Otherwise, a good proportion of the population will remain locked out from enjoyment of the full range of the

Exhibit 2-3

Learning to Value: A Vocabulary of Key Terms

Competency: developed ability to experience satisfactions among alternatives

Consciousness: awareness of the full range of behavioral alternatives among which choices for investing time and energy may be made; first step in values education

Evaluation: comparison of the satisfactions to be gained from different kinds of behavior

Satisfaction: result gained from putting an alternative to the test; measure of the worth of an activity

Value: guideline to behavior based on tested alternatives

Value axes: arrangement of values within major areas of human endeavor and learning in terms of receptive and innovative behavior

Values education: learning about the alternatives for personal commitment of time and energy, developing competency to make truly meaningful choices among alternatives, and testing out choices in terms of competing satisfactions

Value-oriented content: subject matter that lends itself to teaching worthwhile alternatives in which to invest time and energy; may be new content or familiar content reoriented

Valuing: making a choice among tested alternatives to determine which is likely to be most rewarding

arts. And everyone will suffer from a life less rich and varied than it would be if more talent for innovation were released.

Access to the Arts and Humanities

Appreciation of the cultural heritage calls for increased exposure to and experiences with it. An enriched environment is the starting point. Children must hear or read good literature, listen to good music, be helped to encounter good pictorial art. But more is called for. Children must not only listen and look. They need experiences in interpreting their cultural heritage, through dramatization, movement, pantomime, and so on. They need time to talk about their experiences. And they need opportunities to try their own hands at writing, composing, and painting.

Teaching for appreciation today tends toward emphasis on individual choice among a range of approved options, without much attention to organized instruction as such. This is particularly true in the areas of literature and music. Art appreciation tends to get itself mixed up with performance or creative activities; again, however, little time is given to teaching directly for appreciation. Chapter 5 will examine some of the new arts programs being developed across the country, which address the problem of how to help children gain more direct access to their cultural heritage.

Creative Behavior as Something Learned

Good literature, music, and art belong to everyone, and access to this heritage should be open to every child. But our cultural heritage is never static; thus, children must be educated for creativity as well as for appreciation. A balance needs to be sought between profiting from the cultural heritage and adding to it. Appreciation of the arts and creative behavior are both needed to make a complete child — and to enrich and sustain our cultural heritage.

Additionally, learning to innovate or create is closely allied with becoming more appreciative. For example; sound teaching principles are involved in bringing writing together with reading or in relating listening to good music to trying to compose music of one's own.

Efforts to do more with creative behavior in the classroom are discussed in Chapter 6.

THE MORAL-ETHICAL-POLITICAL REALM

A third group of values are those that are involved in learning how to deal with authority in the moral-ethical-political realm. There is little doubt about the importance of the school in building an understanding of the democratic system of goverment and in developing an allegiance to it. In the past, these have been the primary goals of schools' political education programs. An equal obligation — but one that has received somewhat less attention — is the encouragement of a concern for independence and an impulse to reform. In a truly democratic society, respect for duly constituted authority must be tempered by the will to change its operations when and as the need arises. (See Exhibit 2–4 for three value axes in relationship to social demands.)

Respect for and Devotion to Tradition

Perhaps too much reliance has been placed on learning the democratic way of life simply through growing up in a school environment that provides for student participation in some aspects of decision making.[3] Electing class officers, framing rules to live by, engaging in group activities, and functioning in an atmosphere of mutual caring are all useful and desirable classroom experiences. But more could be done. The range of national heroes and heroines called to children's attention could be broadened to include more than explorers, pioneers, and presidents. Children may be capable of learning more about our system than we think they can — and from sources whose impact on the lives of the young we may have left largely unexamined. If we take citizenship education, as it used to be called, at all

---

[3] Major studies in this field include Robert D. Hess and Judith W. Torney, *The Development of Political Attitudes in Children* (New York: Anchor Books/ Doubleday, 1968); and Davd Easton and Jack Dennis, *Children in the Political System* (New York: McGraw-Hill Book Company, 1969).

Exhibit 2-4

What Is Demanded of the School by Today's Society

The world of everyday living

Children are to learn what they have to know in order to make the most of things as they are. (Accommodation)

Children are to learn to ask hard questions about the whys and wherefores of daily existence. (Criticism)

The cultural heritage

Children are to learn how to gain access to the riches of their arts heritage. (Appreciation)

Children are to learn how to add to this heritage. (Creation)

The moral-ethical-political realm

Children are to learn to be devoted to democracy. (Allegiance)

Children are to learn how to bring about needed social and political innovations. (Reform)

seriously, we will want to try to do a good deal more in this important values area. New approaches are reported in Chapter 7.

The Never-Ending Need for Reform

Loyalty, homage to great men and women, and a strong sense of mutuality and unity form an important cluster of values, but so do innovation, emancipation, liberation, independence, autonomy, and reform. Allegiance to the democratic way of life needs to be coupled with a steadfast insistence upon the right of independent thinking. A people remains free only as long as the chance for change is built into the process of lawmaking. Resistance to the enforcement of inequitable laws is not only a right of free citizens but their responsibility. In a culturally diverse and professedly open society, standing up for the right to differ becomes an obligation all of us must assume.

This is sometimes difficult to accomplish in a classroom setting. In the paired value axes set forth in this book, the pressure on schools is always stronger toward the more passive side of things — toward accommodation rather than criticism, appreciation rather than creativity, and allegiance rather than reform or innovation. But schools must try to present both sides. Children should be brought up with the images of political activists and reformers before them as well as pictures of George Washington and Christopher Columbus. In Chapter 8 are reported some of the more adventurous directions in which some schools are moving in the teaching of values related to reform and innovation.

WHEN WE GO TO TEACH — SOME PROBLEMS

Of what use is schooling if it does not deal directly with values or guidelines to behavior or enable children to move from the level of unconscious behavior to that of choice? Dewey, Piaget, Raths, and Kohlberg (and most other thoughtful commentators on the human condition) have declared in favor of the examined life. Rousseau was speaking of the weight of learned but unexamined behavior when he declared in the opening sentence of *The Social Contract* that "man is born free, but everywhere he is in chains."

The question is really not whether teachers should concern themselves with values in the education of children. Of course they should, and of course they do. By its very nature, schooling is value centered. The real question is this: with which values shall the schools be most concerned? Before they can recast the curriculum for children toward more meaningful attention to values, educators are going to have to identify clearly what they value. That is what we have tried to do in this chapter, in proposing three categories of values.

First, all of us value mastery of basic skills and understandings in the world of everyday living. This calls for encouraging a compliance or willingness to learn on the part of children. We also value questioning behavior and critical thinking. Together accommodation and criticism form the first of three primary units of values.

Second, we value our cultural heritage. All children should have the right of access to the arts and humanities as avenues to enjoyment and exaltation; all children also deserve a chance to learn to behave creatively. We want the young to appreciate our cultural heritage and to become contributors to it. Thus, appreciation and creative behavior are paired as another value axis.

Third, we value a truly democratic society, in which respect for authority is balanced by a commitment to independent thinking and innovation. Allegiance to the democratic way of life must be fostered, along with a desire for reform and a concern for independence. Both allegiance and reform, then, make up the value axis in the moral-ethical-political realm.

As we see it, values education is not something to be scheduled twice a week. Education for value development — the essence of schooling — is an hour-to-hour, all-day, every-day enterprise interwoven with every aspect of study. To phrase this point of view in the plainest of terms, values education is what learning to be human is all about. Thus, we call for attending to the guidelines to behavior that inhere in and arise out of study of the subject matter contained in the total curriculum.

The bulk of this book is devoted to reporting more fully what is being proposed as new content for a value-centered curriculum for children. But before ending this chapter, we want to note a few of the problems in teaching values. Education for values is not easy.

Halfway Measures

"Tell me what you like, and I'll tell you what you are," said John Ruskin to a Yorkshire audience. In developing his point, he made clear his belief that the entire object of true education is to make people not merely *do* the right things, but *enjoy* the right things — not merely industrious, but to love industry — not merely learned, but to love knowledge — not merely pure, but to love purity — not merely just, but to hunger and thirst after justice.[4]

Self-awareness is what it takes to bring doing and loving into consonance. Yet sometimes we behave as if our job were done when we have made sure that basic skills have been learned. If we think our challenge is to teach children merely how to read or to develop a liking for reading good books, we may neglect the need to make sure that children actually do read a variety of enjoyable and worthwhile books. How can children know what alternatives amount to unless they have experienced the consequences of acting on them? Valuing calls for awareness of alternatives, development of competence to choose among them, and experience with the consequences of choice. All three steps are part of the process. And teachers must be committed to teaching all of it and not quitting somewhere along the line.

Imbalance Between Receptive and Innovative Values

Teachers also need to avoid an imbalance between the receptive and innovative sides of values education. (See Exhibit 2–5.) Teaching for mastery, hard as it is, may be simpler than teaching for a critical mind; appreciation may be easier to aim for than creativity; and standing up for America may be learned sooner than when to say, "Let's start over."

What teachers have to do is to teach for both kinds of values at the same time. More than half a century ago, when Lewis Terman began to advocate better education of the gifted, he contended that their needs were stronger than those of other children for attention to the innovative side of things.[5] His biographer, May Seagoe, summarizes his proposals as follows:

The gifted need an emphasis on creativity, intellectual initiative, critical thinking, social adjustment, responsibility, and unselfish leadership. They need instruction through concepts and principles rather than

[4] John Ruskin, *The Crown of Wild Olives* (New York: Hurst and Company, n.d.), p. 85.

[5] Lewis B. Terman, *Genetic Studies of Genius*, 5 vols. (Stanford, Calif.: Stanford University Press, 1925–1959).

Exhibit 2-5

**Receptive Versus Innovative Values: Some Problems
in Achieving Balance**

Variable	Response from receptive end	Response from innovative end
Amount of knowledge available for teaching	Always a great deal of information to be taught	Little to go on; information is open, changing
Familiarity of content to teachers	Teachers know what is to be taught	By its very nature, content is likely to be new
Ease and efficiency of teaching methods	Drill-and-practice and group instruction often seem preferable	Greater use of project or activity approach and individualized instruction
Room for self-direction by students	Focus on common learnings; less apparent need for planning with students	More opportunities for independent thought and student planning
Acceptance by parents and public	Generally seen as proper content of the curriculum	Some concern that too much emphasis will be given to this area

through concrete facts. They often learn inductively rather than deductively. They respond on the basis of logic and reason, not social custom. They should have a maximum of new ideas, a minimum of review and drill. They work best independently, with self-direction rather than constant supervision, but with continuing understanding support. They need to build self-confidence and a desire to excel.[6]

Today, if we smile at the idea of reserving such practices for some children instead of opening them up to all, it simply means that we have finally arrived at the insight that receptivity alone will not produce an inquiring mind.

Reliance upon Familiar Content

Finally, teachers must be careful not to rely on outdated content in education for values. Society is restless in its demands upon the school. As new outlooks and expectations come into being, curriculum content has to be reviewed. Much of this content, perhaps most of it, will remain relevant at any one time. But new things that may be worth learning emerge and deserve a chance to prove themselves.

That is what this book is all about. In succeeding chapters, proposals for recasting the curriculum to provide room for new, value-oriented content are reported on, and some additional proposals are made.

Those of us who deal with children every day have always been deeply committed to helping them develop moral guidelines. But now that we know more about how values develop in the lives of children, we are readier than we may have been in the past to declare in favor of teaching those guidelines that will enable children to become personally fulfilled and socially effective persons.

ACTIVITIES

1. Which of the conflicting trends identified in the opening pages of this chapter (talk versus action and so on) seem to you to be subject to

---

[6] May V. Seagoe, *Terman and the Gifted* (Los Altos, Calif.: William Kaufman, 1975), p. 103.

most debate? Can you think of other conflicts that must be resolved before we can decide which values to teach children?

2. The dimensions of human existence proposed in Exhibit 2–2 are familiar enough: everyday living, the cultural heritage, and law and order (or authority). Could the content of a values curriculum for children be categorized some other way? If so, could you divide each of these new categories into pairs of values? Try your hand at this.

3. Select an area of basic skills and propose eight or ten learning activities to develop critical competence in that area. To what extent will these activities also further mastery of skills (accommodation)?

4. The definition of the cultural heritage presented in this chapter may strike you as narrow. Does it encompass the full range of the arts and humanities? Does it take account of cultural pluralism? Review the section in terms of these questions.

5. What are the characteristics of an activity intended to teach children to behave creatively? Illustrate your answer by developing a set of activity options in one or more of the arts areas.

6. History contains many instances of reform movements that improved things for people. Choose one of these and propose classroom experiences and activities related to it that would be suitable for children to engage in.

7. Examine various lists of rules that have been created with or by children. What do you see as the pros and cons of such undertakings?

8. The innovative values are less attended to than the receptive (see Exhibit 2–5). Elaborate on the reasons for this. Should anything be done to change the situation?

Part II

Values in the Curriculum: What Children Need to Know

The World of Everyday Living

The Cultural Heritage

The Moral-Ethical-Political Realm

Values in the Curriculum: What Children Need to Know

The World of Everyday Living

The Cultural Heritage

The Moral-Ethical-Political Realm

Chapter 3

Knowledge of the Everyday World

Children come into the world ready to make the most of it. Nature has prepared them to wrest satisfaction from whatever they find around them. As they grow older, children spend most of their waking hours trying to make more and more sense out of what is happening. In due time, they begin to distinguish experiences that are more rewarding from those that are less so. All in all, they work as hard as they can to cope successfully with everyday living.

By the time they enter school, children have learned a great deal. They can communicate verbally and in other ways as well — by smiles, nods, and frowns; by coming close or turning away or leaving the scene. They can solve many problems on their own and can find out quite a lot of things for themselves. They have come to know where grownups fit into the picture and how to get their help when it is needed.

Children are equipped by nature to learn readily in many areas of living. The language faculty, for example, enables the young to develop a set of rules from the talk they hear around them. On the basis of this grammar, they can generate sentences to forward a great range of purposes. Noam Chomsky, whose studies pioneered in clarifying what he calls "the amazing feat of language learning," has theorized that the mind is composed of a series of innate faculties. This approach runs counter to the "empty organism" doctrine, in which the mind is thought of as a formless substance waiting to be shaped and human nature is viewed as almost entirely a product of environmental impact. Chomsky's proposals encourage a new optimism about the "cognitive capacity" of the individual. Opening up before us, as Chomsky puts it, is "a theory of freedom" that may lead, under the right circumstances, to the release of "a vast creative potential as yet unexplored."[1] (See Exhibit 3–1 for a list of possible faculties and functions to be derived from this theory.) Such a prospect is supported also by ethologists like Konrad Lorenz, who has called for scientific study of humankind's innate cognitive faculties.[2]

The right circumstances include, of course, schools that are quick to build on what children have already learned and that can help children bring all their faculties into play for further learning. As a minimum, schools ought to provide an environment at least as stimulating to children as any of the other places where they live and learn.

THE STARTING POINT

Learning to value one way of being and behaving over another demands the development of competence to test out different options. Thus, the school's first task is to induct children into the world of everyday living. Adjustment to the demands of this world (which we have termed *accommodation*) opens up a range of alternatives to the child who masters basic skills and understandings. Only then is free choice among options likely to be meaningful.

[1] Noam Chomsky, *Reflections on Language* (New York: Pantheon Books, 1975), pp. 123–125, 132–134.
[2] Konrad Lorenz, *Behind the Mirror: A Search for a Natural History of Human Knowledge*, trans. R. Taylor (New York: Harcourt Brace Jovanovich, 1977).

Exhibit 3-1

Cognitive Capacity: Innate Faculties for Learning (After Chomsky)

Faculty	Representative functions
Developing language	Creating a grammar and making sentences
Common-sense information processing	Identifying, naming, and categorizing items in the environment and in experience
Engaging in inquiry and solving problems	Finding out how things work; making and applying rules
Creating, solving puzzles, and playing	Making or expressing something; resolving ambiguities; being fanciful about possibilities
Relating to others	Defining roles of people; taking part in community living; resenting undue exercise of authority by others
Working	Determining needs, nature, and conditions of productive behavior
Willing and doing	Deciding and doing what one wants to do

Source: Derived from ideas projected by Noam Chomsky, *Reflections on Language* (New York: Pantheon Books, 1975); particularly chap. 1, "On Cognitive Capacity." Copyright © 1975 by Random House; used by permission.

In the past, many children were not given genuine opportunities to choose among competing ways to invest time and energy. A key reason for this was that schools sometimes emphasized certain aspects of learning — the maintenance of classroom decorum and the practice of basic skills, for example — to such a degree that they failed to nurture sufficiently the natural curiosity of their students. And surely natural curiosity — "the need to know" — is an essential ingredient of any values education program.

The Need to Know

When he found that notes inviting him to join in family outings had passed him by, Emile decided it was time for him to learn to read. "Present interest," concluded Rousseau, "that is the great motive impulse, the only one that leads sure and far."[3] Jack Houston, growing up in rural Mississippi in the early 1900s in William Faulkner's chronicle of the Snopeses, did not enter school until he was fourteen and "there was nothing else about the farm for him to learn." Up to this point, learning had been a full-time occupation. However, when he came through the schoolhouse door, no sense of need came with him. He showed up not "deliberately intending to learn nothing but merely convinced that he would not, did not want and did not believe he needed to." Learning was something that went on out of school wherever and whenever there was something he had to know more about; in school, he could rest from his labors. As a result, Jack "was competent for citizenship before he could vote and capable of fatherhood before he learned to spell."[4]

The need to know impels the natural learner, the out-of-school learner. Our challenge is to harness the innate energy of children, once they are in our charge, without lessening the will to learn. Reading and writing are surely not as hard to learn as listening and speaking. The problem seems to lie in the urgency of need.

[3] *The Emile of Jean Jacques Rousseau: Selections*, ed. William Boyd (New York: Teachers College Press, 1956), p. 52.
[4] William Faulkner, *The Hamlet* (New York: Vintage, 1940), p. 209. Copyright © 1940 by Alfred A. Knopf, Inc. Quoted by permission of the publisher.

First Things First

Sometimes learning how to behave in school may take precedence over learning anything else. Consider, for example, the way an after-lunch group "sharing" session with five-year-olds can be conducted. "I am going to buy new shoes Saturday," one child states. "Good for you, Bridget," the teacher declares. "I like a child who speaks right up. Who wants to be next?" Roberto says that his cousins are coming to stay, Rachel tells of a trip to Pittsburgh that will be delayed because the car is in the shop, and Darlene reports that her Uncle Willie may get out of jail next week. "Jason, we're waiting for you." Jason sits up and moves back into the circle.

Taking turns, listening to others, asking polite questions ("What was Uncle Willie in for?"), following directions, not wandering off — all aspects of proper classroom behavior — can sometimes take on greater importance than finding out about something a student wants or needs to learn. Of course, learning how to learn is important. But one way or another, core and content have to be brought together.

Use as Well as Practice

However skills are introduced (and practice may play an important part initially), it is their use that leads students to the satisfaction of being really competent at something. In one school that was recently visited, the instructional materials center was located in the middle of a half-acre of open teaching space. The materials specialist enthusiastically spoke about her program for library skills. But as the visitors moved from one group of students to another, they found most of the children engaged in pencil wielding, with workbooks, lesson cards, and textbooks before them. Other books, while in evidence, were being held in reserve. The children could turn to their library books only if time remained after they had finished their assignments.

The development of reading skills as well as library skills was being short-circuited in this instance. Apparently no one, including the materials specialist, seemed to appreciate the real value of the central collection in the teaching of children. Skills teaching that stops short at practice only is one of the reasons that many children never experience the satisfactions that come from true mastery.

Values education starts with everyday living, then, because the need to know is exercised most naturally on the world immediately around the child. The teacher's challenge is to maintain this innate drive, while making sure that the learning of school routines does not get in the way of other kinds of learning and that practice is subordinated to use in the teaching of basic skills. Most important of all, values education starts with everyday living because a child gains access to so many alternatives once the basic skills and understandings of this area have been mastered.

The world of everyday living is usually thought to include the fundamentals of language and mathematics. In this book its definition extends to social and physical skills as well, for children must learn the fundamentals of those areas, too, if they are to be really free to test out a variety of worthwhile ways of being and behaving. Thus, basic skills are to be found in all three primary domains of learning. (See Exhibit 3–2.)

MASTERING THE SKILLS OF BOOK LEARNING

Accommodation to this aspect of everyday living is the first stage in children's formal schooling. It always has been and perhaps always will be. If children are to experience the satisfactions to be derived from many competing ways of being and behaving, then they must develop a degree of mastery that enables them to move along in their learning. This is what teaching the fundamentals of book learning is all about, and it is why ensuring the successful teaching of the three R's is always a matter of public concern.

A special sense of urgency seems to exist in efforts today to get through to children regarded not long ago as more or less unteachable. In the field of conservation, efforts to save emperiled species sometimes require what conservationists call *radical* and *manipulative* measures; to save a child in peril of not learning, we may be tempted to make use of extreme methods ourselves. At least, that is the conclusion that one might draw from an examination of some of the new approaches to skills teaching.

Exhibit 3-2

Basic Skills in Three Domains of Learning

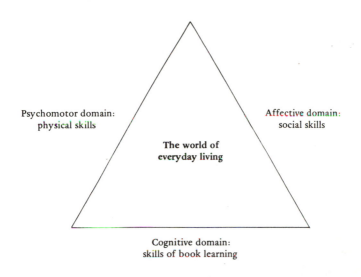

Psychomotor domain:
physical skills

Affective domain:
social skills

**The world of
everyday living**

Cognitive domain:
skills of book learning

Source: Adapted from Benjamin S. Bloom, ed., *Taxonomy of Educational Objectives: Cognitive Domain* (New York: David McKay Company, 1956); and David R. Krathwohl et al., *Taxonomy of Educational Objectives: Affective Domain* (New York: David McKay Company, 1964).

Identification of Skills to Be Developed

Curriculum revision often begins with a definition of what is to be taught. In the past, the result was sometimes a mixed bag of general objectives. Here is a sample set on food and nutrition drawn from a popular how-to-do-it curriculum textbook published over fifty years ago:

The ability to help care for a school garden

A clearer notion of why food is stored in winter

Some understanding of what is done in canning

A better understanding of what a child ought to eat

Some notion of the extent of our dependence upon the outside world of food

To know the function of cereals in the diet

To recognize the forms in which cereals occur

To increase the consumption of oatmeal[5]

Admirable enough in themselves and surprisingly comprehensive, these do not specify precisely what it is that ought to be learned and thus what it is that must be taught.

Today curriculum developers are more explicit about what they are seeking to teach. In practice this means spelling out in much detail exactly what the learner is supposed to be able to do. One recently developed reading program sets for its objectives the mastery of the following skills:

Identifying vowel sounds for the letter *y*
Identifying three sounds for vowel letters *ei* and *ie*
Identifying three sounds for vowel letters *ea*
Identifying vowel diphthongs in words
Identifying vowels modified by *r* in words
Using rules for the sounds of *c* and *g*
Writing medial consonant digraphs

The program then goes on to specify how children should be expected to perform on tests that check their learning of these skills.

[5] Henry Harap, *The Technique of Curriculum Making* (New York: The Macmillan Company, 1928), pp. 114–115, 121.

Given a list of words, the pupil identifies vowel sounds for the letter *y* with 95% accuracy.

Given a list of incomplete words, the pupil identifies medial consonant digraphs to complete these words correctly with 95% accuracy.[6]

How much more specific can one get?

In mathematics, specification may take the form of listing concepts for a particular lesson.

Zero and one in division
Steps in division
Estimating in division
Remainders in division
Short form in dividing
Zero in the quotient

Specific objectives may also be listed.

To divide by a 1-digit divisor, no remainders
To divide by a 1-digit divisor with remainders
To divide by a multiple of ten
To divide by a 2-digit divisor
To divide using money notation[7]

Presumably, tests would aim at measuring the success of this carefully targeted teaching.

Individualization of Teaching

The more precise identification of objectives has had much to do with the rebirth of the movement to individualize instruction. Earlier efforts such as the Winnetka and Dalton plans in the United States and more recent ventures such as Summerhill and the Leicestershire

[6] Marie G. Hackett, *Criterion Reading: Teacher's Guide* (New York: Random House, 1971), pp. 1, 31, 48.

[7] Eugene D. Nichols et al., *Holt School Mathematics* (New York: Holt, Rinehart, and Winston, 1974), dittoed lesson, Content Level 55.

schools in Great Britain may have led the way.[8] But today's challenges to the historic dependence upon group instruction are varied and vigorous.

The rise of educational technology has led to the systematic development of study materials and teaching techniques that refocus attention on the individual. In some programs the study materials are highly elaborate, as in *Individually Prescribed Instruction* (IPI). The mathematics portion of this widely disseminated program, for example, is

> divided into nine levels — A through I. Most levels are subdivided into units. There are units on numeration, place value, addition, subtraction, multiplication, division, combination of processes, fractions, money, time, measurement, and other special topics. Each unit is designed to develop specific skills called behavioral objectives, which the students are expected to master. The entire curriculum has more than four hundred behavioral objectives.[9]

Pretests and posttests accompany the units, with the results of the former used by the teacher to write individual prescriptions of lessons and learning activities to be undertaken before the final test is administered.

Another program that has been widely studied, *Individually Guided Education* (IGE), calls for teachers to prepare their own teaching materials. However, in the Wisconsin version of IGE, teachers are given some help in developing behavioral objectives in reading. The Wisconsin Design for Reading Skill Development specifies behavioral objectives for use in teaching the skills of word attack, comprehension, study, self-directed reading, interpretive reading, and creative reading. Again, hopes for success are high.

1. Ninety per cent of pupils whose measured ability is above average (IQ > 110) will be independent in Word Attack with respect to phonetically and structurally regular words by the end of the fourth year in school.

---

[8] Maurice Gibbons, *Individualized Instruction: A Descriptive Analysis* (New York: Teachers College Press, 1971).
[9] Donald Deep, "An Operational IPI School: The Teacher's Changing Role," in *Developmental Efforts in Individualized Learning*, ed. Robert A. Weisgerber (Itasca, Ill.: F. E. Peacock Publishers, 1971), p. 158.

2. Ninety-nine per cent of such students will achieve independence by the end of their fifth year in school.[10]

Many other teachers besides those using the IGE program are learning to organize individualized teaching programs around behavioral objectives. Indeed, this has become a favorite inservice activity in recent years.[11] Teachers today have a variety of sources that they can draw on for guidance in developing programs because most major textbook publishers have begun to provide new and carefully sequenced study materials that call for a good deal of self-direction on the part of children.

Another and perhaps the ultimate form of individualized teaching is contingency management (or behavior modification) as it is defined and used by trained clinicians. It may not be feasible — or even desirable — to apply reinforcement techniques to all children in a group setting. But a good many teachers are finding that directive teaching, tied to highly specific and limited objectives, can succeed with some individual children who have previously been unreachable.[12]

Revival of Achievement Standards

In the past, the practice was to accept unsuccessful learning as normal for many children. Every year children who had been identified as nonlearners early in their school career were expected to fall further and further behind. By grade six, it was assumed, some groups of children — those from underprivileged racial or ethnic minorities or from welfare or working-class or rural families — would be likely to exhibit a learning deficit of two to three years below established

[10] Herbert J. Klausmeier et al., *Individually Guided Education and the Multiunit Elementary School: Guidelines for Implementation* (Madison, Wis.: Wisconsin Research and Development Center for Cognitive Learning, 1971), p. 73–74.

[11] See Philip G. Kapfer and Glen F. Ovard, *Preparing and Using Individualized Learning Packages for Ungraded, Continuous Progress Education* (Englewood Cliffs, N.J.: Educational Technology Publications, 1971).

[12] See Dwight L. Goodwin and Thomas J. Coates, *Helping Students Help Themselves* (Englewood Cliffs, N.J.: Prentice-Hall, 1976).

norms. And for the most part, teachers believed that such school failure was in the nature of things. Factors over which they had no control were to blame.

This is no longer the situation today. An increasing number of schools now aim at teaching for mastery. All children, for example, are expected to complete the twenty-three books of one programmed reading series by the end of their third year.[13] A few may need a bit more time, but nobody is expected to stall at book 7 or book 12 or book 19 and simply stay there.

Schoolwide test scores have taken on greater significance to the public. Test data showing differences among schools are commonly released to the newspapers by local school systems.[14] State testing programs have been strengthened.[15] There is growing concern about lowered scores on achievement tests administered at the national level.[16] Pressure to get better results all the way up the line has led many states to the widespread installation of proficiency testing at the secondary school level.[17] More and more, then, the public is holding schools and school systems accountable for the successful teaching of the fundamentals to all children. And the educational profession is generally in accord with this posture.

In the varied new approaches to teaching the fundamentals that we have reviewed in this section, there are certain common elements. (See Exhibit 3–3.) Yet these elements are not equally easy to incorporate in new programs. All teachers can be taught to write objectives, of course. In any school setting, time and space and materials can be organized for a degree of individualization. But whether all

---

[13] *Sullivan Programmed Reading Series,* 3rd ed. (New York: Webster-McGraw-Hill, 1973).

[14] See Malcolm Provus, *Discrepancy Evaluation: For Educational Program Improvement and Assessment* (Berkeley, Calif.: McCutchan Publishing Corporation, 1971); and Frank J. Sciara and Richard K. Jantz, eds., *Accountability in American Education* (Boston: Allyn and Bacon, 1972).

[15] *State Educational Assessment Programs* (Princeton, N.J.: Educational Testing Service, 1971).

[16] See periodic reports of College Entrance Examination Board (888 Seventh Avenue, New York, N.Y. 10019) and of National Assessment of Educational Progress, a project of the Education Commission of the States (Suite 700, 1860 Lincoln Street, Denver, Colo. 80245).

[17] For a comprehensive report on proficiency testing, see *Educational Leadership,* 36 (May 1979), pp. 537–560.

Exhibit 3-3

New Approaches to Teaching the Fundamentals: Some Common Elements

Element	Aspects to be found in most programs
Specification of skills	Attempt to analyze skills area scientifically
	Definition of skills in terms of behavior, performance level, competency, criterion of achievement
	Arrangement of skills in order of importance for presentation
Individualization of teaching	Organization of children to let them proceed at own pace
	Development of study materials for self-teaching: some programmed materials
	Provision in study materials of pretest, optional activities, posttest
Standardization of achievement	Expectation that lessons or units of study will be mastered: 85 percent or better
	Reporting of progress in terms of level reached in sequence of study materials
	Expectation that all children will complete program in due time

teachers can successfully teach for mastery in terms of revived achievement standards still remains to be thoroughly assessed.

A few of the new approaches to basic skills teaching may well be regarded by some persons as *too* radical and manipulative. But the programs do exist, and they show that on the whole educators are trying to move ahead as well as they know how in teaching the skills of book learning to all children.

COMING INTO COMMAND OF THE BODY

Children do not live by books alone. If the young are to be free to experience and choose among alternatives in all aspects of everyday living, then they must have command of other areas besides the realm of word and number. One of these is obviously that of the body. Children need to be able to perform with ease and satisfaction the varied physical activities possible and appropriate to their developmental level. Let us examine some current physical education programs to see what progress is being made in this regard.

Movement Education

Movement education is one of the most widely welcomed curriculum modifications on the current scene. It takes as its premise the following:

> Children should be lithe and agile, with easy-flowing movement; they should look good and attractive in action. Yet when many five-year-olds start school they are stiff, tense, and awkward in action. Lots of them need as much help with physical skills as they do with academic skills, yet they are literally taught to run before they can walk.[18]

Sitting and standing, walking and running, lifting and carrying, throwing and catching, hopping and skipping and jumping — all are made up of more or less complementary components. Study and

[18] Jack V. Fenton, *Practical Movement Control* (Boston: Plays, Inc., 1973), p. 5.

practice can relieve tension and improve performance through co-ordination of these components. Appearance also improves when greater competence in movement has been developed.

Although their programs differ, the enthusiasts for movement education all urge intentional teaching rather than relying on an active play base alone, for "a study of physiology is not worth a snap of the fingers if the teacher does not apply its principles in the schoolroom."[19] This older advice has been resuscitated by the new advocates of teaching for more adequate body management. Play may be where physical education begins, but it is not where it stops.

Games, Gymnastics, and Sexual Integration

A major concern in recasting the content of physical education in today's curriculum is equalization of opportunities for girls to do well in outdoor and gymnasium activities. In a set of teaching proposals published seventy years ago, the issue of sex differences was recognized and confronted: although girls might be expected to avoid some games, "the attitude of the parent and teacher should be to extend the field of plays and games for girls."[20] Thus, it was proposed that up to age twelve, program differentiation be kept to a minimum. This is the position educators have generally assumed ever since.

Recent attempts to achieve sexual integration in the physical education program have taken several new forms. Some schools have eliminated from their schedules the rougher, more competitive contact games. Other schools have attacked head on the problem of differences between girls and boys in strength and stamina by introducing body-building regimens, physical fitness–testing programs, nutrition education, and the like.[21]

At the same time, the repertoire of games thought appropriate to

[19] W. W. Charters, *Teaching the Common Branches* (Boston: Houghton Mifflin Company, 1917), p. 319.

[20] George E. Johnson, *Education by Plays and Games* (Boston: Ginn and Company, 1907), p. viii.

[21] Strangely enough, the most direct challenge to sex bias in the realm of children's physical activities has occurred outside of school. We are referring, of course, to the suits against the exclusion of girls from Little League baseball.

both sexes may be undergoing liberalization. The increased television coverage of Olympics gymnastics competition, for example, has helped to popularize a sport in which both girls and boys can excel. Further thoughts on this prospect are discussed in the section on sports.

Expressive Movement: Dance and Drama

The learning of skills that have to do with body management, gymnastics, and games will obviously help children feel more comfortable with their bodies. But can the same claim be made for the expressive side of physical education? How much do the skills involved in dance and drama really contribute to physical competence? No doubt dance and drama contribute to creativity, but that is not our concern here.

Dance as defined by Great Britain–based dance theorist Rudolf Laban and his followers can be quite as skills-centered as any other aspect of movement education. In dance as in other athletic endeavors, space, time, and force are the common elements to be studied and related through the skillful use of the body in motion. In teaching dance, attention is given to locomotion (stepping, running, rolling), elevation (hopping, skipping, leaping, jumping), turns (spinning, pivoting, whirling about), gestures (moving arms, legs), rising and sinking (reaching up, dropping down), opening and closing (with arms, legs), and advancing and retreating (reaching out, drawing back). In addition, use of body parts, symmetry, flow, and shape are explored, along with concern for how and where the body moves. American advocates of dance education for children also accept this view of dance as both a set of physical skills and a creative activity.[22]

The combination of dance and drama movements in improvisational pantomime may seem likely to offer less attention to skills development. But the British see no problem in maintaining the same concern for skills here as in the rest of the program. Body and sensory awareness exercises, while providing underpinnings for free

---

[22] See Joan Russell, *Creative Dance in the Primary School* (New York: Frederick A. Praeger, 1968); and Geraldine Dimondstein, *Children Dance in the Classroom* (New York: The Macmillan Company, 1971).

improvisation, can also enlarge the movement repertoire. Indeed, movement and drama together can provide a firm base for remedial therapy as well as for developmental education.[23]

Sports: Yes or No

Support for a sex-unbiased games program has often been accompanied by disfavor of sports in general. Certainly, sports can be full of undue stress and strain for the young of either sex. This is particularly true of team sports. Adult interest in team sports for children is often focused on winning regardless of cost. Moreover, the star system in team sports often starts too early (high school scouts would no doubt love to have a chance to identify talent in the fifth or sixth grade). As a result, team sports are likely to be both overly competitive and exploitive.

But instead of rejecting all sports, perhaps educators should be doing more to encourage and broaden individual sports programs. Tennis would seem to be a natural. Why should only the children of the well-to-do have a chance to learn the rudiments of this game? Swimming, taught to children in a good many suburban schools, would seem worth offering to children in all kinds of schools. Field sports and perhaps other individual sports might also be added to this list. Finally, schools could be more inventive about developing and testing out modified team sports, which might give new excitement to physical education programs and provide valued physical competencies as well.

Outdoor Education

An increasing number of American families are turning away from motel vacations to take up camping, and many individuals are seeking to develop skill in living out-of-doors. Schools, too, may wish to

[23] See Betty Lowndes, *Movement and Creative Drama for Children* (Boston: Plays, Inc., 1971); and Audrey Wethered, *Movement and Drama in Therapy* (Boston: Plays, Inc., 1973).

accept the challenge of helping children engage in outdoor activities such as the following:

fishing	boating	ice skating
hunting	canoeing	skiing
archery	sailing	sledding
camping	riding	water skiing
hiking		

A week-long camping trip for fifth- or sixth-graders has become part of the school program in every section of the nation. But an extension of this once-in-a-schooltime experience is being sought by many schools because they see outdoor experiences as worthwhile alternatives to more formalized physical activities. Here, again, the skills called upon in the exercise of unfamiliar activities must be developed to the point where choice can carry with it the hope of some reasonable amount of immediate satisfaction for the young learner. Otherwise, options cannot really be said to exist.

This review of the elements in an up-to-date physical education program for children may be too inclusive to suit some teachers. No doubt teachers will want to impose upon these proposals some commonsense criteria to determine which of the elements are most worth including and emphasizing — and why. (See Exhibit 3–4 for a proposed scoreboard for these elements.)

But no matter which activities are selected for inclusion, we are committed to providing a broader and more skills-oriented base for the development by children of the kind of physical competence that will make possible a meaningful choice among options.

LEARNING TO LIVE AND WORK TOGETHER

At school, mastering the basic cognitive skills comes first, or at least looms largest, in the minds of children and adults alike. Learning physical skills follows second because of the increased interest in making children proficient in the physical realm. What comes next?

Much has been said about how getting along with others is basic

Exhibit 3-4

Scoreboard for Elements in New Physical Education Program

	Criteria for inclusion in program				
Element	Development of coordination/dexterity	Development of strength/stamina	Immediacy of appeal	Sociality	Life usefulness
1. Body management	X				X
2. Games	X		X	X	
3. Gymnastics	X	X	X		X
4. Dance and drama	X		X	X	X
5. Individual sports	X	X	X		X
6. Team sports	X	X	X	X	
7. Outdoor education	X		X	X	X

to success both in and out of school. Today more is known about what it takes to learn to live and work together effectively — and thus educators are proposing new, more closely targeted attention to the teaching of social skills. There are options here, too.

Openness to Others

"Why do you always say something bad about other children's paintings, Sherry?" asks one of the half-dozen six- and seven-year-olds working around a double table with big brushes and poster paint. After a pause, Sherry replies, "I don't always." Others get into it: "I think you do." "Yes." "Yes, you do." Adds another child, "*Your* paintings aren't that good, you know." Sherry seems willing to think about it.

Although Sherry's teacher, Mrs. Lane, does not follow any organized program to encourage expression of feelings among students, she makes it possible for her twenty-one children to get together in numerous gatherings that invite such exchanges. A block corner attracts six children, who are reconstructing an elaborate marble chute related to a group study of acceleration and deceleration. In the reading corner, each of the nine children there is absorbed in a book of his or her own choosing but aware, too, of what the rest are reading. Other children sitting side by side at work tables are comparing notes on mathematics and science activities. At a round table in the middle of the room, Mrs. Lane is hearing a child read; nearby are others who are waiting their turns.

In this room, circle time occurs several times a day, offering opportunities for interaction at several levels. Mrs. Lane often asks questions to facilitate the children's interaction: "Have you any work to share? Are there problems we should talk about, do you think? Do we all know what we need to do next?"

As the example of Sherry illustrates, children have so much to learn about themselves and others that can only be learned through openness and interaction. All the children in a classroom are or can be resources for helping one another become aware of new ways of being and behaving. Living and learning together, children have a chance to experience the satisfactions that come from trying out and becoming practiced in a variety of ways of relating to others. Only then are they really free to choose between less and more rewarding ways of dealing with feelings, both their own and those of others.

Mutual Trust and Understanding

"I think people should be born grown-up. Then they wouldn't have to go to school," says first-grader Steven. "The part of school I like best is going home."[24]

The pathos of Steven's position is felt even more strongly when we review the difficulties of helping children transfer skills learned on their own to school situations. For some children the community playground or the backyard or the street is where you learn who you are and whom you can trust; in school, it may be hard to tell what the score is.

Most of the skills children must learn in order to live and work together effectively have to do, of course, with unfamiliar others. Facing two dozen strangers every day is not easy. But most children do learn to take joining new groups in stride; and they as well as inexperienced teachers soon discover how quickly such a group settles down to business as its members come to know and trust one another. Children need help in learning that interaction within a group can provide bonds such as:

Self-esteem, status, and stature
Mutuality of respect for individual differences
Friendliness between individuals and groups of boys and girls
Rapport among group members
Rapport between children and adults[25]

Programs of Social Skill Development

It does not take long, given openness to others and provision of many opportunities for joint endeavors, for a program of social skill development to begin to show results. Social skills develop as occasions for use are provided. But teaching comes into it, too.

In one of the earliest and most seminal explorations of this area, Hilda Taba and her staff reported many instances of deliberate

[24] Arlene Uslander et al., *Their Universe: The Story of a Unique Sex Education Program for Kids* (New York: Delacorte Press, 1973), p. 74.
[25] Adapted from Mary Jane Loomis, *The Preadolescent: Three Major Concerns* (New York: Appleton-Century-Crofts, 1959), p. 63.

teaching of social skills that occurred in the Intergroup Education in Cooperating Schools Project. Children in one class, for example, held a conference on some of the points to be kept in mind in small-group work:

1. What is your job for the group?
2. Does each person in the group know definitely what he is to do?
3. What information do you have? Is it enough?
4. Who is the leader? Has he made definite plans?
5. Let's decide now how to put the work together and how long it will take.
6. Let's decide now what you will do with your work.

In another situation, children were helped to identify the problems faced by newcomers to the school, of whom there were many:

Being threatened and beat up.
Not knowing rules.
Finding it very hard to make friends.
Not knowing the names of children.
Not being asked to join clubs and groups.
Finding it hard to get used to classroom procedures.
Being ridiculed because they did things differently.[26]

Setting up a committee to do something about these matters led to improvement in the lot of children new to the school and no doubt did much for everybody concerned.

Today many schools are employing organized approaches to try to make sure that social skill development is not left to chance. One of the most comprehensive programs is that of the Human Development Training Institute, which specifies content in terms of both scope and sequence and proposes learning activities that make full use of group living as a context for social learning and the children themselves as vital resources in the process.[27]

The problem-solving class meetings advocated by William

---

[26] Hilda Taba et al., *Elementary Curriculum in Intergroup Relations* (Washington, D.C.: American Council on Education, 1950), pp. 183, 138.

[27] Harold Bessell and Uvaldo Palomares, *Methods in Human Development: Theory Manual*, rev. ed. (LaMesa, Caif.: Human Development Training Institute, 1973).

Glasser[28] have been found useful by many schools as a framework for focusing attention on such familiar concerns as truancy and vandalism. Individual teachers have used the Glasser meetings to good effect in helping younger children deal with bullying, tale bearing, and other types of problem behavior.

Psychotherapy has been drawn on for techniques that have seemed promising to school people. One notable source has been transactional analysis as developed by Eric Berne.[29] In addition to those programs specifically aimed at young children,[30] some of the programs meant for adolescents and adults list activities that have been found adaptable to the needs of younger learners.[31] Drug abuse or prevention programs have also drawn on transactional analysis among other sources in developing activities for use with children.[32]

Social skill development has always been of concern to teachers of children. Today teachers know a good deal about how to forward it by giving children opportunities for getting together that allow them to develop openness to interaction and mutual trust and understanding.

But there is now new hope of even greater success through the use of organized programs that go beyond simply learning from group experience. We will return to the promise of such approaches in Chapter 4, in the section on fostering critical thinking about the process of socialization.

In social skill development as in teaching the skills of book learning and body management, the goal is to bring consciousness and choice into the arena of reality. Young choosers must have genuine

[28] William Glasser, *Schools without Failure* (New York: Harper and Row, 1969).

[29] Eric Berne, *Transactional Analysis in Psychotherapy* (New York: Castle Books, 1961); see also Thomas A. Harris, *I'm OK — You're OK: A Practical Guide to Transactional Analysis* (New York: Harper and Row, 1969).

[30] See Alwyn Freed, *T.A. for Kids (and Grown-Ups, Too)*, 2nd ed. (Sacramento, Calif.: Jalmar Press, 1971).

[31] See Muriel James, *The People Book: Transactional Analysis for Students* (Reading, Mass.: Addison-Wesley Publishing Company, 1975); and Dorothy Jongeward and Muriel James, *Winning with People: Group Exercises in Transactional Analysis* (Reading, Mass.: Addison-Wesley Publishing Company, 1976).

[32] For example, Gerald Edwards, *Reaching Out: The Prevention of Drug Abuse through Increased Human Interaction* (Garden City, N.Y.: Innovative Designs for Educational Action, 1972).

competence in social skills if they are to be able to know how satisfying one way of being and behaving is as compared with another.

WHAT DIFFERENCE DOES IT MAKE?

In this chapter, we have discussed what is being done to recast the curriculum in teaching basic skills so that learning to value can become a part of the lives of all children. Let us review our reasons for beginning the sequence of six chapters on value-oriented curriculum innovations with one on accommodation to the competencies called for in everyday living. Then, in closing, we will try to relate Chapter 3 to the thesis and scheme of the book as a whole.

The Basis for Further Learning

As a framework for reporting what has been going on, this chapter has divided the world of everyday living into three parts. In the cognitive or intellectual realm, we have found many program innovators to be specifying book learning skills that they claim have to be mastered for effective functioning. In the psychomotor domain, we have reported on numerous programs that identify physical skills that ought to be learned if children are to function at their best. And in the affective or feelings domain, we have noted new concern for the deliberate teaching of vital social skills. Taken together, we may conclude that learning basic skills in these three areas should equip children to operate pretty successfully in the world of everyday living.

And, of course, this is the whole idea. Unless children possess the basic skills, they can hardly be expected to be choosers and testers of new and possibly more rewarding ways of behaving. Learning to value as a goal for the school becomes a farce and a fraud if the school fails in teaching the basic skills. Wherever they are to begin with, that is where children who lack basic skills are likely to remain. They will never have a chance to learn their way out.

When educators lament the fate of nonlearning children in our schools, they are not thinking only or even primarily of the difficulty they will have in getting ahead in the world. That will be a problem true enough. But they are more immediately concerned about

children's lessened opportunities for making the most of all their experience in living. Children who can't puzzle out new words may
never know what they are missing in the world of books. Children
who can't keep from tripping over themselves may never learn what
control of their bodies could open up for them. Children who always
find it hard to make friends may never realize what social constriction cuts them off from. (See Exhibit 3–5, p. 80.)

Something More than Chance

Let us return now to Chomsky's "theory of freedom" discussed
earlier in this chapter. According to this theory, children are believed
to be born with innate capacities or faculties for learning many kinds
of things. But far from being overoptimistic about the prospects of
maximizing children's potential for learning, Chomsky notes that
real barriers stand in the way of full and free development. "We
must not," he argues, "overlook the fact that for most of the human
race, material deprivation and oppressive social structures make these
questions academic, if not obscene." In moving from physical im-
poverishment toward the level of freedom that may be required for
productivity, "human history has hardly begun for the majority of
mankind."[33]

And favored though Americans are, we would contend that much
the same thing could be said about the prospects of full development
for many children in the United States.[34] Only recently has our
society resolved to do something more in the education of the poor
than leave successful learning to chance. To help all children grow
up conscious of the choices open to them and capable of acting on
their choices, education for competency is what is needed.

Accommodation — Just the Beginning

In this chapter, we have reviewed new developments in the various
skills areas that seem to be aimed at helping children make the most

[33] Chomsky, *Reflections on Language*, pp. 124–125.
[34] See Alexander Frazier, *Adventuring, Mastering, Associating* (Washington,
D.C.: Association for Supervision and Curriculum Development, 1976), chap. 1.

Exhibit 3-5

Alternatives that Require Competency in Basic Skills

Skill group	Examples of skill-based alternatives
Skills of book learning	Reading for pleasure or for self-education
	Further schooling of any kind that requires study and research
	Careers: most professions (law, engineering, etc.), many crafts (carpentry, plumbing, etc.), many businesses (sales, service, etc.)
Physical skills	Games and sports of many kinds
	Pursuits calling for strength and stamina: some kinds of household or yard work, operation of heavy equipment and machines
	Careers: some crafts (bricklaying, auto mechanics, etc.), outdoor occupations (construction, earth movement, etc.), some services (police work, fire fighting, etc.)
Social skills	Relationships with wide range of others: personal friendship, work relations, civic or other bonds
	Further learning in many fields of interest: ethnic-racial contributions, gender commonalities and differences, age-youth contrasts, etc.
	Careers: professions (ministry, social work, teaching, etc.), service occupations (job counseling, sales, etc.)

of things as they are. Accommodation to everyday living is what we have called this process. It is where the schools must always begin with children.

But it is not where they end. In the chapters to come, we will review newly vigorous efforts in teaching critical questioning (Chapter 4), appreciation of the cultural heritage (Chapter 5), creative behavior (Chapter 6), allegiance to the democratic way of life (Chapter 7), and social innovation or reformism (Chapter 8). In Chapter 9, we will try to show more specifically how schools can rework their curriculums to add a greater value dimension to them.

A value-oriented curriculum for children is in the process of being developed in our nation toward the end of freeing more of our children to learn what it takes to become fully functioning and self-determining members of a genuinely open society. Consciousness and choice are important components of this program, but competency is its base.

ACTIVITIES

1. Besides Noam Chomsky, who has contributed to our understanding of the preprogramming that may ready children for learning? Where do Konrad Lorenz and other ethologists fit in? Could the work of Jean Piaget be interpreted in such terms? Look at the faculties suggested in Exhibit 3–1. Would Lorenz and Piaget add others to the list?
2. Check on the extent to which children in one or more classrooms accessible to you are learning skills through use or through practice and drill. Do you see ways in which the time devoted to practice might be cut back to allow more time for learning through application?
3. Selecting a limited reading or mathematics skills area, prepare a learning package for it with behavioral objectives, pretest, developmental activities, and posttest. Try it out on one or more children. What are the advantages and/or limits of this approach?
4. Mastery may be a goal we should hold to in the teaching of reading, but in physical education we have to temper our teaching to take account of several factors. What are these?
5. Examine the proposed scoreboard for elements in the new physical education program (Exhibit 3–4). Do you agree with the ratings? Do you feel other criteria should be added? Revise the chart to fit with your idea of what is important in this field.
6. Propose your own list of social skills that ought to be learned by children. Suggest sample activities that might help in developing the skills.

KNOWLEDGE OF THE EVERYDAY WORLD

7. How do you feel about organized programs in affective education? (See footnotes 27–32 for examples.) Investigate one of the new programs and discuss its good and/or questionable features.
8. Do you think it is desirable to try to combine the skills domains outlined in Exhibit 3–2? Make a list of activities in which intellectual, physical, and social skills could be learned at the same time or in relationship to one another. When is a targeted-on-one-realm approach appropriate? When should teachers try to use a combination approach?
9. Competency in basic skills is essential if children are to be able to make real choices among a broad range of attractive alternatives. How does this position resemble the approaches described in Chapter 1? How does it differ?

Chapter 4

The Ability to
Think Critically

Children are seldom content with learning what and how things work; they also want to know why. This is the question that children most often ask. Answers need not be elaborate, but unless they are to the point, a child may ask why all day long.

Sometimes the persistence of young questioners is hard for busy adults to deal with. Yet checking things out is the only way children can be sure that they really are getting a hold on the world around them. Even then, as Piaget indicates, "trying to make more sense out of experience may seem possible only at the expense of contradictions."[1]

[1] Jean Piaget, *The Construction of Reality in the Child*, trans. Margaret Cook (New York: Ballantine Books, 1971), p. 431.

Puzzlement is the lot of the active learner. Eventually, however, much of what passes for reality in everyday living ceases to arouse questions, as children come to accept the facts of life as the way things are and must be.

If the first task of schooling is to teach children what they have to know to choose wisely among life's present options, the second and complementary goal is to strengthen children's faculty for asking hard questions about the range of these options. Along with accommodation, then, schools must strive to cultivate critical-mindedness.

Awareness of and escape from unconsciously learned constraints has long been a goal of modern humanity.[2] This can be seen in both the writings of philosophers such as Hegel ("The way of liberation is the development of the spirit as free theoretical intelligence and free practical will."[3]) and the works of literary observers. Thus, in Thomas Hardy's *Tess of the d'Urbervilles*, the emancipated son of a clergyman, who is seeking to break through class constrictions, tries to put himself close to "the great passionate pulse of existence," where he can sense true reality "unwarped, uncontorted, untrammeled by those creeds which futilely attempt to check what wisdom would be content to regulate."[4] Today the same theme remains vital in literature. In Saul Bellow's Pulitzer Prize–winning novel *Humboldt's Gift*, the narrator dreams of writing a book about the everlasting struggle between awareness and unconsciousness, in which boredom with things as they are is the enemy to be overcome.

In this chapter, we intend to look at some ways in which educators have tried to build a base for critical thinking. We will then examine three areas where consciousness raising has moved beyond reliance on methods and organization. Today the call is for a vigorous recasting of curriculum content to encourage children's natural urge to ask questions, particularly in regard to such crucial topics as the environmental crisis, the world of work, and social stereotyping.

[2] One might even argue that it's been a goal ever since the Age of Reason in the eighteenth century.

[3] G. W. F. Hegel, "Learning as Dialectical Growth," in *Toward a Philosophy of Education*, ed. T. O. Buford (New York: Holt, Rinehart, and Winston, 1961), p. 341.

[4] Thomas Hardy, *Tess of the d'Urbervilles* (Garden City, N.Y.: Doubleday, [1891]), p. 146.

PAST EFFORTS TO ENCOURAGE
CRITICAL THINKING

In most classrooms, children probably spend more time answering adult questions than seeking answers to questions of their own. Yet we as teachers profess to value critical thinking highly and have made much of it in our literature on methods. We like to believe that given a chance, children will continue to ask why until they find an acceptable answer. We believe we know how to foster and build on this natural urge to know, and we have conventionalized our procedures into ways of organizing for study that have a long history of support in elementary education. (See Exhibit 4–1 for a list of procedures often used by teachers to promote critical thinking.)

The Role of Interest

What impels children to ask questions? Interest is the oldest as well as the easiest answer. Children not interested in something rarely bother to ask questions about it. But is interest alone enough to carry children through a study in depth? Where or when does hard work come in?

Interest versus effort has long been a topic of discussion and disagreement among educators. Dewey sought to put the issue to rest by relating interest and goal setting. In Dewey's view, a child's interest, impulse, or desire is the starting point of all learning. The task of teachers is to extend the first promptings to learn into long-term purposes that can be reached only by the application of plenty of elbow grease. Prolonged periods of study, experimentation, and reflection will follow as children find worthwhile goals to pursue. "When anyone becomes interested in a problem as a problem and in inquiry and learning for the sake of solving a problem," Dewey declared, "interest is distinctively intellectual."[5] In short, interest and hard work do not have to be at war in the life of the child.

Problem solving is generally thought to be the highest level of question answering or critical thinking. And to the extent that children can become proficient in the process, they may be considered to be well on the way to achieving a balance between accommodation and critical awareness in the field of everyday living.

[5] John Dewey, *Interest and Effort in Education* (Boston: Houghton Mifflin Company, 1913), p. 84.

Exhibit 4-1

Procedures to Encourage Critical Thinking

Type of critical thinking	Learning activities	Examples of study topics

Wondering	Framing questions
	Collecting information:
	  Reading
	  Interviewing
	Reporting
	Discussing
		Are girls smarter than boys?
		Do people have to be poor?
		Pollution: why isn't more being done to reduce it?
		Do television commercials tell the truth?
		Can work be fun?

Inquiring	Framing questions
	Collecting information:
	  Reading
	  Interviewing
	Reporting
	Discussing
		Children's food habits and preferences
		Adult attitudes toward allowances
		Cause of change in autumn foliage
		Noise pollution: how serious is it?
		What people like about their jobs

Debating	Defining issue
	Collecting information:
	  Arguing pro and con
	  Weighing evidence
	Discussing
	Deciding
		Should children have to go to school?
		Television viewing vs. reading
		Living in the country vs. living in the city

Type of critical thinking	Learning activities	Examples of study topics
		Energy resources: solar vs. nuclear power
		Child care: should families have some help?
Discovering	Collecting information: Reading Observing Hypothesizing Experimenting Reporting Discussing	What plants need for growth
		Relationship of length of lever to weight of object to be moved
		How fire and oxygen affect each other
		Who is the strongest child in class
		How land erosion takes place
Problem solving	Studying situation Analyzing Hypothesizing Testing Reporting Discussing	How to bring about changes in school lunch menu
		How to raise money for extra field trips
		How to overcome fear of snakes
		How to keep play area clean
		How to improve handwriting

THE ABILITY TO THINK CRITICALLY

The Activity Movement

Seeking answers to questions that matter to them will lead children to learn more easily than they otherwise would. At the turn of the century, this was an established principle reflected in a wide range of normal school textbooks. In Gordy's *New Psychology* ("35th thousand in print!"), the head of the pedagogical department of the Ohio State University identified two burning questions:

> (1) How can we develop those permanent interests that shall induce the mind to attend to the first things in the right way?
>
> (2) How can we interest our pupils in the subjects we teach?[6]

The answer to these questions was self-activity, for in the words of one educator in 1899, "the powers of the human being are developed, strengthened, and matured only on condition of proper exercise, of self-activity."[7]

Observing, inventing, experimenting, discovering, doing — these were the self-activities that had their origin in interest.

> A child goes out to find in what kind of soil toad-stools grow. Having found some toad-stools and examined the kind of soil in which they are growing, he forms a hypothesis which is, be it supposed, verified by his later searchings. This fact enters more firmly into his system of ideas than it would have done had he been told outright.[8]

Indeed, one departmental head of a midwestern teachers college considered self-activity the crucial element in learning because it "prevents school life and school work from degenerating into hateful tasks imposed by the arbitrary authority of the teacher." He even went so far as to claim that "the loquacious teacher is a mind-killer."[9]

---

[6] J. P. Gordy, *New Psychology* (New York: Hinds, Noble, and Eldridge, 1898), p. 125.

[7] Daniel Putnam, *A Manual of Pedagogics* (Boston: Silver, Burdett, and Company, 1899), p. 113.

[8] J. A. H. Keith, *Elementary Education: Its Problems and Processes* (Chicago: Scott, Foresman, and Company, 1907), p. 72.

[9] Chauncey P. Colgrove, *The Teacher and the School* (New York: Charles Scribner's Sons, 1911), p. 246.

The Project Method

By the end of the 1920s, the interest-based activity movement had found a form all its own — the project. Frederick G. Bonser, the broadest-based curriculum thinker of the period, defined the project method as one in which "subject matter will not be learned as a meaningless task but mastered as a step necessary in an enterprise pursued by children because of their interest in it." Ideally, selection of project topics would combine "the spontaneously expressed purposes" of children and life objectives of true importance to concerned adults.[10]

In the hands of William H. Kilpatrick, Bonser's colleague at Teachers College, Columbia University, the project method became institutionalized as the best of all possible ways of working with children. Four kinds of projects — the producer's project, in which something is to be made; the consumer's project, in which something is to be appreciated; the problem project, in which an intellectual difficulty is to be clarified; and the specific learning (or drill) project, in which a skill is to be acquired — were defined with authority and persuasiveness by Kilpatrick in what remains the quintessential methods book of modern times.[11]

Units of Work

A project that incorporated the interests of an entire group was called a class project or group study or, if it seemed to belong within some framework of learning, a unit of work. The latter term was adopted by the authors of the major text on general curriculum development in the 1930s. Caswell and Campbell found the unit format large enough to encompass both individual and group studies, short- and long-range studies, and studies rooted in subject matter as well as those arising from personal experience. (See Exhibit 4–2.)

Theories about interest, self-activity, the project method, and unit organization all arose from a desire to relate learning and teaching

---

[10] Frederick G. Bonser, *The Elementary School Curriculum* (New York: The Macmillan Company, 1922), pp. 90, 93.

[11] William H. Kilpatrick, *Foundations of Method* (New York: The Macmillan Company, 1925), pp. 347–355.

Exhibit 4-2

Characteristics of Units of Various Types

Type of unit	Illustrative topics or themes
Subject matter units	
1. *Topical*	
Sequential relationship between items of subject matter	American Revolution, Colonial Period, invertebrates, fractions (Length: longer than individual assignment, but not uniform — depends on topic)
2. *Generalization*	
Relationship of all materials to one generalization, law, or principle	All bodies of the universe move in an orderly manner; the sun is the source of all energy; people tend to move from place to place in search of better ways of living (Length: varies)
3. *Significant aspect of culture or environment*	
Relationship of aspect of culture or environment to human development or contemporary life	Industrial Revolution, immigration, education, crime, machine production (Length: varies according to importance given to topic or theme)

Type of Unit	Illustrative topics or themes
Experience units	
4. *Center of interest*	
Interest of children in activities and objects that may be classified under one heading	Indians, Eskimos, boats, trains, airplanes, games, fire department (Length: may extend over long period, perhaps a full year)
5. *Pupil purpose*	
Purposeful interest of pupils in achieving a given end	Interest in fire — how fire department operates
	Interest in sickness — how to eliminate sources of contagion
	Interest in new types of goods — how they are made, how they may best be used
	(Length: tends to be short for younger pupils, longer for older)
6. *Pupil need*	
A need that the pupil recognizes	Making purchases, selecting food, reading, keeping personal accounts (Length: tends to be short)

Source: Adapted from Chart VIII in Hollis L. Caswell and D. S. Campbell, *Curriculum Development* (New York, American Book Company, 1935), pp. 428–431. Used by permission of American Book Company.

more successfully. Today our vocabulary may be a bit different, but our commitment to teaching for active learning continues.[12]

However, there is at least one difference. An earlier faith that personal investigative efforts, properly supported, would lead to breadth of understanding has somewhat eroded in recent years. Although method and organization remain important, we no longer believe that emphasis on method alone is enough to ensure the kind of critical consciousness that children need. Today we are inclined to want to make certain that children experience meaningful encounters with selected fields of knowledge. Some content is more worth studying than other content. This is the direction in which the new value-centered curriculum is plainly headed. The next sections will explore how curriculum can be made more value-centered in three significant content areas.

UNDERSTANDING THE ENVIRONMENTAL CRISIS

All children need to think more about the environment if they are to grow up able to deal with environmental problems intelligently. Thus, this section presents and compares a good many approaches in this value-laden area.

Appeal to Emotions

In the science suite of one middle school is a student-made chart:

*ENDANGERED SPECIES OF THE
UNITED STATES*

Mammals	*Reptiles and amphibians*
Indian bat	American alligator
Utah prairie dog	Puerto Rican boa
Eastern timber wolf	Texas blind salamander
Florida panther	Inyo County toad
Columbian white-tailed deer	San Francisco garter snake

[12] See Alexander Frazier, *Teaching Children Today: An Informal Approach* (New York: Harper and Row, 1976).

Birds	Fishes
Hawaiian dark-rumped petrel	Shortnose sturgeon
Layson duck	Montana west slope cutthroat trout
California condor	Colorado River squawfish
Southern bald eagle	Big Bend gambusia
Kirtland's warbler	Blue pike

There are also posted lists of endangered insects, plants, and trees and a series of "Things to Do," which the teacher may have had a hand in preparing. One of the suggested activities: "Reread Little Red Riding Hood or The Three Little Pigs. Rewrite the story from the wolf's point of view."

Pathos, heartbreak, uneasiness, anxiety, fear, anger, outrage — people's reactions to the abuse of natural resources are dependably broad and deep. And children are always among the first audiences to which alarmed conservationists turn when a new atrocity hits the front page. Save the seals, the pelicans, the polar bears! Of course, we would not want to discourage efforts to touch the hearts of the young.

But learning to value in environmental matters calls for something more than an appeal to the emotions. It calls for more even than a simple choice between or among competing goods. Consciousness of options has to be coupled with critical analysis of their promise. Nothing people can now imagine may seem likely to be good enough in the long run. It is at this point that critical thinking and creative planning as described in Chapter 6 have to be brought together.

The Urgent Issue

In a suburban Cleveland elementary school, a group of fifth-graders went for a half-day visit to the Nottingham Filtration Plant on Lake Erie. The children prepared for this trip by viewing a sample of pond water under a microscope, testing tap water for chlorine content, researching the history of several cleanup and conservation efforts, and making up charts and compositions on the subject, "How Does Man Become Responsible for Himself and His Environment?"

In this particular Cleveland suburb, the study of pollution needs little extra motivation, for only a few years ago the Cayuhoga River caught fire in downtown Cleveland — and no one quite knows what it is going to take to bring Lake Erie back. The urgency is such that the need to modify school curriculum to devote more time to environmental education is taken for granted by educators and parents alike.

Interdependence: The Ecosystem

The urgency of doing more with environmental education has been accepted by most people today. "To meet this challenge," Larry L. Sale and E. W. Lee contend, "we must plan and teach environmental concepts and processes at every point in the educational progression but especially during the formative years — in the elementary school."[13]

But in planning how to teach about the environment, educators are confronted by a good many issues. The list that follows was developed by R. T. Tanner, although the order and part of the wording are the present writer's:

1. Scope and definition of environmental education — what should be included
2. Where environmental education belongs in the curriculum — which level, which subject field(s)
3. Sequence — what comes first and so on
4. Content versus methodology — studying pollution or helping to clean up a creek
5. Positive versus negative approaches — emphasizing deterioration of the environment or its development
6. Cognitive versus affective domains — increasing knowledge or deepening feelings
7. Relevance to urban children — plight of the whooping crane or reduction of air pollution
8. Environmental education versus conservation education — need to build a broader base.[14]

Educators seem to have decided in favor of developing a more comprehensive program with greater stress on the cognitive side of

[13] From *Environmental Education in the Elementary School* by Larry L. Sale and Ernest W. Lee, p. 177. Copyright © 1972 by Holt, Rinehart, and Winston, Inc. Reprinted by permission of Holt, Rinehart, and Winston.

[14] R. Thomas Tanner, *Ecology, Environment, and Education* (Lincoln, Nebr.: Professional Educators Publications, 1974), pp. 18–54.

things. As a result, many classes are learning about ecology or the ecosystem.

In the *Teacher's Handbook* for the carefully planned and plotted Science Curriculum Improvement Study (SCIS) is found this description of how to introduce the sixth-year unit on ecosystems:

> To begin their investigations, your pupils build aquarium-terrarium systems that contain separate areas of water and soil. They plant grass, clover, and pea seeds in the terrarium and later add crickets. To the aquarium they add algae, *Anacharis, Daphnia,* snails, and guppies. As they observe events in the aquarium-terrarium systems, the children review concepts introduced earlier in the SCIS life science sequence. The term *ecosystem* is then introduced to refer to the system composed of a community of organisms interacting with its environment.[15]

Among the liveliest members of the community are no doubt the fifty crickets and thirty guppies to be "ordered by means of a prepaid form letter (Shipment S)."

The reason for trying to help children gain a more scientific understanding of interdependence is plain. Cleaning up the creek is more than just a nice thing to do some Saturday morning early in May. It is a matter of life and death for us all — adults and children, crickets and guppies. We are all in this together.

Resource Development

Environmental education is serious business. At the core of the environmental issue are questions about the survival of humanity and of the world as we know it, questions such as:

Has technological man a future?
Are we approaching an end to growth?
Are science and technology getting out of hand?
How can technology best be controlled and directed?
What is the probable lifetime of a technological civilization?[16]

---

[15] Robert Karplus and C. A. Lawson, *Teacher's Handbook,* SCIS (Berkeley, Calif.: University of California Press, 1974), p. 84.

[16] John T. Hardy, *Science, Technology, and the Environment* (Philadelphia: W. B. Saunders Company, 1975), pp. 286–320.

Exhibit 4-3

Approaches to Environmental Education

Approach	Sample topics or aspects for study
Restoration and protection	Wild life and wilderness conservation Sources of pollution Threatened species of birds, animals, and plants Legislation: past, present, and future Heroes and heroines of conservation movement
Management and control	Monitoring function: air, water, noise level Population control Limits to industrial expansion Maintenance of life-environment balance What the future holds
Resource development	Parks: mountains, wooded areas, deserts, lakes, seashores Trails, bikeways, historic and scenic roads Energy sources: coal, oil, water, the sun, nuclear power Decentralization: new towns and cities, new transportation facilities Urban redevelopment, community planning

In considering questions like these, society seems to be faced with a choice between uncontrolled growth, which could spell self-destruction, or large-scale planning, which might diminish personal freedom in ways hardly to be imagined.

Yet, is there not a middle way by which an educated populace could propose and support, upon a proper base of conservation and management, a new effort toward making the most of our natural resources for mutual enrichment? And should not schools be helping children become aware of this middle way? Activities that have to do with resource development and future planning ("Describe the kind of city that you would like to live in. What kind of services would you want from that city and how could they be supplied?"[17]) ought to be a part of elementary education. And surely children would profit from learning some of the planning elements or principles that go into thinking about resource allocation, highway construction, land use, urban renewal, and the like. (For other ideas on the subject, see the section on planning in Chapter 6.)

Environmental education can be approached from several different perspectives (see Exhibit 4–3), and teachers should feel free to use more than one approach. Certainly we must continue to test out a variety of ways to help children become aware of the need to do more than merely adjust to environmental problems as they are or choose among options all of which may be exploitative and wasteful. Critical-mindedness is something to which we have long been committed in the education of children. But its exercise here requires us to keep abreast of new content in developing curriculum oriented toward social effectiveness as well as individual fulfillment.

LEARNING ABOUT THE WORLD OF WORK

Teachers have always paid a good deal of attention to the topic of work in the education of children. Elementary-age children have been taken on countless excursions to fire houses, police stations, and post offices, as well as visits to farms, dairies, bakeries, greenhouses, and supermarkets.

But now teachers are being urged to rethink their intentions. The

[17] Topic for investigation proposed at end of Chapter 8, "Designing the Environment of the Future," in Sale and Lee, *Environmental Education*, p. 158.

claim is being made that more needs to be done to raise the consciousness level of children to numerous aspects of the work world, including the eventual need to decide what occupation to pursue. All of this has come to be known as *career education*, a term that may strike some of us as odd or even outlandish when applied to elementary school children. However, aspects of career education are related very closely to our concern for helping children learn to value.

All of the new proposals for giving more attention to career education agree that greater awareness of the nature of the work world precedes choice making and preparation as the prime target in the education of children. But what does awareness encompass?

Usefulness of All Work

The usefulness of work — of all work — would seem to be a good place to begin because it is here that we lay the foundation for defining criteria that may enable a child eventually to cross class as well as race and sex barriers to freer choices among worthwhile ways to make a living. If the goal of career education is to broaden the base of choice making, then it ought not to ally itself with the idea that the school operates chiefly as a sifting or finding mechanism "to insure obedient and compliant workers for an industrial establishment," as Gordon I. Swanson notes may once have been true.[18] All persons who do well in school may be capable of going to college and preparing for the conventional professions. But should they? Or, more to the point perhaps, can going to college be regarded as good for persons who choose to work in the skilled or semi-skilled trades as well as in the professions? Learning to value in this regard is a very complex process indeed.

As curriculums are recast to pay more attention to the contributions of various occupations, we may expect that some of the new programs will sound pretty academic. A properly informed child, one source proposes, will be one who

> understands that the world of work is composed of occupational units (factories, institutions, enterprises) designed to meet cultural needs;

[18] Gordon I. Swanson, "Philosophical Bases for Career Education," in *Career Education*, ed. Joel H. Magisos (Washington, D.C.: American Vocational Association, 1973), p. 46.

explains why various occupational units have evolved; illustrates by example how a particular type of occupational unit, e.g., construction company, meets a specific cultural imperative; explains why more industrialized cultures have a greater variety of occupational units; describes why more industrialized cultures have a greater variety of service and leisure occupations. . . .[19]

The units of a new elementary social studies program in a midwestern school district include the following: goods and services, consumption, labor, trade, specialization and labor, industrialization, economics, and technology. A far cry from community helpers perhaps but intended to provide children with more food for critical thinking.

The Many Kinds of Work

Much more needs to be done to help children become aware of the varieties of work. One way that teachers have done this in the past has been to teach children about the interrelationships among fields of work. Here is a report by a second-grader indicative of this approach:

CORN
by Adam

> Corn is a Vegetable. It comes from many places. My grandpa grows corn too.
> To get corn you have to plant seeds first. The corn grows on a stalk. The Farmer brings the corn to a place where they put the corn in cans. And then they bring the corn to the stores. Then you buy it.
> Corn belongs to the fruits and vegetables area. And I do not like corn cooked in any way.

Adam may sound as if he knows more about corn than he cares to. But he clearly has some knowledge of the kinds of work it takes to produce, transport, process, and market foodstuffs.

[19] Larry J. Bailey and R. W. Stadt, *Career Education: New Approaches to Human Development* (Bloomington, Ill.: McKnight Publishing Company, 1973), p. 361.

Another familiar approach is to bring in adults to talk about what they do. An elementary school in Detroit found that using both parents and outsiders worked well. When second-graders did a unit on health workers, the dentist, doctor, and optometrist who came to see them were strangers; the nurse and nurse's aide were parents. The fourth-graders, studying transportation workers, started with a skilled mechanic, a cab driver, and a truck driver from the parent group and added a gas station manager, a bus driver, and a flight attendant from outside.[20]

In recent years the supply of books written to introduce children to the varied jobs found in different lines of work has increased greatly. Typical are the *Come to Work with Us* books by Jean and Ned Williams put out by Children's Press. In the publisher's words, *Come to Work with Us in a Telephone Company* (1971), a fair sample of the series, tells about "an unusual and intricate place with operators, installers, line repairmen, and so many more people at work." The series also includes books on a bank, a dairy, a hotel, a newspaper, a hospital, and a toy factory.

The best thinking today seems to advise stressing larger job clusters in developing career awareness among children. The federally funded Comprehensive Career Educational Model (CCEM) study, conducted at the Ohio State University's Center for Vocational and Technical Education, proposes that goods and services be stressed in kindergarten through grade three and that grades four through six concentrate on the following five job clusters: industry, commerce, social science (government, education, and health and welfare), service, and arts and humanities.[21]

Work Well Done: A Source of Satisfaction

Children learn about the sense of accomplishment that can be gotten from doing work well in a variety of ways. In one third grade much is made of caring responsibly for the class's live animals — guinea

---

[20] Ira M. Bank, "Children Explore Careerland through Vocational Role-Models," in *Developing Careers in the Elementary School*, ed. Norman C. Gysbers et al. (Columbus, Ohio: Charles E. Merrill Publishing Company, 1973), p. 141.

[21] Walter W. Adams, "Knowledge about Work: A Career Information Model and System," in Magisos, *Career Education*, pp. 141–156.

pigs, rabbits, and a couple of ducks. Members of the duck detail, whose job is the most demanding, have been signed up all the way until the end of the term.

DUCK HELPERS

Week of	Names
April 19	Cory, Brian E., Mike
April 26	Julie, Jeffrey, John
May 3	Jessie, Romy, Robin
May 10	Rifka, Susan, Steffen
May 17	Wendy, Debbie, Brian L.
May 24	Nils, Renee, Malcolm, Kirsten

Posted also is a set of procedures to be followed in taking care of Daffy and Dilly Duck:

1. Put ducks in green bucket.
2. Remove feeding dishes.
3. Remove dirty paper. Throw away.
4. Put in clean paper, folded to fit.
5. Put in fresh food.
6. Put ducks back.
7. Wash hands with soap!

Learning the satisfaction of chores well done is all part of the day's work for these children.

In another elementary school class, the teacher's intention is equally well meaning but the device used seems open to question. In this class is displayed a chart marked off by weeks, with the names of all the children down the left side. Gold stars go in the squares each week for children who can say, "I did all my work this week." Ellen, Jennifer, Emily, Mark, and Julia are good workers apparently, but Jason, Richard, Buddy B., and Caleb have more blanks than stars after their names. Appeals to pride in terms of extrinsic rewards do not always work.

Good workers both in school and out generally feel pride in assuming responsibility, completing tasks on time, going beyond minimal demands, initiating improvements in the way things are done, and otherwise making the most of work activities, whether assigned or sought. Teachers have learned many sensible and successful ways to keep such ends before children. The new emphasis on career education highlights the need to do even more if possible, for learning to value the worthiness of work requires such a reality base.

What Jobs Call For

Older children may want to investigate specific jobs in which they have at least a passing interest. The materials available to help with such exploration include books, records, filmstrips, and picture collections. Among the former, the *I Want to Be* series written by Eugene Baker and published by Children's Press seems representative. In the list of more than fifty titles, the jobs covered range from animal doctor and architect to weather forecaster and zoo keeper.

Some children may be interested in collecting information about a number of different jobs, with the idea of comparing them in relation to such factors as amount of education required; satisfactions, including pay; job security; demand for workers in the field; kind of job development possible; and problems, if any, in entry and progress.

It is this last factor that gives rise to some of the hardest value-centered questions about career employment practices in our times. (See Exhibit 4–4.) Raising the awareness of children to some of the key issues in the work world may seem premature to some of us. Certainly these issues are a result of inequities of great magnitude. Perhaps, as the National Institute of Education indicates, all the

> unintended consequences of career education have not been adequately examined. For example, will improved knowledge of the economic system help young people think critically about the world as it is, and inspire them to create a better world, or will the effect be to destroy important beliefs, leaving little in their place?[22]

The alternative to such risk taking is to leave the young locked in by the constraints of ignorance. Can we doubt where we must make our stand?

[22] *Career Education Program: Program Plan for Fiscal Year, 1975* (Washington, D.C.: National Institute of Education, Department of Health, Education, and Welfare, 1974), p. 7.

Exhibit 4-4

Some Questions About the World of Work

1. Why are so few nonwhites found in some lines of work?
2. Why do women go mostly into a few kinds of work?
3. Why aren't all jobs given to the most qualified persons?
4. Why should anyone be unemployed?
5. Why does unemployment affect some areas harder than others?
6. Why do some kinds of work pay so much more than others?
7. Why shouldn't any job pay enough to live on?
8. Why are some jobs respected and others looked down on?
9. Why do some jobs require so much education?
10. Why are some jobs called *professions?*
11. Why are examinations needed to get into some fields of work?
12. Why should being rich or poor determine what jobs you can prepare for?
13. Why shouldn't you be able to work at what you want to?
14. Why are more women joining the work force every year?
15. Why shouldn't children work part-time if they want to?

BECOMING AWARE OF WHY PEOPLE DIFFER

Alerting children to the meaning of the environmental crisis is an aspect of values education that has had widespread support. The only questions raised have come from persons who have wondered whether concern for wildlife might not become an unconscious substitute for broader social concern. Enlarging children's sense of how vital and varied the work world is has also been well received. The few doubts that have been expressed have arisen from the anxiety that children from poor backgrounds might be left to aim too low or the suspicion that talent retrieval for the establishment was the behind-the-scenes goal of career education.

But helping children become aware of why human beings differ socially — who supports this aspect of consciousness raising and choice making? Are there any programs in this area? Can elementary school children really study the process of socialization critically with any real profit? Is this kind of thing appropriate for young children to study anyway? Why not wait until later?

Actually schools are already helping children take a closer look at some aspects of socialization. Racism and ethnic bias are being attacked head on in a good many school programs. Sexism is also being studied in a growing number of schools. Concern about classism, if we may use a new term,[23] has begun to come through in some approaches to career education. The new political education programs, to which we shall attend in Chapters 7 and 8, are also paying increasing attention to class differences as related to political action.

Perhaps the chief barrier to doing more with a value-oriented study of socialization is finding a definition of social stereotyping that makes sense and also points toward things we can do something about. At present, theory in this field seems to be composed of all kinds of miscellaneous concepts that hardly belong together. About all that can be agreed on for sure is that, first, most social behavior is learned where children grow up and, second, differences in such learned behavior can be modified if children have opportunities to learn new ways of being and behaving — and want to make changes. Yet for our purpose these concepts may be enough. They will serve

---

[23] For a discussion of classism, see Donald R. Thomas, *The Schools Next Time: Exploration in Educational Sociology* (New York: McGraw-Hill Book Company, 1973), pp. 67–69.

as a starting point for helping children broaden their perception of the value choices possible in this critical area.

Racial-Ethnic Bias

People differ from one another in many respects — in size, shape, and color; in where they live and in where they go to pray; in the languages they speak at home; in the size and organization of their families; in the foods they like and the festivals they celebrate. As children, most of our differences are ones we are born with or into. And most of the time we do not think too much about them. In fact, we may be surprised when we discover that everybody is not just like us. We may be even more surprised to find that some people don't want us around because we are not like them, or that we ourselves may feel uncomfortable with others who are different from us in one way or another.

To help children learn to appreciate the variety offered by subcultures and to take pride in their own subculture if they belong to one and, at the same time, to be effective in trying to free children from the constraints that may come with being born into a given family or neighborhood, teachers need to know more than they now do. Here is a list of attitudes that deserve to be better understood and dealt with by all of us, adults as well as children:

Obedience to authority: overly solicitous concern for doing things the way others want us to rather than sponsorship of creative behavior

Dependency: group as reference rather than our own sense of what is right

Hostility to the new: uneasiness about something unfamiliar because it might harm us or not work well

Reclusiveness: withdrawal from interaction with outsiders who might laugh at, tease, or torment us

Unfamiliarity with language: impact of different home language on proficiency in standard or school English.

Differentiation of Gender Roles

Every day, in school and out, events conspire to teach children how to behave like boys and girls:

> A number of kindergarten children are working at a carpentry bench. A girl shows her teacher (male) her handiwork. "These nails aren't hammered in far enough," he says. "I'll do it for you." A boy shows the teacher his handiwork. "These nails aren't hammered in far enough," the teacher says. "Take the hammer and pound them in all the way."[24]

Some schools are helping children look at the storybook restrictions on what girls can do. Physical education programs that differentiate between the sexes are being reexamined. Where upper graders have choices between home and practical arts, sex bias in enrollment is being monitored.

But the biases that count for most are tough to tackle: "Books and reading mean more to girls than to boys." "Boys like math and science; girls don't." "School is a good place for girls but not so good for boys."

How can children be helped to realize what notions like these can do to them? While waiting for the entire curriculum to be recast to make it sex fair and genuinely challenging to every child, teachers may want to turn their attention to the following socially derived attitudes toward learning new things:

Boredom: tedium of sticking with tasks needed for learning that seem unrewarding in themselves

Irrelevance: subject to be learned doesn't tie in with anything that seems valuable to child and perhaps to parents

Not worth trying: result to be achieved by learning seems inconsequential; too much effort seems required

Conformity: in child's family, neighborhood, and group of friends no person likes subject or has done well in it

Distaste: tasks involved in learning seem too sissified or roughneck

---

[24] Barbara G. Harrison, *Unlearning the Lie: Sexism in School* (New York: Liveright, 1973), p. 9.

Some of the attitudes identified in the preceding section on racial-ethnic bias may also operate here.

Toward Social Declassification

The old ways of identifying socioeconomic status no longer work too well. Income level, number of rooms in dwelling, and amount of education have ceased to serve as sure-fire guides to social class. Type of work remains as one criterion. But that is as much a matter of history as anything else. The enlargement of the middle class is changing the social landscape. Class no longer seems to be a useful guide to much of anything. Our whole society, as Paulo Freire predicts, may be moving away from drawing on the ideas of the past for its needs to a more problem-posing posture of working it out as we go.[25]

Moreover, we are learning to think of strengths instead of weaknesses in social assessment. The children of migrant workers, if we choose to view them this way, can be seen as heirs to a rich oral culture and possessors of skills that may be less well developed among stay-at-home children. For example, there is narrating:

> A child who grows up on the road listens again and again to heightened versions of incidents that occurred in travel or in previous work situations — the freeway pile-up in Southern California last year, the forest fire or the big flood, the Colorado strike three summers ago, the history of the grape boycott.
>
> He hears and learns ballads that celebrate the exploits of men who were shot down or cut up — and the hard times of women who remained true while their men were away at war or serving time in the pen.
>
> He learns to make the most of reports of his own experiences, fixing them up a little so his companions listen more closely. He likes to tell tales he has learned in school. "Then Papa Bear said, 'Somebody done been in my porridge.'"[26]

[25] See Paulo Freire, *Pedagogy of the Oppressed* (New York: Herder and Herder, 1970).

[26] Condensed from Alexander Frazier, "Developing Expressive Powers," in *The Ripe Harvest: Educating Migrant Children*, ed. Arnold Cheyney (Coral Gables, Fla.: University of Miami Press, 1972), pp. 141–142. Copyright © by University of Miami Press; used by permission.

Casual dress, informality in manners, and a new regard for forth-rightness, including candor about sex relations, are among the be-havior trends that have blurred such lines as there may once have been between blue-collar and white-collar workers. You don't have to be middle class any more to have money. You don't have to be working class to have a good time.

As noted before, raising children's consciousness of the constraints that can come from the remnants of classism can be related to career education. It can be tied in, too, with consciousness of racial-ethnic and sex biases. As we shall see, it can have strong ties with political education. The following are some of the negative attitudes toward people in other classes that teachers may want to help children deal with in learning about the impact of classism:

Falseness: pretend to be better than they are; can't trust them; two-faced

Irresponsibility: big talking but don't come through on their prom-ises; can't depend on them

Narrowness: suspicious of newcomers; doubtful of changing ways; want to keep things as they are and always have been

Snobbishness: overly concerned about manners, dress, and so on; prefer to keep to themselves

Fecklessness: never have a penny; spend beyond their means; happy-go-lucky; careless about what lies ahead

Obviously much yet remains to be explored before teachers can be sure of how best to help children understand what social declassifica-tion may mean to them.

This section has dealt with ways in which the curriculum is being recast to provide children with opportunities to think critically about the process of socialization. In each instance, as we have examined teaching about racial-ethnic bias, gender roles, and classism, we have ended by proposing a set of attitudes that children should be helped to understand. These attitudes present the negative side of issues. Perhaps we can close more positively by proposing that children be helped to develop in common certain enabling attributes that can transcend the constraints of social stereotyping. (See Exhibit 4–5.) Social constraints on learning may be expected to diminish and perhaps disappear as children are able to get together in pursuit of

Exhibit 4-5

Enabling Attributes that May Transcend Racial-Ethnic, Sex, and Class Differences

Attribute	Statements that reflect attribute
1. Desire to do one's best	"Let me try." "This looks funny. What did I do wrong?" "It's not as good as it ought to be." "I need more practice, I can see that." "I'll do better next time."
2. Enjoyment of planning and working with others	"We've done that already." "Can you help us tomorrow, Mrs. Jay?" "And we will need something to cut the wire." "What do we have to do next?" "It will take us a week, I think."
3. Risk taking in pursuit of goal	"Maybe this will work." "This will have to do. I don't have time to fool around." "Why don't we use corrugated cardboard instead?" "Let's try it and see." "What if it doesn't work? So what?"

Exhibit 4-5 (cont.)

Enabling Attributes that May Transcend Racial-Ethnic, Sex, and Class Differences (cont.)

Attribute	Statements that reflect attribute
4. Persistence in pursuit of goal	"Well, we'll just have to start over." "Think how good it will feel to have it finished." "We're making progress." "I'll try again tomorrow." "Just two more and then I'll have read all the Hardy books!"
5. Sympathy with the wants of others	"It's Tommy's turn to talk." "No wonder you don't feel so good." "Then what happened?" "Do the best you can, and it'll be all right." "Let's walk home together. Okay?"
6. Willingness to suffer consequences of wrongdoing, mistakes, or failure	"Yes, I said I would. But I forgot." "I just goofed off." "We just made a mess of it." "It was my fault. I started it." "Do you want me to say I'm sorry?"

Attribute	Statements that reflect attribute
7. Good-humored reception of personal attacks	"I do talk too much." "You don't like me very much, do you?" "My mother would agree with you." "I will try not to be so slow." "I'm sorry."
8. Welcome of unfamiliar ideas	"Say, that's a good idea!" "Who would ever have thought of that?" "Tell me more." "I would like to read that book, too." "Maybe it would work better than this."
9. Generosity in judging others	"All the pictures are good, I think." "Why not divide the cost equally?" "They were both to blame." "Let's play ball!" "Look — he didn't mean to hurt your feelings. He just got excited."
10. Assumption of responsibility for well-being of needful others	"Who hid Billy's glasses?" "I'll share mine with you." "You just hold its mouth open. I'll do the rest." "Jessie don't feel good, Mr. Wagner." "Lean on me."

THE ABILITY TO THINK CRITICALLY

111

common purposes. Perhaps it is only as children are free to learn that they can learn to be really free.

THE CRITICAL APPROACH

The curriculum is being recast to support a much broader base for learning to value. In the preceding chapter and in this, we have summarized what seems to be going on in the field of everyday living. Chapter 3 was given over to the new demand for true mastery in skills teaching. This chapter has dealt with the ways in which content has been reconstituted to increase children's critical awareness of selected problem areas.

Method Is Important

We have long thought that some ways of teaching encourage critical thinking better than others. Our faith in the motivating power of interest, independent study, the project method, and unit organization, as we have tried to make clear, is enduring. There is no doubt that children who have a chance to think for themselves will learn to do so. The rewards that come from self-activity, to use the old-fashioned term, foster and sustain the desire to do one's best and the derring-do and doggedness of the true inquirer. Indeed, the attributes learned through self-activity are those that are most needed for the liberation of children from old ways of thinking.

Learning to value the could-be or might-be over the present range of options calls for many chances to experience the satisfactions that can come from independent and imaginative thinking. The questioning child becomes critically aware as interaction with agemates and adults sharpens the first questions and challenges the first answers.

Critical thinking looms large as a goal in the emerging curriculum for values education. Is it possible to help more children break through the restrictions that impede free choice among ways of being and behaving in all aspects of living? Our answer — and society's — is that we must try.

But choices also should be open among options not yet realized.

These are choices not yet available to anyone, either young or old. Genuine emancipation from choice restriction in everyday living can come only as people are able to imagine things as they might be. This may well be the ultimate challenge to be faced by those who would develop a value-oriented curriculum for children.

Content Comes First

In this chapter, we have contended that study of areas of major concern to society is the best way to think critically, and we have examined the way the curriculum is being revised in three such areas: the environmental crisis, the world of work, and social stereotyping. What is needed, of course, and what the new value-oriented curriculum hopes to achieve, is the coupling of a method that encourages critical thinking with selected content that will yield children new insights into the facts of life — insights that will make for richness and rightness in their choices of what to demand of themselves and of their society.

ACTIVITIES

1. Select one of the procedures aimed at critical thinking shown in Exhibit 4–1. Taking a topic of your own choice, prepare a set of activities for study by children.
2. Of the three approaches to environmental study summarized in Exhibit 4–3, which seems to you of most importance? Why?
3. The aquarium-terrarium proposed for study of the ecosystem on page 95 is remarkable on several counts. Analyze it in terms of the chapter's description of what is needed to stimulate critical thinking (interest, self-activity, and so on). What maintenance problems would you anticipate?
4. Examine the social studies textbooks used by a school to which you have access. What evidence do you find of attention to the nature of the work world?
5. What more can be done to develop appreciation of the usefulness of work? Propose a series of group experiences toward this end.
6. To what extent should children be encouraged to explore possible job choices?

7. Examine the questions in Exhibit 4–4. Would you modify or omit any of these? Propose additions to the list. Can children really be helped to deal with such questions? How?
8. History is being rewritten to provide more attention to racial-ethnic problems and to the contributions of minority group members. Would the same approach be useful as a way of providing fairer treatment of women and the working class?
9. What kinds of changes do you think ought to come about to make the school experience sex fair? Propose a list of changes with your rationale for supporting them.
10. The chapter makes the claim that America is moving toward social declassification. From your own experience, what evidence do you have to support or counter this claim?
11. Examine the list of enabling attributes offered in Exhibit 4–5. Do you find these acceptable as behavorial goals for all children? Are you able to find racial-ethnic, sex, or class biases in the mix?

Values in the Curriculum: What Children Need to Know

The World of Everyday Living

The Cultural Heritage

The Moral-Ethical-Political Realm

Chapter 5

Appreciation of the Arts

Children everywhere in the world come into possession at birth of an arts heritage that in some ways is remarkably similar from one culture to another. Even before they can stand alone, infants may respond to songs and dance music. Among the earliest delights of all young children are naming-rhymes and counting jingles. Chants that have to do with playing games and teasing, stories of family or tribal events, and folk, fairy, and other tales told or read aloud are common elements in the oral culture of humankind. The visual arts, while operating in less striking ways, are also pervasive. Toys, dress, furnishings, buildings or shelters, pictures, art objects — all serve to excite and educate the senses that have to do with sight, touch, and spatial relationships.

WHY TEACH THE ARTS

When children in literate societies enter school, their experience with the arts takes on new dimensions. Most exciting, of course, is access to literature. Children soon discover that books offer an open sesame to riches almost beyond their imagination.

In the visual arts, which include both arts and crafts, children find themselves surrounded by materials and are encouraged to try their hands at any or all of them: poster paint, large sheets of newsprint, easels, brushes, clay, lengths of wood, wool for weaving, textile scraps, and pots of paste and old newspapers for papier-mâché.

Children bring a lot of music with them. But in school they sing new songs, learn folk and square dances, hear kinds of music they may not have heard before, and master some simple instruments. They learn to search out and appreciate unfamiliar pieces from a library of good recordings. In time, they may be able to read music, play instruments of greater complexity and variety, and even compose music to be performed by themselves and others.

In brief, school is where children can gain access to those aspects of the arts heritage that are not automatically encountered simply by growing up in our society. Children may continue to enjoy what is available in the popular culture. Television, radio, comics, picture magazines and books, films, tapes, and records surround people with a varied and everchanging set of resources that add zest to being alive. But the larger human heritage is entered into only through the doorway of formal learning. For most children this occurs in school, although private lessons in some of the arts (primarily music and dance) provide special training to a few children.

Can teachers do a better job of helping children learn to appreciate their cultural heritage? That is the concern of this chapter. The school's responsibility for educating the young to make the most of their formal arts heritage — what is termed *school culture* in contrast to *popular culture* (see Exhibit 5–1) — is already well established. Our treatment of learning to value in the arts area acknowledges the historic role that teachers have accepted of teaching children first for competence in understanding the arts and then for innovativeness or creativity. In this chapter, we shall review current efforts to recast the curriculum to bring about an even greater appreciation of the arts. In the next chapter, we shall note what is happening — and what more should happen — in educating for cultural innovation.

Exhibit 5-1

Range of Arts in the Cultural Heritage

| Arts category | Forms to be found within category | |
	Popular culture	*School culture*
Literature	Nursery rhymes (oral)	Myths, legends
	Folk tales (oral)	Folk tales, fairy tales
	Comics	Poetry
	Magazines	Drama
	Newspapers	Stories, novels
	Picture magazines and books	Biographies, auto-biographies
	Films	Travel books
	Radio programs	Essays, including humor
	Television programs	
	Records	History
		Philosophy
		Informational books of many kinds
Visual arts	Photography	Oil paintings
	Commercial art	Water colors
	Clothing design	Prints
	Furniture design	Murals
	House furnishings	Sculpture
	Flower arranging	Pottery
	Arts and crafts	Architecture
		Gardening
		Landscaping

Exhibit 5-1 (cont.)

Range of Arts in the Cultural Heritage

Arts category	Forms to be found within category	
	Popular culture	*School culture*
Music	Jazz	Chamber music
	Rock and roll	Symphonies
	Soul music	Ballet music
	Country music	Other orchestral works
	Dance music	
	Musical comedies	Electronic music
	Dance: square dance, disco	Folk music: ballads, dances
		Operas, operettas
		Choral works
		Solo works: instrumental and vocal
		Dance: folk dance, ballet

KNOWLEDGE OF ALTERNATIVES

What does competence in appreciation call for? As far as literature is concerned, no one has defined it better than Samuel Taylor Coleridge. "I learned from him," wrote Coleridge of a beloved master at Christ's Hospital School, "that poetry, even that of the loftiest and, seemingly, that of the wildest odes, had a logic of its own, as severe as that of science; and more difficult, because more subtle, more complex, and dependent on more and more fugitive causes." Reading literature requires more than ability to recognize or pronounce words. "In the truly great poets, he would say, there is a reason assignable, not only for every word, but for the position of every word." Looking about him in his later years, Coleridge would complain that the young, "these nurslings of improved pedagogy," had been taught mainly to "dispute and decide" rather than to understand.[1]

John Ruskin also emphasized the need for

> the kind of word-by-word examination of your author which is rightly called "reading"; watching every accent and expression, and putting ourselves always in the author's place, annihilating our own personality, and seeking to enter into his, so as to be able assuredly to say, "Thus Milton thought," not "Thus I thought, in misreading Milton."

Ruskin, too, had scorn for teachers who failed to demand close attention to the meaning of literary texts. Modern education, with its emphasis on "thus I thought," resulted in "giving people the faculty of thinking wrong on every conceivable subject of importance to them."[2]

The point to be garnered here is that *understanding* is the basis of appreciation. A work of art, whether it be a poem, a painting, or a piece of music, needs to be studied. Casual acquaintance is not enough. If choice among alternatives in the world of the arts is to mean anything, then the alternatives have to be truly accessible to the young reader or viewer or listener.

[1] S. T. Coleridge, *Biographia Literaria* (New York: E. P. Dutton and Company, 1906), pp. 4, 6.

[2] John Ruskin, *Sesame and Lilies* (New York: Thomas Y. Crowell and Company, n.d.), p. 65.

Enrichment and Ennoblement

The end of appreciation is something more than mere comprehension. The process of entering into a work of art enlarges one's outlook on the world. "Anyone who looks at life in all its aspects will see how far the remarkable, the great, and the beautiful predominate in all things," Longinus claimed in extolling the benefits to be gained from reading Homer and Plato, "and he will soon understand to what end we have been born."[3]

Is poetry still good for something? T. S. Eliot would contend that it is, for poetry "may effect revolutions in sensibility such as are periodically needed; may help to break up the conventional modes of perception and valuation which are perpetually forming, and make people see the world afresh, or some new part of it." Moreover, poetry may alert people to "the deeper, unnamed feelings" of their subconscious and cause them to confront themselves.[4]

Children can get caught up in poetry of many kinds. As Bernard Berenson noted, visual arts experiences can "console and ennoble and transport us."[5] And music, too, can enrich the lives of those who gain access to its beauty.

No doubt these thoughts may seem a bit grandiose when we think of teaching elementary school children. But knowledge of the arts can have a profound effect on young lives, as novelist William Dean Howells acknowledged in describing his own encounter with Greek and Roman mythology as a ten-year-old.

> . . . If it had ever been a question of sacrificing to Diana, I do not really know whether I should have been able to refuse. I adored indiscriminately all the tribes of nymphs and naiads, demigods and heroes, as well as the high ones of Olympus; and I am afraid that by day I dwelt in a world peopled and ruled by them, though I faithfully said my prayers at night, and fell asleep in sorrow for my sins.[6]

[3] Longinus, *On Great Writing*, trans. G. M. A. Grube (New York: Liberal Arts Press, 1957), p. 47.

[4] T. S. Eliot, *The Use of Poetry and the Use of Criticism* (Cambridge, Mass.: Harvard University Press, 1933), p. 149.

[5] Bernard Berenson, *Aesthetics and History* (Garden City, N.J.: Doubleday and Company, 1948), p. 25.

[6] W. D. Howells, *My Literary Passions* (New York: Harper and Brothers, 1895), pp. 10–11.

A Point of Departure

One reason to help develop competence in the arts is to provide prospective new contributors to the cultural heritage with a foundation from which to launch ventures of their own. The miracle of Greek mythology was its creation of a world in which humans could feel at home. It was a world founded on reality and peopled by gods and goddesses whose behavior, if not always reasonable, was at least comprehensible.[7] Howells, whose fascination with Greek mythology we have noted, in turn created in *The Rise of Silas Lapham* and *A Modern Instance* a mythology of his own about the gods and goddesses of American business enterprise. His books, and those of his good friends Mark Twain and Henry James, made people newly aware of a world in which getting on financially and socially seemed to be the principal occupations of upper middle–class Americans, both at home and abroad.

Each generation creates a new picture of reality. The arts are integral to this process. The characters, the images, the motifs that help redefine what life is like transcend the world as it has been known. Thus, people come to understand more than they did about how life is or how it can be. In looking ahead at the end of World War II, critic Isaac Rosenfeld saw the task of the creator to be helping humankind find out more about joyous living, for the war itself had taught enough about the world of horrors.[8]

A Better Environment for All

One further good reason for teaching well in this area, selfish though it may seem, is that learning to appreciate the arts redounds to the benefit of us all. If we really want a well-funded public broadcasting system to develop, for example, we ought to get busy and teach more about what television — the most powerful and pervasive of today's visual arts — is doing to us and could do for us. Libraries, art museums, city or county orchestras, and public television stations

---

[7] Edith Hamilton, *Mythology* (New York: Mentor Books, 1953).
[8] Isaac Rosenfeld, "The Meaning of Terror" (1949), in *An Age of Enormity* (Cleveland: World Publishing Company, 1962).

come into being because enough individuals to matter find that they do not want to live without them.

Why do we need to teach the arts? As has been pointed out in this section, children cannot really choose among arts alternatives unless they develop competence in dealing with a range of options for enjoyment. Although popular culture is easily accessible, the larger heritage offers dimensions for the enrichment and ennoblement of human experience that ought to be recognized as the birthright of all children. Nor can children learn the arts on the run, so to speak, as they themselves become writers, readers, singers, or watchers of television, for creative behavior needs a base to depart from. Finally, a more widespread appreciation of the arts can lead to a more satisfying culture for all members of society.

Now we will have a look at what is happening — or should be happening — in the area of teaching children to appreciate their cultural heritage. Our review will encompass literature, the visual arts, and music.

ENTERING THE WONDERLAND OF BOOKS

Literature is a vital part of the cultural heritage. Thus, knowledge of it cannot be left to chance. Today children are fortunate in having ready access — through public libraries, school book collections, and bookstores — to a profusion of books on all sorts of subjects. Many excellent children's books are available in paperback; as a result, children are buying books for themselves — something truly new.

Good books and children who can read are the starting points. But learning to value in the field of literature takes a lot of doing by both students and teachers. If children are to be able to choose rewardingly from what is available to them, they need to know how varied the possibilities are. Children can learn to read without actually having read much. Growing competence in reading widely and well yields the kind of satisfaction that makes it possible for the young reader to choose intelligently among all the books that might be read, and between reading good books and investing time in other pursuits.

The only way to guarantee that children will have many satisfying experiences in reading a range of good books is to treat literature as a subject field worthy of study like any other. Commitment to reading widely will come as children discover how much they gain from guided experiences in making the most of many kinds of good books.

Some persons devoted to both books and children may still insist that children can be counted on to come to love reading if they grow up surrounded by a lot of good books and are encouraged to read whatever is of interest to them. But we would argue that such an approach does not provide for any child what a well-organized literature program can provide. Random reading is not enough. Some books are plainly more worth reading than others. In addition, literature programs are concerned about depth of understanding. Good books are worth thinking about — and talking about.

The debate over how to organize the new literature programs has been in full swing since the mid-sixties.[9] What is the best framework for such programs? Let us examine some of the proposals that have attracted attention.

Classics, Old and New

Many literature programs are based on the idea that there are certain key works — classics — that should be part of every child's experience with books. Teachers interested in this kind of organized literature program choose particular works — such as the Andersen fairy tales, *Peter Rabbit, Pinocchio, Treasure Island*, and *Tom Sawyer* — to present to children, hoping that other teachers will do the same. By the time they complete their schooling, children will have had an experience with literature that has been shared by many other children over the years.[10]

Programs such as these often include new books along with the old. Younger readers might be given a chance to read and talk about *Madeline* and *The Bears on Hemlock Mountain*, while older children might be offered *The Hobbit, Island of the Blue Dolphins*, and *The Wind in the Willows*. The list of fine books seems to be ever increasing. To the books that have won Newbery and Caldecott awards might be added many other outstanding titles worthy of inclusion in broadly based literature programs for children.

---

[9] See Alexander Frazier, ed., *Ends and Issues: Points of Decision in the Development of the English Curriculum* (Champaign, Ill.: National Council of Teachers of English, 1966).

[10] See Mary J. Lickteig, *Introduction to Children's Literature* (Columbus, Ohio: Charles E. Merrill Publishing Company, 1975), pp. 310–331.

A study of the works of outstanding authors of children's books is another useful way to organize literature programs. Robert Louis Stevenson and Beatrix Potter have more than one good book to their credit, and so do Robert McCloskey and Marguerite De Angeli. Like other readers, children are happy when one good book leads to another, and studying an author's output offers linkage of this kind.

Themes as a Basis for Study

Literature programs can also be organized around themes. The books that are chosen to be read all relate to a particular theme. There are many possible sources of themes, for example, the area of human virtues. What books could help children think and talk about courage (or friendship, loyalty, honor, endurance, love of country)?

Themes may be drawn from human relations. Ethnic and racial problems have become a major concern in children's books as in society at large. Family patterns, rural-urban contrasts, relations between generations, contrasts between different cultures, and war and peace are other aspects of social interaction around which worthwhile reading and discussion programs may be organized.[11]

Books also may be presented in terms of general content or purpose — books of adventure; stories of romance; humorous books; books on sports, hobbies, or careers; and so on. For older children, books may sometimes be grouped by historical periods or by region, and perhaps related directly to social studies.[12] Books occasionally may focus on very large themes — people and nature, people at work and play, children around the world.

Since literature encompasses all of human experience, deciding which works to present to children is always more or less arbitrary. The main concern ought to be relevance to the reader. Themes can help in the selection of suitable titles from among all the many and varied high-quality books that children might rewardingly read.

---

[11] See Virginia M. Reid, ed., *Reading Ladders for Human Relations* (Champaign, Ill.: National Council of Teachers of English, 1972).

[12] See Dewey W. Chambers, *Children's Literature in the Curriculum* (Chicago: Rand McNally and Company, 1971), pp. 37–71; and Jane Yolen, *Children's Literature: An Issues Approach* (Lexington, Mass.: D. C. Heath and Company, 1976).

Types of Literature

Conscientious teachers often call the attention of children to particular types of literature. They may want to introduce an unfamiliar kind, such as biography, or help children learn to appreciate a genre that at first may seem somewhat forbidding, poetry for example. They may feel obligated to make sure that children know the most popular fairy tales or fables or myths. Or they may wish to present a literary form as the basis for writing or some other kind of creative experience.

These are all good reasons for studying various types of literature. Some teachers, however, believe that a more formal effort ought to be made to bring awareness of literary forms to children.[13] In one approach, teachers may agree among themselves that certain types of literature will be highlighted in the early grades of school and others in the later. In another, the same types may be represented in children's reading every year, but with increasingly mature works selected for study as the children progress in grade level. Children might thus be expected to grow into an understanding of the characteristics of each genre without undue attention to the more technical differences between, say, kinds of poetry or varieties of nonfiction.

Elements of Critical Analysis

Can children learn to deal with literature in terms of critical analysis? Any careful reading of a good book may be presumed to involve attention to many of the elements of critical reading. If the work is fiction, plot development, characterization, and the role played by setting will certainly be examined. For any work, language and how it is used will be discussed.

But some persons have argued that a more direct attention to critical analysis is needed if children are to be helped to develop dependable criteria for book selection. Concern for structure may encompass analyzing a story or poem in terms of episodes, noting use of symbols to tie episodes together, or becoming familiar with basic types of plots — the journey of search, the series of tests of strength,

[13] See Mary Lou White, *Children's Literature: Criticism and Response* (Columbus, Ohio: Charles E. Merrill Publishing Company, 1976), pp. 1–7.

Exhibit 5-2

Literature: Its Varied Media

Types of literature	Appearance in different media					
	Print	*Print-and-picture*	*Comics*	*Films*	*Radio and television*	*Records*
Folk tales, fairy tales	X	X	X	X	X	X
Myths and legends	X	X	X	X	X	X
Poetry	X				X	X
Drama	X	X	X	X	X	X
Stories, novels	X	X	X	X	X	X
Biographies, autobiographies	X	X	X	X	X	
Travel books	X	X		X		
Essays, including humor	X		X		X	X
History	X	X		X	X	
Philosophy	X					
Informational books in general	X	X				

the mystery that may be solved, and so on. Attention to language may go beyond choice of words to include a focus on figurative language, sentence variety, and paragraph development.

Critical analysis is part of any program of literature study.[14] It can also become the framework within which pieces of literature are selected for study.

The New Media

We have looked at several ways to organize the study of literature so that children will have good reasons for going deeply into what books have to offer. Children can read selected works of a high order without too much attention to anything but the books themselves; they can read in terms of theme or type of literature; or they can learn to analyze books by use of a set of critical concepts that they may also find useful in their later years. Most programs probably draw on more than one of these approaches.

An aspect of literature that is sometimes neglected in the classroom is the function of the new media. The nonprint media tend to be relegated to the popular culture, as noted in Exhibit 5–1. Yet at their best, they are often carriers of the formal heritage of true literature. Perhaps one of the newer challenges in developing appreciation will be to assist children in relating types of literature to varieties of media. (See Exhibit 5–2 for an attempt to express such relationships.)

LEARNING TO SEE THE VARIETIES OF ART

Since 1965 when the National Endowment for the Arts was funded and monies also became available from the newly passed Elementary and Secondary Education Act, many new ventures in teaching appreciation of the visual arts have been undertaken. No single definition of what art appreciation involves has emerged; instead, schools have utilized a variety of approaches, some of which we shall examine in this section. One thing is clear: educators have moved beyond the assumption that free-time experimentation with a miscellany of art materials is sufficient introduction to the arts.

---

[14] *Ibid.*, pp. 223–236.

Art appreciation calls for conscious art encounters of sufficient duration for the experiences to have an effect. The authors of a popular textbook on art education express in question form what they believe to be the steps or phases of the process:

What do you see? (Description)
How are things put together? (Formal analysis)
What is the artist trying to say? (Interpretation)
What do you think of it? (Judgment)[15]

Some teachers might want to substitute for the third question one less likely to be confusing: "What is the artist trying to do?" Also, keeping in mind the remarks of Coleridge and Ruskin quoted earlier in this chapter, a teacher might want to substitute "How well does the artist do it?" for "What do you think of it?" But there does seem to be general agreement that if children are to develop the ability to choose consciously and intelligently among art experiences, they must spend more time in looking at what is around them and thinking about what they see.

One well-planned program is organized around six categories of activities:

Learning to perceive
Learning the language of art
Learning about artists and how they work
Criticizing and judging art
Learning to use art tools and materials
Building productive artistic abilities[16]

For this program, its sponsors have developed over a thousand learning tasks or things to do, stated in behavioral terms.

What we are concerned with here is the development of a framework for formal study of our art heritage. Such a framework can be based on many different ways of analyzing the field. (See Exhibit

[15] Charles D. Gaitskell and Al Hurwitz, *Children and Their Art*, 3rd ed. (New York: Harcourt Brace Jovanovich, 1975), p. 464.
[16] Guy Hubbard and Mary J. Rouse, "Art — Meaning, Method, and Media: A Structured Program for Elementary Classrooms," in *Programs of Promise: Art in the Schools*, ed. Al Hurwitz (New York: Harcourt Brace Jovanovich, 1972), p. 18.

5–3.) No single approach is likely to be totally satisfactory; thus, seeking a combination in terms of the needs of students, available resources, and teacher competence would seem to be advisable.

Access to Art Treasures

Museums are not located within reach of all children. But the art treasures of the world are newly accessible in ways that emancipate instruction from dependence upon the real thing. Through color reproductions of paintings, water colors, and prints and through photographs of art objects from all over the world, everyone can become acquainted with great art to some degree. In André Malraux's words, books of high-quality art pictures have become "museums without walls."[17]

The school's first obligation is to build a good collection of photographs, slides, books, and a variety of original works — prints and paintings and perhaps some pieces of sculpture. What then? How should children and the school and other collections be brought together?

An example of a specific appreciation study is provided in a report from University City, Missouri (a suburb of St. Louis). The basis of the study was a touring photo exhibit of African Art sent out by the National Gallery of Art in Washington, D.C., and augmented by art objects borrowed from local collections.

> A teaching packet was prepared for use prior to the exhibit in elementary classes. A set of slides showed African art objects; a script described the slides; a tape presented selected music from African tribes; transparencies included maps of Africa for geography studies; and information sheets on Africa were available for distribution.[18]

More than 4,000 children toured the exhibit.

[17] André Malraux, *Museum without Walls*, trans. Stuart Gilbert and Francis Price (Garden City, N.Y.: Doubleday and Company, 1967).

[18] Stanley S. Madeja, *All the Arts for Every Child: Final Report on the Arts in General Education Project in the School District of University City, Missouri* (New York: The John D. Rockefeller Third Fund, 1973), p. 68.

Exhibit 5-3

Some Bases for Organizing Art Appreciation Experiences

Basis	Examples of study topics
Periods or movements	Etruscan art French impressionists Hudson River School Pop art
Forms	Landscape painting Portrait painting Genre painting: domestic scenes and stories Sculpture: African bronzes
Functions	Ceremonial and religious artifacts Record of historic events Public buildings, plazas Decoration in general
Elements	Color, line, shape Proportion, symmetry Composition Texture
Media	Oil, water color, photography Clay, marble, bronze Woodcut, silk screen, etching Wood, stone, steel (buildings)

Basis	Examples of study topics
Problems	Preservation of works
	Public acceptance of the new
	Support of the artist
	Learning about art of other lands and peoples
Themes	Nature
	Great persons or events
	National contributions to the arts
	Famous buildings
Trends and issues	Abstraction vs. representation
	Romanticism vs. classicism
	Surrealism
	Functionalism (architecture)
Artists	Rembrandt
	Cézanne, Monet
	Orozco, Rivera
	Georgia O'Keefe
Selected works	"Primavera" (Botticelli)
	Ceremonial mask (Nigeria)
	"Between Rounds" (Eakins)
	Larkin building (Wright)

Visual Aspects of the Environment

Art treasures form an important part of the cultural heritage. But they have to be sought out to be enjoyed. A broader base for appreciation can be found in our everyday surroundings. Perhaps art appreciation can be considered as part of environmental education, which is usually defined as the study of the interaction between and among living things and their physical setting. But it seems simpler to propose another kind of education-in-environment, one that focuses on the visual aspects of what is all about us.

Many of these aspects are being examined by children today as the curriculum is recast to include community study. In seeking to relocate art education in the total environment, we may want to paraphrase Malraux and speak of the *school* without walls. Elsewhere at some length we have argued for adventuring beyond the school as one way to revitalize children's learning.[19] What follows is a list of some of the visual aspects of the outside-the-school environment that would seem to be worth studying:

Individual buildings: Every community has buildings of interest because of their period, style, or design. Contrasts may also be studied among new buildings. Differences in function reflect themselves in a variety of ways that deserve study.

Plazas and malls: Civic centers, convention centers, and shopping malls can be studied to see how they allocate space in new ways to take account of such elements as traffic flow, parking, exhibit or sales areas, and weather protection.

Urban renewal projects: How can good older buildings be preserved and combined with needed new buildings? What guidelines are being followed locally? How do these compare with those in use in such cities as Philadelphia, Savannah, and St. Louis?

Apartment complexes and subdivisions: Contrasts in design of low-cost, middle-income, and expensive housing can be noted, as well as design of common facilities — recreational areas, greenbelts, and schools.

Commercial parks: Layout and location of areas reserved for business-industrial development may be studied in relation to access to throughways, airports, population centers, and so on.

[19] See Alexander Frazier, *Adventuring, Mastering, Associating* (Washington, D.C.: Association for Supervision and Curriculum Development, 1976), chap. 2.

Parks and gardens: Landscaping and gardening involve design principles that may be derived from on-the-spot study.

Preserves: When should watercourses, forests, swamplands, and other natural areas be set aside for preservation? What restrictions may be needed to curtail or govern public use?

Highways and parkways: Changes of great magnitude have come about since the first national roads were built. Many localities provide examples of earlier roadways that point up changes in adjustment to terrain, relationship to waterways, use of land, and the like.

City, county, and state planning: Right of way, zoning, annexation, and other regulations can be studied to see how they affect community land use. Do the laws of different divisions of government complement one another adequately?

The planning arts, to which we shall return in the next chapter, are aimed at altering for the better also the use of a community's natural setting and built environment. Most of us only half see what is happening or changing around us. With proper teaching, children should begin to be aware of the principles involved in community design and thus may become better able than we have been to support the development of a total environment that will be visually as well as socially rewarding.

Artists and Craftspeople at Work

Another approach to learning to appreciate the arts is to observe artists and craftspeople at work. If the idea of a school without walls — "the everywhere school"[20] — were to prevail, then the studios and workshops of a community might be enlarged to admit children as watchers and learners. Of course, adults engaged in turning out art products can hardly also be full-time teachers. But they can be resources for learning, as many schools have discovered. A study trip to a crafts cooperative, for example, may provide children with a chance to see leather workers, jewelry makers, potters, and weavers actually at work.

[20] Carol Testa, *New Educational Facilities: An International Survey* (Boulder, Colo.: Westview Press, 1975), p. 14.

Another way for children to learn about arts and crafts at first hand, which has been much tested in recent years through federal funding, is to relocate artists and craftspeople in the schools. There they can show children what art is all about by working in a corner of a classroom for at least part of the day or the week. Children will learn by watching how a painting or other project is planned, how work on it progresses, and how changes are made along the way to a finished product.

More often than not, when artists and craftspeople come to school, they find they cannot remain in the corner. They venture out and become part-time artist-teachers. Their projects gain junior partners. And children find themselves learning through participation as well as through observation. Among the cooperative activities reported from schools with artists in residence have been these:

Sculpture: a bright orange, dextron-tubing, geometric sculpture ten feet high, twelve feet long (cost: $32); also a twelve-foot-high chrome eagle — Troy, Alabama

Town planning: a model of a new city, Purium — Venice, California

Clay: 600 pounds of clay dumped on a twenty-foot spread of plastic sheeting, with blindfolded children working to shape it as they wished — Providence, Rhode Island[21]

Playground structure: children, acting as clients, and a university architecture class worked together on a three-story structure with platforms, lookout tower, climbing poles, slide — University City, Missouri[22]

Playground sculpture: metal, plastic forms, bedsheets, and lights were used to stimulate children to design their own "arrangements" — Columbus, Ohio[23]

Such cooperative art projects apparently tend to take on a certain size in comparison to work that is individual in nature and has a

[21] Foregoing examples drawn from Bennett Schiff, *Artists in Schools* (Washington, D.C.: U.S. Government Printing Office, 1973), summarized from various pages.

[22] Madeja, *All the Arts,* pp. 56–60.

[23] J. David Boyle, ed., *Arts Impact — Curriculum for Change: A Summary Report* (University Park, Pa.: Arts Impact Evaluation Team, Pennsylvania State University, 1973), p. 13.

product that can be stored in a locker or stacked atop a cabinet until the next day.

In the long run, of course, serious artists and craftspeople, however effective their efforts might be, can hardly be expected to devote a great deal of time to working with children unless teaching is to become a major means of their support. In that case, problems of professional training and certification have to be dealt with.

There are many viable approaches to art appreciation. Children can learn to appreciate art through the study of art treasures. They have much to gain, too, from becoming increasingly aware of the visual aspects of their total environment. Some things they undoubtedly learn best from direct observation of artists and craftspeople at work, as well as through working with adult professionals in the planning and production of art works.

Many school districts are recasting the curriculum to provide more opportunities for children to learn what art is all about. As in literature and music, making choices in this realm of the cultural heritage cannot be broadly based unless or until the chooser knows what there is to select from and has experienced a range of satisfactions greater than is open to most children without formal help. Valuing some art experiences above others or learning to value many kinds of art experiences is something that has to be learned. Such is the point of view behind the new programs for art appreciation.

HEARING THE MUSIC OF MANY DIFFERENT DRUMMERS

This morning members of the Camerata Trio are interacting with children of the Union Springs school in a variety of ways. In a special class, Charles Forbes holds up his cello and asks if anyone knows what it is. "A guitar?" ventures one child. In the kindergarten, Paula Hatcher plays her flute for dancing. Pianist Glenn Jacobson is playing lead in a first-grade rhythm band.

In the afternoon the trio performs for an assembly. Jacobson introduces each piece:

"Usually, when you play the piano you use your fingers. Here's a piece that starts out differently." And he plays a Henry Cowell bit using forearms on the keyboard. Then, he plays East Indian drums and Forbes picks up a cello pizzicato accompaniment and there is music in the school.[24]

The children beat time on the floor with their hands, caught up in the complicated rhythm.

> And so, in Union Springs, Alabama, a group of some 80 elementary school children listen, enthralled, to Henry Cowell, East Indian music, Twelfth Century Medieval motets, and a late baroque trio.[25]

The Camerata Trio is in residence as part of the Artists-in-the-Schools program to which we have already referred.

Is it too much to hope that all children will have a chance to hear such a variety of music — and have a chance, too, to interact on occasion with adult performers? People are able today, technologically speaking, to experience more kinds of music than ever before. Children grow up with radios in their homes, in their cars, and at their ears. By the time they are four or five, many have their own radios or record players. Records and tapes are on sale even in supermarkets. And in communities of any size, FM radio stations provide a richness of resources to choose from that is new to listeners both old and young.

All Kinds of Music

The task of deciding which music to bring to children in school cannot be left to occasional visitors like the Camerata Trio. Nor can schools afford to wait for a publisher to put together a multimedia music education program. At this point in time, schools have to do most of the planning themselves if they are to meet the challenge of providing children with a broader base of in-depth experiences with music.

In developing music appreciation programs, there are some questions that deserve consideration about the dimensions or directions in which the curriculum needs to be recast:

[24] Schiff, *Artists in Schools*, p. 56.
[25] *Ibid.*, p. 57.

Old music and new: Are children getting enough exposure to the classical heritage? Do they also have a chance to hear avant-garde music — electronic and the like?

Varieties of contemporary music: If children are experiencing today's music, are they sampling all of it? Can more be done in serious terms with jazz, rock-and-roll, the blues, pseudo-folk?

African and Eastern music: Do children have a chance to hear the instruments that make African music so vital and varied?[26] Do children realize that the United States, according to Ravi Shankar, has led the world in appreciation of India's great classical music?[27]

Vocal music: Do children learn about the varieties of vocal music: songs of many kinds for solo and ensemble singing, choral works, dramatic singing in operas, operettas, and musical comedies?

Instrumental music: Do children hear a variety of musical instruments often enough to begin to distinguish and enjoy the differences among them?

Individual and group performances: Do children have a chance to hear solo performances of high quality? Do older children hear distinguished orchestras with differing interpretations of standard works?

We are assuming that children's experience with many kinds of music will come through performances by the children themselves, attending or participating in live performances by other persons, and listening to recordings. Undoubtedly, reliance on recordings will have to be heavy in any program that tries for depth as well as range. Thus, as central and classroom record collections are developed, teachers will need to work closely with specialists who know the record output.

Elements and Forms of Music

As children learn to read music, understand something about rhythm, and gain some sense of the differences in the way musical

---

[26] See Frances Bebey, *African Music: A People's Art*, trans. Josephine Bennett (New York: Lawrence Hill and Company, 1975).

[27] Ravi Shankar, foreword to Peggy Holroyde, *The Music of India* (New York: Praeger Publishers, 1972), p. 14.

compositions are put together, they acquire knowledge that can contribute to their competence in understanding, responding to, and talking about many kinds of music.

Approaches to teaching the elements and forms of music vary. In one method, young children begin with "the rhythmic swing and pulsations in music."[28] Free body movement, imitative and dramatic activities, games and dances, playing simple instruments — all help to develop a surer sense of rhythm. Further teaching of music will thus be assured of a firm foundation.

Teaching may also be based on one of the several organized programs that have gained adherents over the years. In the Kodaly method, for example, three-year-olds chant nursery rhymes, mark the beat by clapping it out or stepping it off, play percussion instruments of several sorts, and learn a repertoire of songs and singing games. The Orff approach makes use of specially designed instruments so that beginners can make music of their own. The Carabo-Cone program is based on learning through movement, guided games, and play.[29]

If the teacher so desires, a direct assault may be made on teaching the basic elements — melody, rhythm, harmony, tempo, dynamics, tone color, and form.[30] Procedures and lesson plans for developing specific concepts in all these areas can be prepared for use by whoever wants to make sure that children really do learn something about music as well as have a good time with it.

The Uses of Music

What is music good for? Finding answers to this question is another way to help children learn music appreciation. Music appears in every culture as

> a kind of expression of the most basic values and feelings of people. Thus, whatever it is that music does for people, it somehow involves

---

[28] Marguerite V. Hood, *Teaching Rhythm and Using Classroom Instruments* (Englewood Cliffs, N.J.: Prentice-Hall, 1970), p. 7.

[29] Robert E. Nye and Vernice T. Nye, *Essentials of Teaching Elementary School Music* (Englewood Cliffs, N.J.: Prentice-Hall, 1974).

[30] Marylee McMurray Lament, *Music in Elementary Education: Enjoy, Experience, and Learn* (New York: The Macmillan Company, 1976), chaps. 6–10.

man's quest for an understanding of the world and of himself. On a larger scale, music (along with the other arts) is a vehicle for the expression of what is happening in the culture of the performer, composer, or listener, an expression of things in that culture that cannot be readily verbalized.[31]

People have sent messages across distances by pounding on drums. People have marched off to war to stirring music and down the aisle to the joyous strains of a wedding march. People — great crowds of people — have raised their voices in national anthems. People have sung work songs or chants to keep their work rhythm straight as they pulled in nets or pried rails back into line. People have sung songs of worship in camp meetings and cathedrals, and they have celebrated harvests with festive dances. People have expressed their grief in tender ballads and their love in songs and dances both tender and gay. People have delighted in playacting that brought song and dance and spectacle to the stage. They have been eager everywhere to listen to good music sung and played for itself alone. Wherever and whenever possible, people have gained satisfaction and joy in making music for themselves and for others.

Can children be helped to understand all this? Certainly, the functions of music can be spelled out, albeit in a somewhat simplified way. (See Exhibit 5–4 for a chart that brings the functions of music together.) The usefulness of a functional approach to music may need to be tested out, with particular reference to its bearing on children's becoming producers as well as consumers of music.

If children are to be able to get the most out of music, they must have experiences with many varieties of music. They need to understand some of the elements and forms of music. And they should be aware of the ways in which music functions in people's lives. Only when children are conscious of how varied music is, develop enough competence to gain satisfaction from a good many kinds of music, and have opportunities to experience these satisfactions again and again, can their choice of what to listen and respond to be said to be really free.

[31] Bruno Nettl, "The Role of Music in Culture: Iran, a Recently Developed Nation," in Charles Hamm, Bruno Nettl, and Ronald Byrnside, *Contemporary Music and Music Cultures* (Englewood Cliffs, N.J.: Prentice-Hall, 1975), pp. 71–72.

Exhibit 5-4

The Functions of Music

	Type of music	
Function	*Vocal*	*Instrumental*
Communicating (over distance)	Yodels	Drum messages Band music (at sports events)
Marching, parading	Marching songs	Marches: military, wedding, funeral, parade
Uniting together	War songs Patriotic songs	Dances: tribal
Working	Work songs and chants	Recorded music in stores and factories
Worshiping	Masses Oratorios Hymns	Processionals
Celebrating, rejoicing	Victory hymns and chants Holiday songs	Victory dances Festival music Folk dances

	Type of music	
Function	*Vocal*	*Instrumental*
Grieving	Ballads Lamentations	Funeral marches
Romancing, courting	Love songs	Dances of many kinds
Playacting	Opera Operetta Musical comedy	Incidental music for plays and background music for movies
Pleasing self and others, entertaining	Art songs, popular songs Choral works	Chamber music Ballet Symphonies Solo works of many kinds

WHAT WE ARE AIMING AT

Knowledge has been the catchword of this chapter. A lot has to be learned by children about literature, the visual arts, and music for choice among alternatives in these areas to mean anything. As a result, many schools have committed themselves to more thorough-going programs in the arts. Literature is being recognized as a subject field, and a number of approaches to its organized study are being tried out. The visual arts are receiving more serious attention; programs have been developed to help children learn more about the art treasures to which they are heirs, develop visual awareness of the total environment, and profit from observation of and participation with adult artists and craftspeople. Schools have also been allocating more time to encouraging children's growing musical competence.

Such familiarity is the base needed for genuine appreciation of the arts. By helping children experience the satisfactions to be derived from a wider range of options, we enable them to choose the more rewarding as against the less rewarding aspects of their cultural heritage and to enjoy a greater variety of experiences than would have been open to them without our teaching.

Let us close this discussion by looking briefly at some of the concerns we must keep in mind as we recast the curriculum to give children more chances to enjoy their cultural heritage.

Talk Is Not Enough

Appreciation of the arts can become a matter of throwing words around without too much interest in depth of experience. Is this book fiction or nonfiction? Is this painting impressionist or expressionist — or something else again? Is this piece of music a sonata or a concerto? All too often in the past, the main goal of art appreciation courses was to teach children how to label art. Experiencing the art came second, or not at all.

Ease of identification of form, period, and the like — and the vocabulary that goes along with it — should come as a product of many experiences, and not as a precursor. Children will learn the appropriate terminology if the right questions are asked: What is this book saying to us? What is this picture showing us? For whom was this music written — and why?

Coleridge and Ruskin were not opposed to talking about literature as long as the talk had the right target. What does Milton say? What is there to learn from Plato and Homer? In contrast, the art historian E. H. Gombrich described the breed of gallery goers who walk through with catalogs in hand:

> Every time they stop in front of a picture they eagerly search for its number. We can watch them thumbing their book, and as soon as they have found the title or name they walk on. They might just as well have stayed at home, for they have hardly looked at the painting.

Labeling art works may be an outcome of study but ought not to be an end in itself. We would like art study "to open eyes, not to loosen tongues."[32]

The Need for Both Content and Skills

The competence basic to appreciation involves a balance between content and skills. Children need to read and think about different kinds of books. They also need to develop proficiency in doing some writing of their own. Children need to encounter and wonder about many kinds of art products. They should also learn how to handle a brush, shape a pot, and weave a length of cloth. Children need to hear and respond to music of all sorts. They also need to learn to make music — to sing, play a recorder, jot down a melody to go with a poem they have written.

In the old days, teachers may have relied too much on doing as a way of developing competence. Of course, writing, painting, and singing contribute to appreciation. But children can write, paint, and sing well without necessarily learning much about Milton, Rembrandt, or Beethoven. Skills — although useful and desirable — are no substitute for knowledge of the arts. Both are necessary in a good arts appreciation program.

[32] From *The Story of Art*, 12th ed., by E. H. Gombrich, published by Phaidon Press, Oxford, England, and E. P. Dutton, New York; copyright © 1972 by Phaidon Press, Ltd. Reprinted by permission of Praeger Publishers, a division of Holt, Rinehart and Winston, and of Phaidon Press.

Experiences that Really Satisfy

We already know a good deal about how to provide children with cultural experiences that really count for something. Live encounters, such as study trips to museums or attendance at children's concerts or children's theatre productions, may be best. Nowadays recordings and filmstrips are wonderful resources as well.

Work stations or centers can also play an important role. They help put everything together where children can get at it; let children choose their own time for completing common assignments; and provide opportunities for children to make what they want with materials in the art center, experiment as they wish with instruments in the music center, and select whatever books they wish to read from the several hundred, ever-changing titles in the library corner.[33]

And yet so much more could be done.

Today children ought to have even more help than they have had in the past in learning to value the satisfactions that can be derived from their cultural heritage. Literature, the visual arts, and music need to be taught in such a way that children — all children — will learn to appreciate what is theirs by right of birth. Only then will they be able to express in action the value they attach to those experiences most likely to enrich immediate living and ennoble the human spirit.

ACTIVITIES

1. Examine the range of arts shown in Exhibit 5–1. Can you add any items to the lists provided for popular and school cultures?
2. What does knowledge of alternatives as a basis for valuing mean to you? What must be present for an alternative to be meaningful in literature, the visual arts, or music? Why?
3. Some persons fear that if children are required to read good books, they may come to hate all reading. Which of the ways proposed for organizing a literature program do you think would be least likely to cause this reaction among children? Why?
4. Select one of the ways to organize a literature program and prepare a

---

[33] For a report on promising practices in individualized instruction, see Delmo Della-Dora and Lois J. Blanchard, eds., *Moving toward Self-Directed Learning* (Arlington, Va.: Association for Supervision and Curriculum Development, 1979).

specific lesson or experience in terms of it. List books to be read, activities to be undertaken, and ways of sharing results of the experience.

5. Examine the bases for organizing art appreciation experiences shown in Exhibit 5–3. Select one of these and prepare a sample lesson.

6. If you were to undertake a program of visual environmental education, what principles would you be trying to develop?

7. Do you think the kinds of music proposed for examination by children are inclusive enough? How would you analyze the field of music to present a better range and balance?

8. Can you think of experiences children could have in school that would help clarify the different uses of music (see Exhibit 5–4)?

9. Do you agree with the factors identified as those that teachers should be concerned with in teaching art appreciation? Which of these would you say is most troublesome? What others might be added?

Chapter 6

Creative Behavior

In the process of helping children learn to value the arts, a balance has to be established between appreciation and creation. In "The American Scholar," Ralph Waldo Emerson expressed this need as a challenge to a young nation. Use books, but at the same time be wary of them, for "the mind of the Past" can weigh too heavily upon us. And not merely in the form of books — through colleges, schools of art, institutions in general. "They pin me down," he declared. "They look backward and not forward. The eyes of man are set in his forehead, not in his hindhead." In a democracy the creative spirit has to be exalted above all else, for "the one thing in the world of value is the *active* soul — the soul, free, sovereign, active. This every man is entitled to; this every man contains within

149

himself, although in almost all men obstructed; and as yet unborn."
(italics added)[1]

Undue subservience to the past was seen by Emerson as a danger to democracy and to the creative spirit. Similarly, those of us who wish to teach children to value their cultural heritage should be wary of an undue reliance on appreciation. Certainly, a broadened base of knowledge and competence in the arts can contribute to a higher level of functioning by children as artists, performers, inventors, or planners. But schools must also make a conscious effort to help children develop their individual powers and potential. Learning to value their own versions or visions of the world ought to be part of the education of all children.

WHY TEACH CREATIVE BEHAVIOR

In teaching children we always begin with the receptive side of things. Children need to experience the range of satisfactions to be found in literature, the visual arts, and music if they are to be able to choose rewardingly from among the options presently open to them. Yet in order for them to have a genuine freedom of choice, children must also become experienced in the satisfactions to be derived from creative behavior, and schools must find room for and learn how to support the development of the artist in each child. Why should we try to teach children to be makers of a world of their own? Let us look more closely at some good reasons.

Encouragement of Selfhood

Appreciation calls for self-abnegation. The first task, as Coleridge and Ruskin agreed, is to get inside a work of art and look out through the eyes of the poet or painter or composer. But not so with creation. Here the self is in charge all the way. As George Santayana noted, the self is in control of every artistic expression. When the

---

[1] Ralph W. Emerson, *Select Essays and Addresses* (New York: The Macmillan Company, 1905), p. 191.

creator shapes an object, the various pieces of the self come into focus to provide both order and meaning.[2]

Creation can also extend the self. In the process of creation, the self is absorbed into, passes through, and emerges from an exercise in imagination as something else again. The first readers of Rousseau's *Julie* were sure that he himself was the heroine's lover. He had written the romance, he remembered, in "a state of almost feverish ecstasy," but readers were wrong in thinking it was based on fact: "They were far from understanding to what an extent I am capable of being inflamed by beings of my imagination."[3] Henry James expressed it more sedately. "The house of fiction" has a number of windows beyond reckoning, all of which have been or can be forced to open as the writer exercises vision and will.[4]

In today's view, selfhood or individuality is good in itself. The Greek ideal of the individual as creator of his or her own world was dimmed by the Dark Ages but came back with renewed force during the Renaissance. Starting in the fourteenth and fifteenth centuries, the cultural realm burgeoned, with the creative arts, the performing arts, the arts of invention, and the arts of planning bursting into bloom all at once. Such self-expression opened up new regions for personal development.[5] Certainly this individuality remains one of the goals of our society today.

Acceptance of Freedom

Freedom is the circumstance in which children must find themselves before their choices can begin to mean much. Yet freedom can be a heavy burden for the individual. As Albert Camus noted, one of the greatest problems or challenges of freedom arises from the fact that creating a world of one's own can be a risky business.[6]

[2] George Santayana, *The Sense of Beauty* (New York: Modern Library, 1955), p. 231.

[3] *The Confessions of Jean Jacques Rousseau* (New York: Modern Library, n.d.), p. 567.

[4] Henry James, *The Art of the Novel: Critical Prefaces* (New York: Charles Scribner's Sons, 1934), p. 46.

[5] Edward H. Weatherly, ed., *Renaissance* (New York: Dell Publishing Company, 1962), p. 14.

[6] Albert Camus, *The Rebel: An Essay on Man in Revolt*, trans. Anthony Bower (New York: Vintage Books, 1958), p. 255.

If valuing requires freedom, so too does creativity. Undue dependence on the past or reliance on things as they have been must be transcended by the creative person. Consumers of art may be content to be passive but not its producers. Poets and composers and painters have always preferred to tackle the impossible.[7] Thus, the creative person learns to accept the burden of freedom and indeed thrives under it.

Renewal of the Arts

We have been looking at the creator rather than the creation. But of course, we are deeply concerned with renewal of the arts. Unless artists emerge from each generation, the richness of the cultural heritage suffers. Art historian Heinrich Wolfflin has reminded us that in each period, however hidebound it may seem, there is always room for the unexpected to make its appearance, and for art "to pass beyond the law-bound towards the unbound and unbounded."[8]

Charles Baudelaire, in defending the apparent outrageousness of Eugene Delacroix, tried to identify in him many qualities derived from the past, contending that the painter resembled Rembrandt in one way, Rubens and Veronese in others. But finally, Baudelaire had to be completely candid. Delacroix "also had a quality of his own, a quality indefinable but itself defining the melancholy and the passion of his age — something quite new, which has made him a unique artist, without ancestry, without precedent, and probably without a successor."[9]

Beyond the Boundaries

In short, renewal of the arts comes as the boundaries are pushed out. And the boundaries lie in the mind more often than in the

---

[7] Nicholas Berdyaev, *Slavery and Freedom*, trans. R. M. French (New York: Charles Scribner's Sons, 1944), p. 243.

[8] Heinrich Wolfflin, *Principles of Art History*, trans. M. D. Hottinger (New York: Dover Publications, n.d. [1st ed. in English, 1932]), p. 341.

[9] Charles Baudelaire, *The Mirror of Art*, trans. J. Mayne (Garden City, N.Y.: Doubleday Anchor Books, 1956), pp. 218–219.

material realm. For example, what are the elements that can be subjected to the will of the composer? Sound and silence, Ralph Hill suggested. The rest is up to the imagination.[10] It was the will to find new possibilities in art, Herbert Read proposed, that gave rise to the rococo movement. Freedom from classical restraints was what was being sought. Stucco versus stone came into it, of course, but basically the movement was "a spiritual manifestation."[11]

Inventions, too, are the product of creative behavior, and as Francis Bacon pointed out, inventions such as printing, gunpowder, and the compass changed the world. Thus, support for scientific discovery can be based on self-benefit. But it is better, in a bid for such support, to argue for the claims of truth; the prize of new knowledge "is the contemplation of things as they are, free from superstition or imposture, error or confusion, much more dignified in itself than all the advantages to be derived from discoveries."[12]

This section has tried to describe how creative behavior functions in the lives of everyone. Creativity encourages the development of selfhood and a respect for individuality. It helps free people from the past and furthers the renewal of the arts. How far may creative behavior take people? Who can say? But it will certainly be beyond past boundaries.

No area of values education has more significance in terms of both individual fulfillment and social effectiveness than that of creativity. Freedom here, as in critical thinking, means emancipation from things as they are or have been, good as these might be. Yet a word of caution is in order. Newness does not automatically lead to cultural enrichment, particularly if it is seen as the sole criterion of excellence. Sometimes, in looking at the variety of approaches to the arts today, particularly in the visual arts, we may be inclined to agree with Harold Rosenberg, interpreter of abstract expressionism. He speaks of contemporary art criticism as tending "to normalize the new" as a means of reducing antagonism to it.[13] Anything and everything may be art — or nothing. There is a risk, then, that the very

---

[10] Ralph Hill, ed., *The Concerto* (Baltimore: Penguin Books, 1952), p. 9.

[11] Herbert Read, *The Meaning of Art* (London: Faber and Faber, 1931), p. 111.

[12] Francis Bacon, *Novum Organum* (New York: P. F. Collier and Son, 1902), p. 106.

[13] Harold Rosenberg, *The Anxious Quest: Art Today and Its Audience* (New York: Horizon Press, 1966), p. 232.

Exhibit 6-1

Activities in Four Areas of the Arts

Area	Activities	
Creative arts	Building	Painting
	Carving	Photographing
	Choreographing	Pottery making
	Composing	Sculpting
	Drawing	Weaving
	Expressing	Writing
Performing arts	Acting	Instrument playing
	Dancing	Reading
	Interpreting	Rendering
	Moving	Singing
	Pantomiming	Speaking
Arts of invention	Constructing	Hypothesizing
	Contriving	Model making
	Devising	Originating
	Discovering	Theorizing
	Experimenting	Thinking up
Arts of planning	Blueprinting	Landscaping
	City planning	Laying out
	Conceptualizing	Mapping
	Designing	Projecting
	Drafting	Visualizing

idea of art may lose its meaning unless creative behavior is grounded in appreciation of society's cultural heritage.

This chapter examines ways in which schools have been working to encourage creativity in children. Included in our survey are programs dealing with the arts of invention and planning as well as the creative and performing arts. (See Exhibit 6–1 for the scope and interrelatedness of these areas.) Learning to behave innovatively in the arts opens up options otherwise closed to the young learner. And such innovative behavior is as vital to the welfare of the total society as it is to the well-being of the individual learner and valuer.

SHAPING EXPERIENCE THROUGH THE CREATIVE ARTS

Teachers have always sought to encourage self-expression in children. Toward this end, they have set aside time for creative writing and made paints and paper and clay readily available for on-call use. Most teachers have tried to introduce new art media thoughtfully and to provide some help to children in learning how to handle tools of one kind or another. And they have been delighted to seek assistance from art teachers or consultants whenever such help has been offered.

For the most part, teachers have had an accepting attitude toward the stories, poems, paintings, and clay animals that their students have produced. By and large, they have not pressed children too hard toward being more creative next time. Believing that creativity is an intimate matter between children and their sense of need for expression, they have been cautious about doing too much for fear that they might interfere in the creative process. Moreover, to be completely honest, they have not always known what to do.

In recent years, a somewhat different outlook has developed on how to promote activities in the creative arts. We now know a good deal about what's involved in creativeness, and we are more willing to take actions to encourage it. Waiting upon inspiration hardly seems enough. If creative behavior is as important as we think it is, then we should be doing more to try to teach children how to create. That seems to be the theme of the new approaches to helping children gain real satisfaction from doing well in a variety of the creative arts.

Purposeful Creation

In many elementary school classrooms, Mother's Day is often an occasion for creative writing. Members of one fourth-grade class were given an opportunity to write their own poems:

Mother's Day, it is the best.
It could take on all the rest.
— Larry

My mother is sweet.
She makes me things to eat.

I would like to take her breakfast in bed
And get pillows to rest her head.

But I have a busy mother who never stays in bed
So I'll have to give her lots of love instead.
— Toni

She cleans,
She sews,
She paints her toes.
— Carol

Every day is Children's Day
But this day is for mother
To honor her for her good deeds
Which can beat any other.
— Robby

Context and purpose can play important roles in stimulating creativity. Indeed, a group of British teachers maintain that the context for writing is of prime importance in any creative writing program. They have developed a series of questions that they believe should be asked about a school's efforts to elicit children's writing:

How much self-initiated writing is there in school? Does the context enable each writer to find his own way of relating what is new to what is known? How much time is there for writing which sifts, orders, and shapes for the purposes of the individual as well as making known to the teacher that what is required has been done?[14]

[14] Carol Burgess et al., *Understanding Children's Writing* (Baltimore: Penguin Books, 1973), p. 137.

The authors cite an example of how such context-oriented writing works. One October morning a group of eight-year-olds visited a local park, which had its own stream and "a bit of wilderness in places." The children took along a good deal of equipment, including a bucket for "large watery specimens." Back in school, the children began to make many kinds of reports — poems, descriptive paragraphs, notes about gnats and fish and weeds (with pictures), three musical compositions. The most highly prized writing, however, came from Raymond, who had been tested for autism, had a speech defect, and couldn't read very well: "I was the boy who carried the bucket." It was "his very first piece of entirely original writing."[15]

Teachers sometimes find that using models for writing is another successful way to introduce context. Thus, after reading a number of fables, children may be encouraged to write some of their own.[16] Or they may read a poem together, particularly one that is structured as a series of images or ideas, and then write similar poems.[17]

Time to Work It Through

When he was a boy in Indiana, Theodore Dreiser used to

> arise as early as three or four o'clock in the morning in the summertime, and after looking at the clouds over the fields or watching the sun rise, examine all the wonders of the morning — bejeweled spider webs, striped and tinted morning glories of ravishing form and color, the yellow trumpet-flowers which covered our porches, our many varieties of roses in full bloom, bluebirds, swallows, wrens — and then stroll away through the clover or timothy to the neighboring woods or open fields.

When the boy came back from his jaunts, he sat "by one of the windows in our living room, and holding in my lap, for love's sake, a small black and yellow mongrel dog, that along with two others had attached itself to us, I used to rock and sing by the hour, enjoying

[15] *Ibid.*, pp. 138–139.
[16] Eldonna L. Evertts, "Literature and Composition in the Elementary Grades," in *New Directions in Elementary English*, ed. Alexander Frazier (Champaign, Ill.: National Council of Teachers of English, 1967), pp. 207–221.
[17] Kenneth Koch, *Wishes, Lies, and Dreams: Teaching Children to Write Poetry* (New York: Random House, 1971).

the morning sun." His mother could not understand why he among her dozen children needed so much time to himself, but she respected his need. Here was a child, "vibrating with an emotional ecstasy in regard to life itself,"[18] who had to have time to take it all in and try to make something of it.

Some of us are learning to provide such time in school. Leslie, aged seven and a half, is in a group where children are expected to do some imaginative writing every day. In Leslie's folder (the children file their work after they have read it to the teacher and sometimes the class) are stories entitled: "Pandas" (illustrated); "Age of Muscle Power"; "The Candy Parade"; "The Good Dog"; "The Old Tree," parts 1 and 2; "Al, the Good Boy"; "The Bad Man"; "Count the Puppies" (illustrated); "The Great Girl"; and "Lincoln" (illustrated). Some of these stories obviously took several days to complete.

In another class, one of older children, the students are encouraged to write books, which are then included in the classroom library and read right along with regularly published works. A recently completed book is *Michael and the Birds*, written by a ten-year-old named Anne. "Once upon a time there was an old man who took care of his grandson. His grandson was 8 years old and his name was Michael. He liked nature very much, but his favorite part of nature was the bird." After his grandfather's death, Michael went to an orphanage where he stayed until he was sixteen. Soon he was twenty and well started on his career as a "naturist." His desire was to fly like his beloved friends, the birds. One day he fell over a cliff.

> Michael was falling yet he was not afraid. He was the closest to flying he had ever been before in his life. He was happy. Suddenly he landed, he was stiff and sore. The joy was over, but he had experienced flying. He had a small feeling of joy in his heart.

He also had assorted broken bones. But after a month in the hospital, he was ready to go again. Further adventures in flying were helped by his inventiveness. His was a long and eventful life, bird-centered to the very end. Of him Anne could finally say: "He loved the birds and learned to be like them in a way."

Writing a book such as *Michael and the Birds* takes time. And the same is true of productivity in any of the arts.

[18] Theodore Dreiser, *Dawn* (New York: Premier Books, 1965), pp. 56, 53. By permission of Harold J. Dies, Trustee, The Dreiser Trust.

Growth in Competence

In the promotional literature of a small private school, the following paragraph appears:

> Our large crafts room is open throughout the day for use by all of the children. Both boys and girls have a chance to master sewing machines, floor looms, and potting wheels. Besides the usual range of activities with chalk, crayons, paints, yarns, papier mâché, and the like, there are opportunities for candle making, copper enameling, batik, and silk screen printing. Children interested in photography can learn to develop and print as well as take pictures. Periodically small groups of children make super 8mm movies.

This all sounds wonderful. But how much teaching goes on in these fine surroundings? Does real competence result? We can testify that in this particular school the teaching is worthy of the facilities.

For creative behavior to develop as it should, attention needs to go directly to how competence is developing over time. Stimulation and occasions for creation, time for working projects through, and good facilities are all important. But the bottom line is whether children are experiencing the satisfaction that comes from gaining ever-increasing control of the medium in which they are expressing themselves.

Criteria for determining this are numerous and can be expressed behaviorally. But the overriding goal in schools with well-planned creative arts programs is an increasing degree of independence. Competence in the creative arts means that children become free to go off on their own — or to books and adults and other sources of their own choosing — for ideas in any of the arts that they wish to explore.

Independence is the goal of creative behavior and perhaps the means of developing it as well. Learning to value creative arts activities calls for a program that provides children with many truly satisfying experiences. Children who have come through an unplanned and impoverished program are likely never to have known the delight that comes from competence-based independence. For such children, other, less rewarding ways of investing time and energy will more often than not win out over seeking more experiences in the creative arts. This can be a sad loss to all concerned. We hope to avoid such losses through well-planned creative arts programs that emphasize context-oriented creation, provide children with sufficient time for creative activities, and encourage the development of competence and independence.

PERFORMING ARTISTIC COMPOSITIONS, OLD AND NEW

The best teacher the distinguished American composer Charles Ives ever had was his own band-leader father, a natural innovator in music education. The senior Ives believed that most persons do not make use of all their native talent. Thus, as part of their training, he would have his children sing a song in one key while he played the accompaniment in another.[19] What he hoped for was their emancipation from the pressure of old ways of doing things.

In attempting to do more with the performing arts in school, teachers must be certain of their priorities and not permit themselves to get weighted down by old ways of doing things. Challenging children to use all their faculties will not get much attention if the teacher's time is tied up with preparing a never-ending series of school assemblies and PTA programs. Pursuit of the goal of developing innovative behavior in performing artistic compositions means that the instructional end must take precedence over other ends.

Complexities of Performance

Performance does not always require appearance before a formal audience. That is a point that needs to be made. Most of the time, singing or playing music or reading a poem aloud or putting on a play is aimed at being meaningful mainly for the individual or group involved. Even then, performance activities are likely to combine a good many elements that make for complexity, particularly in the field of music. Teachers need to do what they can to simplify performance so that the emphasis remains on learning.

One way is to do much more with speech and drama. Children are born storytellers and can be helped to be even better. Reading aloud is a lost art that deserves to be revived. Choral speaking or reading makes an audience out of the performers themselves and offers the best of chances to unite appreciation of good poetry (and prose, too) with growth in power of interpretation. Such activities as pantomiming, improvising, and making up plays have many merits;

---

[19] Charles E. Ives, *Memos*, ed. John Kirkpatrick (New York: W. W. Norton and Company, 1972), p. 115.

yet, they tend to be overlooked when the focus of performance narrows to showcase occasions.

Careful direction is required to make development through drama succeed. Children need to find out for themselves their own way of doing things, but they need a framework of some kind to help them along. For example, Brian Way lists a series of situations in which pairs of children (British) may work together to develop a sense of differing dialects and accents. The list includes:

> Two North Country business men discussing absenteeism among workers because of weather.
>
> Two American tourists grumbling about how the weather spoiled their holiday.
>
> Two Scottish lighthouse keepers swapping yarns about terrible weather at sea.[20]

Learning needs to be thought of as a result of preparation rather than as a product of formal performance alone.

Of course, working together toward a common goal can be rewarding. When Edwin Booth, the celebrated American actor, had an opportunity to be directed by the great Henry Irving in a London production of *Othello* (1881) in which the two men played Iago and Othello and Ellen Terry played Desdemona, he found the experience exhilarating:

> To be on his stage and find all one's own ideas perfectly carried out is delightful! He imparts to the humblest member of his corps a somewhat of the true artistic feeling that animates himself. Rehearsals, which were always an exhaustion and a bore to me, are, on his stage, with him as director, positively a pleasure; it revives all my old interest in my profession. He deserves all the honors heaped upon him and wears them modestly.[21]

Perhaps direction is in itself an art; if so, it might be included in the section on the arts of planning. But cooperative productions provide a variety of other opportunities for learning as well.

[20] Brian Way, *Development Through Drama* (London: Longman, 1967), p. 138.

[21] From *Between Actor and Critic: Selected Letters of Edwin Booth and William Winter*, ed. Daniel J. Watermeier, copyright © 1971 Princeton University Press, p. 187. Reprinted by permission of Princeton University Press.

Need for Individual-Group Balance

"Creative dramatics refers to an informal activity in which children are guided by a leader to express themselves through the medium of drama." This is how one up-to-date school system announced an addition to its arts program. The goal of creative dramatics

> is not performance but rather the free expression of the child's creative imagination through the discipline of an art form. The emphasis is on the development of the child's creative personality — sharing, thinking, feeling. The warm and stimulating atmosphere of the creative dramatics workshop is a highly beneficial one for every child.

We may wonder about the tone of this statement. The goal here seems to be as much social as artistic. Has the focus been lost? Group experiences are important in the lives of children, of course. But these can be provided within many other frameworks. Singing, dancing, and similar activities provide a natural base for social interaction that may sometimes make teachers unconsciously prefer group to individual performance.

We can understand the hold that group performance has on schools. The group remains the unit of instruction in music and drama as in much else. When special teachers in the arts are provided, they generally work with groups of children at the same time. And as for music, choral singing is often almost the whole of the program.

This dependence on group activities can be seen in new ventures, too. Here are some of the experiences reported by one of the field centers in the federally financed and carefully planned Arts Impact Program:

> Fifth and sixth graders performed an exchange concert. The sixth graders played rounds on recorders while the fifth graders sang; the fifth graders played piano accompaniments which the sixth graders sang. . . .

> One girl copied Brahms' "Lullaby," "Camptown Races," and "America" to be played on recorders. The class discovered (in two minutes) that she had omitted the sharp signs. After the correction, the class created an accompaniment and tape recorded the package to be played for the entire school. . . .

A critical incident arose in connection with a dramatization of "Goldilocks and the Three Bears." After hearing the story read to them, the children wished to dramatize it; one boy, the "slowest" child in the class, a boy who never had voluntarily joined in a class activity, insisted that he should be Father Bear. He was given a chance and was the star of the performance.[22]

The point we are trying to make is that recasting the curriculum to provide for higher-level creative activity in the performing arts means provision of chances for all children to work toward greater competence and more innovativeness in interpretation. Group undertakings, although excellent in themselves, are not substitutes for individual performance. Both aspects need to be represented in an effective performing arts program. Indeed, as much attention may need to go to individual performance as to group performance — and possibly more. (See Exhibit 6–2 for the range of possibilities in both areas.)

Creation and Performance Joined

By definition, the performing arts start with a composition of some sort — a song or other piece of music, a poem or speech or story, a play, an opera or operetta, a dance. Thus, talk of developing a program for children that stresses creative behavior in the performing arts may seem a bit overoptimistic. Can we really expect children to interpret works of merit with any kind of excellence? Surely we can hardly claim that most performances by individual children or groups of children will be memorable for boldness of approach or nuances of interpretation.

Obviously, our definition of creative behavior must be broad enough to encompass performance at less than the level of perfection. Yet in a sense, any performance of a set work calls for creative effort. Reciting a poem or singing a song or moving through the measures of a dance takes doing. And such behavior can be learned and is worth learning.

---

[22] J. David Boyle, ed., *Arts Impact — Curriculum for Change: Final Report* (University Park, Pa.: Arts Impact Evaluation Team, Pennsylvania State University, 1973), pp. 56–62, selected instances.

Exhibit 6-2

Types of Performance: Individual and Group

Category of performance	Individual as performer	Group as performer
Speaking/ reading/ reciting	Giving a talk Reading a story aloud Reciting a poem from memory	Taking part in a panel discussion Engaging in choral reading or speaking Reporting on a group project
Acting	Putting on a puppet show Pantomiming a story or situation Impersonating a famous person or character from literature Clowning	Putting on a puppet show Dramatizing a play Role playing a situation Presenting a play Presenting an opera
Singing	Singing unaccompanied Singing with accompaniment Solo singing against choral background	Singing in a small group: duo, trio, quartet Singing in a chorus or choir

Category of performance	Individual as performer	Group as performer
Playing musical instrument	Playing composition unaccompanied	Playing in a small group: duo, trio, quartet
	Playing with accompaniment	Playing in a band or orchestra
	Solo playing against orchestral background	
Dancing	Dancing alone	Dancing in an ensemble or troupe
	Solo dancing with an ensemble or troupe	Large group dancing: square dancing, folk dancing, paired dancing to popular music

Another way to maximize creativeness in performance is to join the composition of works with their performance. This is a familiar technique. Children read their own stories and poems to the class. They prepare and present puppet plays. They make up plays based perhaps on a favorite story and present these to an audience of some kind.

Today one of the areas in which composition and performance are most often joined is the dance. With the rebirth of movement education in this country has come renewed interest in modern or expressive dance. The modern dance heritage is peculiarly American. Its forerunners Isadora Duncan, Ruth St. Denis, and Ted Shawn; its great creative spirits Martha Graham, Doris Humphrey, and Charles Weidman; its more recent innovators such as Merce Cunningham, Alvin Ailey, and Paul Taylor — all have built upon the concept of individual expressiveness and the freedom of dancers to create or choreograph their own dances.[23]

This freedom is manifest in the work of Gladys Andrews, long a leader in the children's dance field. In a fascinating account, she describes some dances made with or by children:

Horse Dance: circus horses, work horses, police horses, race horses, wild horses

Things Are Swinging All Over Town: from study of swinging movement

The Dancing Elephant and His Friends: giraffe, porcupine, monkey, baby bear

Good Morning: celebration of signs of spring

The World Is Made of Many Things: illustrating concepts like small and big, heavy and light

Kite Weather: acting out favorite poem

Dance of the Blackfoot Indians: derived from social studies unit on Indians[24]

Here, for sure, the creative and the performing arts are joined together.

[23] See Don McDonagh, *The Complete Guide to Modern Dance* (Garden City, N.Y.: Doubleday and Company, 1976).
[24] Gladys Andrews Fleming, *Creative Rhythmic Movement: Boys and Girls Dancing* (Englewood Cliffs, N.J.: Prentice-Hall, 1976), summarized from pp. 302–344.

More is being done to extend the scope of the performing arts in the education of children. The new curriculum recognizes and honors the complexities of performance. It seeks a balance between individual and group performance. And it includes activities that unite composition and performance.

Performance of artistic compositions, old and new, offers children an arena for comparing and evaluating many kinds of interpretive experiences, their own and those of other children and adults as well. Whether children will gain enough satisfaction from such activities to insure that performance in an arts area will loom large in their lives we cannot say. Perhaps all we can do is to sponsor rewarding experiences in the performing arts for as many children as possible.

EXERCISING THE ARTS OF INVENTION

In another time, proponents of active learning — or project study — often spoke of the need to integrate the arts with academic subjects. Content of a sober nature (social studies, science, mathematics) could be enlivened and lightened by singing a song, writing a story, or dramatizing an event.

But today, with more understanding of how creativity relates to intellectual development, we see things in a different light. Inventiveness is integral to making sense out of the world. As Jean Piaget has helped us understand, young children, if they are to be eager learners, have to be free to explore, discover, and recreate the elements and qualities of their world on their own terms. And teachers, if they wish to support continued learning, must know how to enrich their students' search for meaning and growth of personal powers.

Creative arts, performing arts, and the arts of invention and planning belong together because they inspire opportunities for children to exercise and develop the faculty Noam Chomsky would identify as inherent in the person: the power of making or expressing something, resolving ambiguities, being fanciful about possibilities. (See Exhibit 3–1.) If we are earnest about opening up options in creative behavior to all children, then we must provide them with satisfying experiences in going beyond things as they are to things as they might be. Inventiveness is a kind of creativity in which Americans have long excelled. American children have a heritage here that predisposes them to think big. With our help, satisfying experiences in inventiveness can become very much a part of their school lives.

Old Questions, New Answers

As boys in Wisconsin, architect-to-be Frank Lloyd Wright and his friend Robie had a "real passion for invention":

> A water velocipede was started — to be called the "Frankenrob." Drawings made for a "Catamaran" that cost too much to happen. The boys made a cross-gun, bows and arrows, and long bob sled on double runners. They painted them — the joy of striping them in colors! They had them "ironed" by the blacksmith according to design. A new style newspaper — a scroll. Another kind of ice-boat. Fantastic new kinds of kites of colored paper. Kites with fantastic tails. A water-wheel.[25]

One cannot list all the marvels that they dreamed up in those years. But of the school where the boys went, Wright in later years could not recall a thing. His memories were all of self-initiated and self-directed learning activities.

The questions children wonder about may be old — how to travel faster on water or ice or, like Anne's Michael, how to fly with the birds. Inventiveness comes from the impulse to find new answers. And today school programs are trying to do more with this impulse. One group of ten-year-olds, for example, designed their own planes, kites, and hang gliders. Afterwards, Beth worked through the steps required to replicate her design:

HOW TO MAKE A HANG GLIDER

1. Find any kind of material.
2. Then you cut out the pattern of the Sky Hawk [shown in 10 diagrams].
3. Then you take a pen and draw around the pattern on the material.

The instructions continue to the end:

19. Now take each string and thread it into the needle and stick the needle and thread into each hole, one string to each hole. And don't forget to tie a knot after each hole! Now you are done.

[25] Reprinted from *An Autobiography* by Frank Lloyd Wright, copyright 1977, by permission of the publisher Horizon Press, New York, p. 55.

Experimentation in General

During the sixties, two powerful movements were at work to further the need for attending to the arts of invention in the school. One was the study of creative behavior as such. Creative children, so identified, were described as being less likely to be thrown by ambiguity or uncertainty; they might even welcome it as a challenge! They were also found to be more likely than most children to involve themselves wholeheartedly in seeking out answers. Inventing was perceived to be part of the creative complex to which the school should give more heed. "In this type of creativity," as art educator Elliot Eisner has noted, "the individual uses objects and ideas in combination so that an essentially new product is developed."[26] Whether as a part of science or as an aspect of art, inventiveness was thought to be one of the primary ends of modern education.

The other movement was the redevelopment of mathematics and science programs on a disciplines-centered base. As this movement's unofficial spokesperson, Jerome S. Bruner wrote with authority of the need to develop ways of communicating to learners the abstract content of some of the national curriculum projects.[27] In time, problem solving, inquiry, and discovery became the favored approaches. Manipulative activities of one kind or another were written into most of the new programs. As Piaget had expressed it, "To understand is to invent."[28]

Today there seems to be agreement on the desirability of fostering the arts of invention in every possible way. Assignments that call for the exercise of inventiveness have become familiar in most of the subject fields, as indicated in Exhibit 6–3. Valuing something developed by one's self over whatever else is available may be what it takes to put inventiveness to the test. Even though the choice may change over time, the experience of being inventive and of learning to value the new and untried over the familiar is of great importance in the education of children. Frank Lloyd Wright's message was that

---

[26] Elliot W. Eisner, *Think with Me about Creativity* (Dansville, N.Y.: F. A. Owen Publishing Company, 1964), p. 45.

[27] Jerome S. Bruner, "The Act of Discovery" (1961), in *Inquiry Techniques for Teaching Science*, ed. Willam D. Romey (Englewood Cliffs, N.J.: Prentice-Hall, 1968), p. 169.

[28] Jean Piaget, *To Understand Is to Invent*, trans. George-Anne Roberts (New York: Grossman Publishers, 1973).

Exhibit 6-3

Activities Calling for Inventiveness: By Subject Fields

Subject field	Sample activities
Social studies	Thinking up ways to increase voter turnout
	Developing a new set of map symbols
	Working up a form to use in recording biographical data on unfamiliar heroes/heroines in American history
Science	Creating new energy sources
	Developing a vocabulary for a new aspect of ecology
	Designing instruments to measure rainfall, wind direction, and other aspects of weather
Mathematics	Developing the basis for a new number system
	Finding new units of measurement
	Working out new ways to add, subtract, multiply, and divide
Language arts	Finding a new stanza or verse form
	Developing a new set of sex-free pronouns
	Finding a way to simplify the spelling of English words

Subject field	Sample activities
Physical education	Designing new gymnastics equipment
	Creating a field game for three teams
	Developing a grid for keeping track of height-weight changes
Visual arts	Finding a new process or material for use in printmaking
	Developing a table loom for younger children
	Discovering new uses for carpet scraps
Music	Developing new percussion instruments
	Composing music by combining a miscellany of recorded sounds
	Working out a way to chart or record dance movements

"experiment, tolerance, and change give a culture strength."[29] And a person, too, we may add.

PLANNING IN SEVERAL DIRECTIONS

In these days, few would deny the need for creative enterprise in looking ahead, evaluating choices, and, once a decision has been reached, mapping things out. Skills of many kinds are involved in the arts of planning. But at the core is the union of intellect and spirit under the governance of imagination. The demand is great for effectiveness in many dimensions of planning. Thus, we need not be surprised that more is being done with planning in the education of children.

Like inventiveness, planning involves a definition of possibilities. But here the young valuer also has to establish priorities. The planning experiences offered in schools today differ in degree of imaginativeness. However, all are designed to help children learn to identify and put a proper value on what matters most in thinking and planning ahead.

Focus on Learning Needs

Careful planning by and with children is increasingly a part of classroom life. The teacher of a group of younger children, for example, getting ready to go to gym, takes advantage of a few minutes of waiting to draw attention to planning needs. "Brian, what are you going to start on when we come back? Billy Jean, you've finished your math. What next? Sandy, how did your writing assignment go? If any of you have a problem deciding what to do next, check with me when you come back." The planning here is integral to learning to make good use of time.

In another group, each child is assigned to go to the library to look up information for a science report. But before they go, the

---

[29] Reprinted from *An Autobiography* by Frank Lloyd Wright, copyright 1977, by permission of the publisher Horizon Press, New York, p. 559.

children are expected to have done some planning. Jon's plan for a space report is representative.

> I want to find out which planet is the closest to the earth. Another thing I want to know is which of the nine planets is closest to the sun. I also want to know which planet is the hottest and which is the oldest.

When he returns from the library, Jon will write out answers to his questions. Planning can have a lot to do with whether anything of value happens in an independent learning activity.

In one third-grade class, the children made plans based on the idea of interrelating — or webbing — a variety of different subject field activities around a single topic. Liz, whose topic was plants, planned to do the following:

Art. Painting, collage, drawings, make a plant store.

Mathematics. Count how many leaves on a plant. Surveys. Measure a plant. Story problems about plants.

Science. Plant a seed and see how long it takes to grow. Put a seed in water and see if it grows.

Music and Drama. A puppet show. A plant dance.

Reading. Research. Read books about plants.

Writing. Concrete poem. Report on plants — what they need to grow.

Several other children also planned to study plants. Perhaps they would pool their ideas somewhere along the line. Rodney, Sam, and Chris were working together to build a web of space activities. Carol and Amelia were planning to study stamps. The ocean, sharks, and crabs (the children had had a group study on land-water relations) were other topics of interest to more than one child.

As planning for learning in many classrooms has become more elaborate, it has tended to focus on individual responsibility for thinking ahead. Programs of individualized instruction, in particular, have allowed children to determine their own rate of progress through study materials, choose among varied materials or activities to realize given goals, decide how to use time during an open work period, and even make study plans for the better part of an entire week.[30]

---

[30] See Jack Frymier, *Annehurst Curriculum Classification System: A Practical Way to Individualize Instruction* (West Lafayette, Ind.: Kappa Delta Pi, 1977).

No doubt the emphasis in recent years on framing behavioral objectives for teaching has spilled over into helping children learn to spell out more precisely their own goals for learning.

Focus on the Future

Can we help children better prepare for the future by encouraging them to imagine what it will be like? Some of us may hesitate to embrace this approach with all the enthusiasm of futurists or futurologists. Yet we can recognize the challenge offered by exercising the imagination on the world of tomorrow. Planning for the future involves many dimensions. (See Exhibit 6–4 for a recent effort to define these.) But it is the process rather than the content of futuristic thinking that most concerns us here.

Today some schools are encouraging children to engage in a variety of ventures to help them project their ideas beyond things as they are or always have been.[31] Here are some of the topics relating to future planning that groups of children have been examining recently:

A new town or city — what will it be like?

Living under the sea

Space station — the year 2000

People to people — two-way television

When everybody lives to be 100

Solar energy — the house of tomorrow

No cars — a plan for public transportation

Child care in the future — when all women work

A world without war

Schools should not limit their inquiries into the future only to these rather familiar topics. The need exists for a range of topics that stimulate the collection of base data as well as the exercise of

[31] See Alvin Toffler, *Future Shock* (New York: Random House, 1970); and Harold G. Shane, *The Educational Significance of the Future* (Bloomington, Ind.: Phi Delta Kappa Educational Foundation, 1973).

Exhibit 6-4

Dimensions of Planning for a Better World

Communications

Mass media, interpersonal communications, understanding of human rights and responsibilities, travel and transportation

Environment

Radioactivity, air and water pollution, solid waste pollution, pollutants in food, pesticides and heavy metals, noise pollution

Science and technology

Population growth, nutrition needs, energy prospects, mineral resources

The world

Peace, international cooperation, survival

Justice, society, and the individual

Housing, employment, health and medical care, equal protection under the law, equal education

---

Source: Drawn in part from J. J. Jelinek, ed., *Improving the Human Condition: A Curricular Response to Critical Realities* (Washington, D.C.: Association for Supervision and Curriculum Development, 1978).

imagination. Greater variety is also needed. Planning an ideal community can become pretty routine the third time around.

Dealing with problems is one area where the arts of planning gets plenty of exercise in school. Projection into the future can be another. No doubt additional topics will be found as this aspect of creative behavior receives greater attention in the curriculum.

Creative behavior, grounded in appreciation of what already exists, can enliven and enlarge the role of the arts in all our lives. Teaching for creative behavior is one way to develop in children a sense of personal identity and ensure freedom from the weight of the past. Innovation is needed just to keep things moving along — to avoid cultural stagnation. Finally, society depends upon the creative spirit in its several forms to take the giant steps that change and better the world for all of us.

Much is being done to foster creativity in the new, value-oriented curriculum for children. In the area of the creative arts, children are no longer simply being provided with chances to write or paint or compose music. They are being taught to those ends — and given the time they need to produce works of merit. In the performing arts, there is a new respect for the complexities involved in doing something worthwhile. There is also recognition of the need to provide opportunities for individual as well as group performance and to seek for union of the creative and interpretive arts.

In addition, much more is being done than in the past with the arts of invention and planning. Thinking up new solutions to old problems and finding out for one's self what one needs to know are newly valued in all subject fields. Thinking creatively in many directions and dimensions has taken on new status as schools work to help develop the competencies society most needs.

WHERE WE NEED TO GO NOW

"Whenever I draw a circle, I immediately want to step out of it." In this statement Buckminster Fuller, one of the truly innovative figures of our time, warns against the constriction that comes with a sense of completion. We must keep our minds open about what can be done to bring to consciousness in the lives of children more alternatives of behavior that include the creative dimension. "One reason humanity loves its children is that the children start off with such potential," Fuller remarks. "Raise high the roof beam, carpenters."[32]

Creativity as Learnable Behavior

Today, as we have noted, teaching for creative behavior has become an acceptable practice. Fear that children will be put off by direct efforts to elicit artistic work has apparently lessened. There seems to be growing recognition that if children are to gain a sense of what creativity is all about, they must develop the kind of competence that is not likely to come except through planned instruction.

Yet we might be wise to wonder a little about whether we may lose our way if we get too far from openness and freedom in natural expressiveness. A planned program should not be repressive. What characterizes effective teaching in all the arts areas is that children find true satisfaction in reaching new levels of competency and a greater independence.

Certainly, a balance needs to be sought between teachers' expectations and children's choices. But perhaps that is the goal in any kind of teaching.

Appreciation plus Innovation

In the past, teachers may sometimes have trusted that children would learn to appreciate their arts heritage as they became artists. As we have reported (in Chapter 5), the movement in appreciation today is toward doing more than that, for the arts are content as well as process.

Although there is a relationship between the study of one's arts heritage and one's attempts to contribute to it, we must be careful not to substitute arts projects originating in science or social studies

---

[32] From *I Seem to Be a Verb* by R. Buckminster Fuller with Jerome Agel and Quentin Fiore; copyright © 1970 by Bantam Books, Inc., pp. 3, 163. By permission of Bantam Books, Inc.

for creative arts activities. Making a mural of the westward movement or a diorama of underwater sea life can absorb an entire term's art time. Moreover, if we press unduly for union of appreciative and creative activities, we might end up with lessons in making models of Greek and Roman columns or painting like Jackson Pollock.

What we are after is a higher level of competence in both appreciation of the cultural heritage and innovation in the various arts. Thus, activities relating these two ends should be strengthening to both.

Creativity in All Learning

The ultimate goal in teaching children to be more creative is to encourage creative behavior in all aspects of children's learning. Let us return to Emerson and his contention that genius is "the sound estate of every man," even though the talent may lie undeveloped within each person. There are possibilities for many kinds of creative behavior, he was telling his Harvard audience. Readers, too, can be creative: "One must be an inventor to read well." Thus, we must strive for creative reading as well as creative writing, and a more creative or inventive approach to everything that is to be studied — science and social studies and mathematics as well as literature. As Emerson noted, "When the mind is braced by labor and invention, the page of whatever book we read becomes luminous with manifold allusions."[33]

We are pledged to do all we can to free the active soul within each child, to nourish in each child what Walt Whitman called "the seed of perfection."[34] That is what the new curriculum for children is all about.

ACTIVITIES

1. "But is it art?" This familiar question is often directed at new ventures. Can you list some recent examples of painting, sculpture, and music about which this question has been asked?

[33] Emerson, *Select Essays*, pp. 192–193.
[34] Walt Whitman, "Song of the Universal," in *Leaves of Grass* (1855).

2. The examples of children's original writing in this chapter are of several sorts, although all are responses to specific stimuli of some kind. Review these examples critically, and then propose an assignment that you feel will get good results. Test it out on a group of children.
3. Consider the time factor in creative arts activities. Why do teachers tend to assign those activities that are easy to complete in a single session? What can be done to make long-term projects more practical?
4. In what ways do the complexities of performance influence what teachers do with children in this area? What could teachers do to achieve more balance among types of performance?
5. What will it take to reduce emphasis on group performance in schools? Make specific proposals toward that end.
6. Examine Exhibit 6–3. Choose one of the subject fields and prepare a list of ten activities that call for inventiveness.
7. Develop five to seven planning activities in each of three subject areas.
8. Do you think that every child has the potential for creative behavior? Are there social factors or influences that may shape or thwart creativity? As you see it, what is the role of the school in developing creativity?
9. Relate critical thinking (discussed in Chapter 4) and creativity. In what ways are they alike? In what ways are they different?

Values in the Curriculum: What Children Need to Know

The World of Everyday Living

The Cultural Heritage

The Moral-Ethical-Political Realm

Chapter 7

Allegiance to the Democratic Way

Children seek out other children for many purposes: as companions for ventures into unfamiliar territory, as collaborators on work or play projects, as players for a team game, as confidants with whom they can share their interests and ideas.

In time and after many experiences in working and playing together, most children learn to relate effectively with one another in a wide variety of contexts. Schooling can help children to develop needed social skills. As indicated in Chapter 3, this is one of the areas of special concern in the new curriculum for children. If they are to be truly free to choose their associates, children must learn to feel at ease with all kinds of others.

But there is a larger realm of association to which the school must also give its attention. And the learnings in this realm go beyond the give-and-take of everyday living together. We are thinking, of course, of the world of governance — of democracy and the principles of self-government. We are thinking, too, of morals and ethics as they relate to and result in social control.

How fortunate we are to have had so much help in recent years in thinking through what it takes to help young valuers function in this realm! The findings of the moral developmentalists, the framework of study proposed by the value clarifiers, and the strategies devised to offset the social constraints on freedom of choice among ways of being and behaving — all of these, as discussed in Chapter 1, have contributed to our understanding of how valuing functions as a learning process in this particular realm. Recasting school experiences to provide more relevant content for education in humane and democratic values has become a major focus of curriculum making for children today. Yet schools can and should be doing more to help children develop social competence and experience the satisfactions that come from being socially effective (in the broadest sense of the word). For there is much that children need to learn in the moral-ethical-political realm.

WHAT CHILDREN NEED TO KNOW ABOUT DEMOCRACY AND SELF-GOVERNMENT

The Nature of Freedom

"Man is born free, and everywhere he is in chains." As noted earlier, in this famous first sentence of *The Social Contract*, Rousseau raised the oldest of questions. Why is freedom so hard to come by? The answer, so far as we have found one, is that a society can exist only if its members give up some of their claims to natural liberty (in return for which they presumably gain greater safety and security and other values as well). Freedom has to be weighed against the guarantees that come with social union. In one sense, freedom is relative. "For freedom is not procured by a full enjoyment of what is desired," Epictetus warned, "but by controlling that desire."[1] The relationship between citizen and society is always at issue, in both the real and

---

[1] *The Moral Discourses of Epictetus*, ed. Thomas Gould, trans. Carter-Higginson (New York: Washington Square Press, 1964), p. 242.

the ideal worlds. Concerns change, laws change; the person gives up an old privilege, the state takes on a new obligation.

Freedom and independence are hard to win and harder still to sustain. To some extent they have to be rewon by each generation. Thus, American children need to be taught to regard democracy as both a summons and a challenge, and they need to learn how to sustain it. The ever-present forces that work for inertia, conformity, and blind acceptance of authority are powerful indeed.

The Nature of Authority

Chains can be mental as well as physical. "Even where democracies now exist," John Dewey pointed out, "men's minds and feeling are still permeated with ideas about leadership imposed from above, ideas that developed in the long early history of mankind." Old ways of deferring to authority are hard to give up. They are found in many places — at home, in school, in business, in the church — "and as long as they persist there, political democracy is not secure."[2]

Do children need to be helped to think about the nature of authority? In his investigation of moral reasoning, Piaget found that children under nine years of age tend to parrot what they consider to be adult standards. The internalization of such standards can get in the way of arriving at independent assessments of guilt or a genuine comprehension of rules. Only as children exchange ideas does the give-and-take of reciprocal relations become meaningful to them. Only then can they appreciate that the rules of the game, observed by all, ensure equality of treatment under the law (or what might be called the administration of simple justice).

Just having to live as closely supervised by duly constituted authority as children almost always are can be onerous. Additionally, their size, age, and ignorance make children potential targets of abuse and exploitation by unconscionable older children and adults. Children need to understand the way adults normally exercise control, so that they can deal with persons who would take advantage of children because they are weak and helpless. This, too, is part of learning about the nature of authority.

[2] John Dewey, *Intelligence in the Modern World*, ed. Joseph Ratner (New York: Modern Library, 1939), pp. 402–403.

The Political Process

It is sometimes assumed that children will pick up knowledge of how the political system functions simply by growing up in it. No doubt much important learning does occur this way. As David Easton and Jack Dennis noted in their report on the political socialization of children:

> The child learns from those who protect him from the hazards of the world and whose authority he is most apt to accept without question. Thus, in an atmosphere of warmth and protection, the young child is susceptible to appeals for his allegiance that enter his consciousness through the auspices of those people closest to him.[3]

But feeling good about or even being loyal to democracy as a way of life is merely a starting point. Children also need to understand the why of self-government and something, too, about its processes.

The Human Struggle

In "The Waste Land" (1922), T. S. Eliot epitomized his era's sense of disenchantment with the human struggle. Another poet, writing nearly a century earlier, cried out against the lack of social concern of *his* generation.

> The age is dull and mean. Men creep,
> Not walk; with blood too pale and tame
> To pay the debt they owe to shame;
> Buy cheap, sell dear; eat, drink, and sleep
> Down-pillowed, deaf to moaning want;
> Pay tithes for soul-insurance, keep
> Six days to Mammon, one to Cant.[4]

That was John Greenleaf Whittier, abolitionist and spokesperson for the American conscience.

[3] David Easton and Jack Dennis, *Children in the Political System: Origins of Political Legitimacy* (New York: McGraw-Hill Book Company, 1969), pp. 322–323.
[4] "For Righteousness' Sake," in *The Complete Poetical Works of Whittier* (Boston: Houghton Mifflin Company, 1894), pp. 317–318.

Alienation from the realities of life and a sense of resignation in the face of inequality and injustice are familiar enough even (and some might say, especially) today. Thus, it is important for children to realize that other responses to the human struggle are possible. Throughout the history of our country, there have been instances when the actions of people have helped alleviate suffering or prevent disaster or avert death, and these deserve to be celebrated. Children should know, for example, about the work of Jacob Riis, author of *How the Other Half Lives* and *The Children of the Poor*, who took his camera with him into slums and factories and schools to record for a complacent, turn-of-the-century America some facts of life that needed to be altered.

Through such efforts, the promise of democracy is brought into focus. The struggle against hunger, disease, ignorance, and enslavement of various kinds should be recognized as part of the American heritage. For the world at large, the American experience, as Daniel J. Boorstin notes, proves that government can be created by self-reliant men and women without recourse to or dependence on gods or heroes. And that such a people-made government can get things done.[5]

Good reasons exist, then, for helping children to understand the nature of democracy and the principles of self-government as these extend to and embody enduring moral and ethical values honored by the ages. Developing allegiance to the democratic way of life and gaining knowledge of the nature of freedom, authority, and the human struggle should not be taken for granted or left to chance. Such premises underlie the emphasis given to political education in the new curriculum for children.

FINDING OUT ABOUT AMERICA'S HISTORICAL HERITAGE

The successful exercise of political power calls for compliance and a sense of common purpose, regardless of whether the ends are evil or good. So contends Robert L. Heilbroner, an insightful observer of

---

[5] Daniel J. Boorstin, *The Exploring Spirit: America and the World Then and Now* (New York: Random House, 1976), p. 31.

the current scene.[6] The question that concerns us here is what role schools should play in fostering allegiance to the nation. In the days of Hitler, when the development of a fanatic loyalty to the state was a key objective of education in totalitarian states, some persons in the United States contended that in self-defense Americans should strive to do more to assure that their own youth became believers in the worth of a free society. "Hitler is making fanatics. We should, at least, make believers."[7]

Today there is no general agreement among educators on how far American schools should go to build belief. But few would argue against attention being given to the origin and development of the United States as a nation. The history of its people, its heroines and heroes, some of the symbols of its political heritage — these can be studied in school without fear of undue indoctrination.

Study of Ethnic Groups

Units on Indians continue to be a popular means of introducing children to American history. In one school, a class of seven-year-olds saw a film on Indian shelters. Then the children drew pictures of hogans, tepees, and pueblos. Other proposed Indian activities, posted above the table where Indian artifacts (beadwork, pottery, and baskets) and books were displayed, included the following:

Write an Indian story.
Give yourself an Indian name — and tell us why you chose it.
Tell about your house.
Tell about the work you do.
Describe your weapons.

On another posted sign was a question:

Who wants to help me add to this list of Indian words?

pow-wow	tribe
papoose	Blackfoot
how	Sioux

[6] Robert L. Heilbroner, *An Inquiry into the Human Prospect* (New York: W. W. Norton and Company, 1974), p. 102.

[7] Gregor Ziemer, *Education for Death: The Making of the Nazi* (New York: Oxford University Press, 1941), pp. 198–199.

A second class of Indian investigators prepared a number of charts on a variety of themes: Indian inventions — snow goggles, hammock, moccasins, snowshoes, and toboggan; Indian crafts — silver jewelry, pottery, and weaving; Indian names — Chicago, Connecticut, Massachusetts, Michigan, and Mississippi; and Indian communication — pictographs for *happiness, swiftness, journey, man, fish, rain,* and *running water.*

This "tepee" approach to the study of Indians may seem a bit outmoded, however. There are larger and more substantial questions that can be asked about Indian history. For example, between 1825 and 1844, most of the Indians in the eastern United States were moved west across the Mississippi, in a series of long and tragic marches. Why and how did this happen?[8]

The study of other ethnic groups can also serve as a useful way to learn about the past. Black history has been receiving increased attention in many classrooms. Some classes have done units on the study of slavery. Others have studied the role of black patriots in American history from Crispus Attucks to Martin Luther King, Jr. The histories of specific European, Asian, or Latin American ethnic groups in the United States can also make useful focal points in the study of America's past.[9]

Heroines and Heroes

Schools have always done a good deal to honor great Americans. But perhaps they have tended to place too much emphasis on George Washington, Abraham Lincoln, and the current occupant of the White House. Attention to the presidents, appropriate as it is, is insufficient. What is needed is a broader view of what constitutes

[8] For a careful report on this particular event, see Michael P. Rogin, *Fathers and Children: Andrew Jackson and the Subjugation of the Indian* (New York: Alfred A. Knopf, 1975).

[9] See Sidney Kaplan, *The Black Presence in the Era of the American Revolution, 1770–1800* (Greenwich, Conn.: New York Graphic Society and the Smithsonian Institution Press, 1973); for review of multi-ethnic study approaches, see also Leonard A. Valverde, ed., *Bilingual Education for Latinos* (Washington, D.C.: Association for Supervision and Curriculum Development, 1978), and Maxine Dunfee, "Unity with Diversity — A Common Commitment," *Educational Leadership*, 36 (February 1979), 344–348.

heroism. The reworking of social studies in ethnic terms has brought new names to the fore — Benjamin Banneker, Phillis Wheatley, Cesar Chavez. But other kinds of bias also need to be overcome.

Broadening the range of greatness to avoid class bias may turn up some persons whose deeds are basically unfamiliar to many Americans — Eugene V. Debs, Sacco and Vanzetti, Big Bill Haywood. These individuals might become heroes to a child from the Bronx, whose relatives are employed in the garment industries and to whom unions are a part of family and neighborhood life.[10] For young blacks, A. Philip Randolph might be a hero on two counts, as a leader in the early civil rights movement and as the longtime president of the Brotherhood of Sleeping Car Porters.[11]

Gender bias and bias against social agitation and dissent may have united to obscure the leadership role displayed by many American women. Jane Addams, founder of one of the best known of the settlement houses, kept Hull House going as a beacon of forward-looking social thinking. Yet what do children know of the movements for which she provided leadership — pacifism, labor unionization, woman's suffrage, welfare legislation in a dozen fields? (See Exhibit 7–1 for a list of some neglected figures in American history with whom children might well become better acquainted.) One reason for the rise in the 1960s of a radical center in America, which was largely working class and ethnic in origin with a Catholic or fundamentalist Protestant orientation, may have been the absence in the education of the young from this background of attention to the social-political achievements of historic radical or liberal leaders.[12]

Symbols of the Past

Honoring the flag and reciting the Pledge of Allegiance are an established part of opening exercises in most schools across the country.

[10] Leonard Kriegel, *Notes for the Two-Dollar Window: Portraits from an American Neighborhood* (New York: E. P. Dutton and Company, 1976), p. 24.
[11] See Daniel S. Davis, *Mr. Black Labor: The Story of A. Philip Randolph, Father of the Civil Rights Movement* (New York: E. P. Dutton and Company, 1972).
[12] See Donald I. Warren, *The Radical Center: Middle Americans and the Politics of Alienation* (Notre Dame, Ind.: University of Notre Dame Press, 1976).

Exhibit 7-1

Some Possibly Neglected Heroines and Heroes in American History

Occupation	Heroines and heroes	
Labor organizers	Eugene V. Debs Samuel Gompers Sidney Hillman	Mother Jones John L. Lewis A. Philip Randolph
Social agitators and dissenters	Jane Addams Susan B. Anthony Victor Berger John Brown Carrie C. Catt Frederick Douglass Emma Goldman W. D. Haywood Martin Luther King, Jr. Horace Mann	Tom Mooney Lucretia Mott Thomas Paine Wendell Phillips Elizabeth Cady Stanton Norman Thomas Harriet Tubman Frances Willard Peter Zenger
Writers and editors	Edward Bellamy John Dewey Theodore Dreiser W. E. B. DuBois Margaret Fuller William L. Garrison Horace Greeley Langston Hughes Jack London	Frank Norris Jacob Riis Upton Sinclair Lincoln Steffens Harriet B. Stowe Ida Tarbell Henry D. Thoreau Walt Whitman John G. Whittier
Government figures	William Jennings Bryan Oliver Wendell Holmes Robert LaFollette George Norris	Frances Perkins Gifford Pinchot Charles Sumner Henry Wallace

What about attending to some other aspects of America's symbolic heritage? One possibly neglected field is that of political documents. Here is a list of key documents to start with, drawn from a compilation meant for the general reading public:[13]

The Mayflower Compact (1620)
Massachusetts School Law (1647)
Benjamin Franklin, The Albany Plan of Union (1754)
The Declaration of Independence (1776)
The Constitution (1787)
The Bill of Rights (1791)
Horace Mann, Report on Education (1845) — extract
Seneca Falls Declaration of Sentiments and Resolutions (1848)
John Brown, Last Speech in Court (1859)
Abraham Lincoln, The Gettysburg Address (1863)
The Fourteenth Amendment (1868)
Preamble to the Constitution of the Knights of Labor (1878)
Platform of the Populist Party (1892)
Declaration of the Conservation Conference (1908)
The Nineteenth Amendment (1920)
Bartolomeo Vanzetti, Statement from Prison (1927)
Franklin D. Roosevelt, First Inaugural Address (1933)
Franklin D. Roosevelt, The Four Freedoms Speech (1941)
Brown v. Board of Education of Topeka (1954)
Martin Luther King, I Have a Dream (1963)
The Twenty-Sixth Amendment (1971)

Some of the documents are familiar, some are less well known. And, of course, most of them will call for carefully planned teaching if they are to carry much meaning for younger or even older children. But should children be denied access, even partial access, to such expressions of America's basic beliefs?

Literature also has its contribution to make — poems such as Emerson's "Concord Hymn," Whitman's "When Lilacs Last in the Dooryard Bloom'd," and Frost's "The Gift Outright"; extracts from

[13] See Irwin Glusker and R. M. Ketchum, eds., *American Testament: Fifty Great Documents of American History* (New York: American Heritage Publishing Company, 1971).

the essays of Paine and Thoreau; and stories for children such as *Johnny Tremain* by Esther Forbes.

A hundred years ago, children in Baltimore, Philadelphia, and elsewhere in the United States learned their history from Samuel G. Goodrich's pictorial version of *Parley's Common School History of the World*. Because it was simply written, it was claimed "that a pupil may commit the whole volume to memory during a winter's schooling."[14] The frontispiece engraving offered a preview in the form of a monument to the great events of all time. The book began with the creation (4004 B.C.) and closed with the American and French Revolutions. The fifty pages reserved for America touched on the first inhabitants, discovery by Columbus, settlement and colonial history, causes of the Revolution, the battles of Lexington and Bunker Hill, the story of Benedict Arnold and Major André, and a few events of the Great Rebellion.

Schools must do more with American history in today's curriculum for children. The "voluntary utopia" of America, as one social scientist has termed it, was not something that resulted from a common ancestry; it was a conscious creation of its people. This creation of "the dream of brotherhood of common ideals and virtues open to all" (even if it was open in its early stages "most cordially to Caucasians"[15]) deserves to be honored in the schools.

Cultural pluralism is to be respected, but maintenance of cultural unity is of first importance. Thus, children need to find out about the origins of America and Americans, the great leaders in American history, and the symbols of America's past. In learning to value their political heritage, children need something more to work with than their own immediate life experiences or awareness of events on the current scene. Competence in this instance rests on a knowledge base to which learners must be receptive if they are to be able to choose wisely between less and more rewarding ways of being and behaving in the moral-ethical-political realm.

---

[14] Advertisement, front pages, in Samuel G. Goodrich, *A Pictorial History of the World, Ancient and Modern, for the Use of Schools* (Philadelphia: J. H. Butler and Company, 1877).

[15] William Zelinsky, *The Cultural Geography of the United States* (Englewood Cliffs, N.J.: Prentice-Hall, 1973), p. 33.

DEVELOPING SOME UNDERSTANDING
OF GOVERNANCE

Children need to learn how self-government works. In the past, teachers relied heavily on children's picking up democratic behavior through working together in a way that taught respect for the rights of others. The give-and-take of everyday living led to appreciation of the need for rules to govern group activities. Children also learned responsibility through taking turns at housekeeping duties. All of this will certainly continue to be thought important in the education of children.

But nowadays many teachers are inclined to want to do more. Political education needs to include some acquaintance with how a system of self-government operates. Competence of a higher order comes as children have opportunities to become skillful in making decisions, sharing in the exercise of authority and control, and performing the varied roles of leadership.[16] Let us examine some of the approaches currently in use in the new political curriculum for children.

Shared Decision Making

All forms of government are or can be oppressive, including democracy. This was the conclusion of the distinguished historian Arnold Toynbee at the age of eighty-two.[17] But power must be exercised in one way or another, and children must be helped to understand it. Children can learn something of the nature of power in a democracy through becoming more conscious of how it can be shared.

One useful approach is to provide children with formal problem situations and invite them to come up with appropriate answers. Authority, consensus, and voting are three good ways to make

[16] See Elliott Seif, *Teaching Significant Social Studies in the Elementary School* (Chicago: Rand McNally College Publishing Company, 1977), pp. 334–367.

[17] Arnold Toynbee, *Surviving the Future* (New York: Oxford University Press, 1971).

decisions, depending on the circumstances. The following is a set of problems proposed for discussion in these terms:

1. The airplane engine has caught fire. A decision must be made about landing.
2. You and two friends are deciding what to do on a Saturday afternoon.
3. The football team is in the huddle. It is time to decide what the next play will be.
4. The people of Ohio want to decide who their governor will be.
5. A family is deciding whether to go to a drive-in.
6. The class is deciding whether to have milk or pop at the class picnic.[18]

The question to be answered is this: in each case, which of the three alternatives is the best way to arrive at the needed decision — and which is the worst?

Law and Order

Key concepts may also provide a framework for political education. In one school district, a social studies chart shows how concepts are worked into the school curriculum.

Kindergarten:	conflict, cooperation, rights and responsibilities
First grade:	change, citizenship, compromise, interdependence, rights and responsibilities
Second grade:	decision-making, justice, law, society
Third grade:	cooperation, social discrimination
Fourth grade:	behavior (political), change, freedom, leadership, power
Fifth grade:	conflict, democracy, differences, government

[18] *Citizenship Decision-Making Project, Mershon Center and Ohio Department of Education* (Columbus, Ohio: State Department of Education, n.d.), Unit II, *Making Political Decisions*, p. 8.

Sixth grade:	compromise, norms, rights and responsibilities, society
Seventh grade:	compromise, decision-making, government, social discrimination
Eighth grade:	citizenship, democracy, government, institutions, law, rights and responsibilities

It is significant that the topic of rights and responsibilities (or law and order) appears and reappears on this list. Clearly, schools are doing more today to help children understand how laws are made and how the apparatus of enforcement functions. Unhappily, the images invoked by the phrase *law and order* for a television-reared generation tend to be violence-related. Crimes against person and property provide a dependable source of cheap drama for a commercially controlled and often conscienceless medium. The essence of the law, however, is settlement of legalistic differences. Civil conflict is not as reliably or immediately dramatic as are encounters between cops and robbers. But for children as for all of us, appreciating the process for the quiet resolution under law of differences that have to do with a broad range of human rights is of vital importance. (See Exhibit 7–2, pp. 198–199.)

Sometimes, as in South Boston or Louisville or Little Rock, these differences make headlines. More often, the conflict at issue is not so tense. Children need and deserve our help in understanding the law as it has evolved in relation to inequities of many kinds — racism, sexism, classism, ageism, and even "species-ism" (or the rights of animals[19]). In addition, protection of people's common rights is a matter of increasing concern in the curriculum for children, as shown by the number of new environmental and consumer education programs.

The Structure of Government

For older students, the common learnings to be sought in political education may be spelled out more elaborately. In one sixth grade, the unifying theme of an integrated or cross-disciplinary curriculum is

[19] See Peter Singer, *Animal Liberation: A New Ethics for Our Treatment of Animals* (New York: Random House, 1975).

"Man in Community," with content organized around seven concepts or elements. Here are some of the study topics:

Need

Meeting local needs through government
The role of cooperation in meeting needs

Conflict

Resolving personal conflicts
Resolving conflict in the process of government
Contemporary world issues: national interests vs. global concerns
Contemporary issues in our community

Change

The Declaration of Independence: unfinished business
The process of change in America

Community

Development of communal societies: components of civilization
Planning for a better community
Cooperation as a civilizing force
Communities of the past

Social control

Working effectively in groups: processes and problems
National needs and global concerns
Understanding the legal process; school rules
Ways of dealing with aggression

Individual uniqueness

The causes of American independence

Adaptation

Problems of the newly independent U.S.A.
Modern challenges in adaptation: a continuous struggle

Ambitious as this framework may seem, it does provide children with an opportunity to come to grips with the basics of government and to explore local, state and federal relationships.

Exhibit 7-2

Human Rights: Some Points of Legislative Concern

Area of rights	Examples of concern
Education	Racial integration of students: busing
	Bilingual education for children whose home language is not English
	Access to higher education by members of minorities
	Equal access to professional schools by women
	Equal access to sports programs by women
Employment	Fair screening practices for entry into civil service and other jobs
	Racial-ethnic balance in given field of work
	Entry of women into all kinds of occupations
	Promotion of minority group members and women
	Full employment of all able workers
Consumer protection	Truth in advertising
	Proper labeling of products in terms of contents, weight, uses, etc.
	Honesty in contracts for goods and services
	Improving quality of commercially sponsored children's television programs
	Prohibition of advertising of harmful or worthless products

Area of rights	Examples of concern
Environment	Provision of parks and playgrounds
	Prevention of pollution
	Protection of wilderness areas
	Regulation of trapping, confining, and experimenting with animals
	Planning use of space, urban as well as rural
The young and the old	Adequate retirement benefits
	Prevention and detection of child abuse
	Fair adoption policies and practices
	Food service for the poor: free meals at school, inexpensive meals for the elderly
	Better care facilities: day care centers (for young and old), nursery schools, nursing homes
Protection in general	Health insurance: Medicare, Medicaid
	Good community health facilities: hospitals, nursing homes, clinics
	Adequacy of police and fire services
	Safe highways and traffic control
	Safety programs in the schools: water, home, bicycle, play, etc.

The results of recent studies of what children know about government have been disappointing to many persons. Although older students do better than younger, it is apparent that schooling in government has not significantly added to children's knowledge of government.[20] Broad-based studies, including some investigations conducted in other nations, indicate that schools in general have been unable to provide a politically relevant education for children and youth, as Byron G. Massialas points out.[21] Even when something is being done, it is likely to be of relatively little social or political significance, he concludes.

Teachers seem to be resolved to do more to help children understand the structure of government. The challenge is to do this in such a way that the reasons for government do not get lost in teaching the details of how it is organized.

The Nature of Leadership

In a unit of older children, issues defined for debate in an election of a governing committee include these:

1. More bathroom passes
2. Longer recess
3. Chewing gum in school

In another group, one of fifth-graders, the study theme is the coming national election. Children are working independently on such activities as writing biographies of candidates, investigating key issues (unemployment, inflation, foreign policy, taxes) for oral reports, and

---

[20] See Charles F. Andrian, *Children and Civic Awareness* (Columbus, Ohio: Charles E. Merrill Publishing Company, 1971); also, for reports of more recent findings, see Pearl M. Oliver, *Teaching Elementary Social Studies: A Rational and Humanistic Approach* (New York: Harcourt Brace Jovanovich, 1976), and J. Bryan Moffet, *Teaching Elementary School Social Studies* (Boston: Little, Brown and Company, 1977).

[21] Byron G. Massialas, ed., *Political Youth, Traditional Schools: National and International Perspectives* (Englewood Cliffs, N.J.: Prentice-Hall, 1972).

doing research on the origins and history of major political parties. A mock election will be the culminating event.

Such activities are familiar enough and relate to the emergence of elected leadership. But there are deeper questions that deserve to be examined: What is leadership good for? How does its nature vary from one situation to another? How can persons learn to be good leaders? These are questions to which attention may need to be more directly given in the education of children today. Passive behavior can disfranchise whole neighborhoods.[22] Thus, no one concerned with wider participation in political decision making can doubt the need for leadership training.

Governance, then, is something to which children should be helped consciously to attend. "The citizen's right to participate in government is not emphasized in the school curriculum," concluded a study of the early 1960s.[23] And the same charge can be made today. Schools must do more, particularly in the study of decision making, law and order, governmental structure, and leadership. Yet these topics alone do not form an adequate framework for developing competence in the moral-ethical-political realm.

DEFINING THE GOOD SOCIETY

Political education has to involve something more than knowledge of our nation's history and the structure of its government. These could become static in orientation. But by its very nature, democracy is dynamic. Children need to be caught up in the ever-present concern for realizing better solutions to moral and ethical problems and issues. Principles become clear as people have many experiences in the use of the "critical method applied to goods of belief, appreciation, and

---

[22] See Curt Lamb, *Political Power in Poor Neighborhoods* (Cambridge, Mass.: Schenkman Publishing Company, 1975); and David Morris and Karl Hess, *Neighborhood Power: the New Localism* (Boston: Beacon Press, 1975).

[23] Robert D. Hess and Judith V. Torney, *The Development of Political Attitudes in Children* (Garden City, N.Y.: Anchor Books, Doubleday and Company, 1968), p. 126.

conduct, so as to construct freer and more secure goods."[24] These are the words of John Dewey, but they might also have been said by Lawrence Kohlberg or Louis Raths or anyone else close to the problem of helping children develop competence in learning to value in this vital realm. "Shareable meanings"[25] (Dewey's words again) are what we are all after. But the way to develop them is hard to find.

Moral and Ethical Problems

The children of our time have vast amounts of data presented to them every day from the world around them. Through television, even the youngest child becomes aware of questions that have to do with the right and wrong of many kinds of events, both private and public. Children do not, of course, understand fully the dimensions of such events. But who would deny that they can be puzzled by reports of graft and corruption in sports, international trade, national elections, food merchandizing, and the like? Schools must assist children in exploring the moral and ethical meanings of such happenings.

This need may represent one of the true frontiers in the new curriculum for children. Educators may hardly know where to turn for help, but they would no doubt agree on the urgency of positive action of some sort. We cannot allow children to come to the conclusion that a world filled with immoral activities is the way things are and always have to be. Simply not facing up to the situation can lead to the worst kind of negative education, as described by Franz Kafka in *The Trial*.

> "No," said the priest, "it is not necessary to accept everything as true, one must only accept it as necessary." "A melancholy conclusion," said K. "It turns lying into a universal principle."[26]

[24] See B. Frank Brown et al., *Education for Responsible Citizenship: The Report of the National Task Force on Citizenship Education* (New York: McGraw-Hill Book Company, 1977).

[25] Dewey, *Intelligence in the Modern World*, p. 273.

[26] Franz Kafka, *The Trial*, trans. Willa and Edwin Muir, Definitive Edition, Revised (New York: Alfred A. Knopf, Inc., 1968), p. 276.

We must do what we can to bring children opportunities to define and exemplify the essential elements of the good life and the good society. "I do not need my freedom when I'm dead," wrote Langston Hughes. "I cannot live on tomorrow's bread."[27]

Our uneasiness here has made us welcome the work on moral reasoning and values clarification. "Moral discussion," as advocated by Kohlberg, may help children think through "situations posing problems and contradictions,"[28] whether these are drawn directly from personal experience, picked up at second hand, posed as "moral dilemmas" by the teacher, or derived from America's own past history as a nation.

Analysis of Current Issues

Children can be helped to examine the elements of the good society through analysis of the issues that are always before us. These are many and various. (See Exhibit 7–3 for a framework that may be useful in thinking about their scope.) Thus, teachers must choose what issues are most worth working through with children.

No doubt interest has its part to play here. Interest is often inspired by awareness of something new. An election year, a world crisis, sports and labor events — these are likely to attract the attention of children through television or newspaper accounts or talk at home.

But interest alone is not enough. As in the treatment of human rights topics, major areas must be deliberately covered. Hopefully, teachers will work together so that continuity can be assured. Currency of interest may be the starting point. However, as issues change, our concern for helping children come to some understanding of the larger moral-ethical dimensions of political and domestic events must be maintained.

[27] From "Freedom," in Langston Hughes, *The Panther and the Lash: Poems of Our Times* (New York: Alfred A. Knopf, Inc., 1971), p. 89. Copyright © 1971; reprinted by permission of the publisher.

[28] Lawrence Kohlberg, "The Cognitive-Developmental Approach to Moral Education," *Phi Delta Kappan*, 56 (June 1975), 157–164.

Exhibit 7-3

Public Events with Moral-Ethical Dimensions

Area	Examples of events
Political events	
Campaigns and elections	"Dirty tricks" in campaigning
	Sources of campaign funds
	Platforms: what parties promise
The legislative process	Pros and cons of pending legislation
	Impact of lobbyists on lawmaking
	Internal organization of legislatures: minority versus majority
Execution of the law	Dissension between executive and other branches
	Selection of goals to be promoted
	Abuse of power by undercover operations
Judicial action	Decisions related to integration
	Law and order rulings
	Fair employment decisions
Foreign policy	Military preparedness
	Relations with Communist world
	Help provided to nations in need
Internal affairs	Welfare needs
	Employment and unemployment
	Environmental issues

Area	Examples of events
Domestic events	
Sports	Franchise policies
	Protection of players' rights
	Relationship of sports and television
Business and industry	International trade: kickbacks, bribes
	Restriction on competition
	Employment practices
Labor	Strikes and walkouts
	Union membership policies
	Union politics and leadership problems
Medicine	Adequacy of health care
	Costs of health care
	Malpractice insurance

HOW TO MOVE AHEAD IN THE
MORAL-ETHICAL-POLITICAL REALM

If children are to grow up to function fully in the political arena, they need to become aware that there are options for action. They can exercise the prerogatives of citizenship or not as they see fit. But before an intelligent decision can be made, they must know what the prerogatives are and also, to the extent that young citizens can do so, they need to have experienced what difference it makes whether they act in a particular way — or not at all.

There is no area of values more vital to a society's well-being than that of political performance. But we need to be alert to some of the challenges that must be met if teachers are to succed in developing allegiance to the democratic way of life.

Avoidance of Prematurity

In their summary of the classic University of Chicago study of children's political attitudes in the early 1960s, Robert Hess and Judith Torney noted the tendency of schools to limit teaching to compliance with authority or "regard for the rules and standards of conduct of school." The curriculum, as they viewed it, "underemphasizes the rights and obligations of a citizen to participate in government. The school . . . does not offer the child sufficient understanding of procedures open to individuals for legitimately influencing the government. Nor does it adequately explain and emphasize the importance of group action to achieve desirable ends." Since that time, as we have tried to indicate, the new curriculum for children has moved to take on some of the burden of teaching a "more realistic view of the operation of the political system."[29]

Schools have moved ahead. But have they gone too far? In planning for children, one of the prime perils is prematurity. Are children — or the particular children with whom a teacher may be concerned — ready to study this or that aspect of the history or structure of government? Will what they learn have enough meaning for them to retain it? Or will it go down the drain with a lot of other school learning that is presented too soon?

[29] Hess and Torney, *Political Attitudes*, pp. 248, 251.

In the sixties, an absorbing interest of many academic curriculum makers was to see how soon they could begin to teach what they felt children eventually needed to learn. The sooner, the better, they seemed to be saying. It is hard to quarrel with the wisdom of giving children as much as possible of what they need to make sense out of their experiences. But some caution is called for here. Children may be able to repeat the definitions they have been taught in relation to the differences among the branches of government. But will they use this information often enough and with sufficient understanding so that three months or six months after initial learning the distinctions will have sharpened — or indeed survived?

Psychologization of Subject Matter

Probably the chief challenge in planning better experiences in political education for children is to find ways to relate what needs to be learned to children's ongoing interests and concerns. In Dewey's view (and those of Johann Pestalozzi, too), we need to psychologize the content.[30] We are presently doing a pretty fair job of tying in political learning with the tasks and opportunities of living together in school. Children share housekeeping duties, operate the traffic patrol, and conduct classroom and schoolwide elections. But most of us have not done as much as we should to give children experience with the larger concepts or competencies that contribute to democratic governance.

When we do, we may be in for a few surprises. Anxiety about the exploitative aspects of television's impact on children should not blind us to the tremendous enlargement in social awareness that comes from an average of three hours a day exposure to the medium. In the human rights area, for example, children may be much readier than we might expect to handle aspects of racism and sexism. And children are almost certain to have some awareness of many of the kinds of public events (listed in Exhibit 7–3) that have moral-ethical dimensions.

We are not proposing a series of new studies on children's awareness of the world around them, useful as such knowledge would be. More immediately to the point is the need for trying out many ways

[30] See "The Child and the Curriculum," in *Dewey on Education: Selections*, ed. Martin S. Dworkin (New York: Teachers College Press, 1959), pp. 91–111.

to present content so as to enlarge and enliven the political education of all children.

Focus on Choices

Learning to value rests on consciousness of options and the checking of consequences through making choices. Yet in the arena of political education, the options open to children are likely to be confined to the little community that is the school. Dewey had faith that if children lived there in truly democratic fashion, they would learn much of what it takes to function effectively in the larger society. We would not want to abandon this position. But many of us would like to extend it.

Today schools are sponsoring many kinds of forays into the surrounding community. Most of these, it is true, are service projects — clean-up campaigns, paper drives, participation in walk-a-thons for worthy causes. But there are other possibilities. School groups have conducted traffic counts and presented their findings to city councils. Children have had a hand in getting more recreational facilities for their neighborhoods. Organized efforts by school children to get more field trips, swimming pool time, library books, and the like are not as rare as they may once have been. In the next chapter, we deal in some detail with the problem of providing children with meaningful activities as part of their political education. Let us be content here simply to note the need as a real challenge.

Recasting the curriculum toward the end of helping children develop allegiance to the democratic way of life is plainly a major undertaking. This concern, however, has not been confined to the elementary school level. Harvard University and Carnegie-Mellon University (Pittsburgh) have sponsored large-scale efforts to develop civic education programs based on the Kohlberg model of moral development at the secondary level, with attention primarily to the fields of social studies and English.[31] Moreover, the general curriculum field has been responsive to the idea that all curriculum making is necessarily value based. As James B. MacDonald has defined

[31] Edwin Fenton, "The Implications of Lawrence Kohlberg's Research for Civic Education," in *Education for Responsible Citizenship*, ed. Brown et al., pp. 120–127.

it, concern for the nature of goodness underlies all curriculum talk and work whether or not it is acknowledged. The fundamental questions, he contends, in proposing any program for children or youth are these: "(a) what is the meaning of human life? and (b) how shall we live together?"[32] Our own intention has been to invite the participation of children in finding answers to these questions, as a way of helping children learn to value in the moral-ethical-political realm.

And, as this chapter has shown, there is much for children to learn in this area. Political education as we have defined it has allegiance to the democratic way of life as its primary objective. The new curriculum for children puts renewed emphasis on finding out about America's past — the history of its people, its heroines and heroes, its political and historical symbols. The new curriculum is also committed to helping children gain some understanding of governance. Decision making is to be shared. Concern for law and order needs to go beyond controlling crime in the streets; children must learn something about the need for safeguarding human rights. Children must also devote more attention to understanding the structure of government and the nature of leadership. Finally, the moral and ethical dimensions of the good society must not be overlooked.

But allegiance to basic principles is not a stopping place. Children must also learn how to bring about needed social and political changes. Reform and reconstruction — or radicalism, if you will — are part of America's dynamic way of life and must remain so if its people are to respond successfully to the changing demands of the real world. Thus, children also need to learn about social innovativeness, as we will try to indicate in the next chapter.

ACTIVITIES

1. Collect several examples of room rules made by children. What do these reveal about the standards of behavior expected by teachers?
2. Should children use cameras, as Jacob Riis did, to record conditions that need to be changed? What kind of assignments might inspire children to try their hand at social reportage?

[32] James B. MacDonald, "Values Bases and Issues for Curriculum," in *Curriculum Theory*, ed. Alex Molnar and John A. Zahorik (Washington, D.C.: Association for Supervision and Curriculum Development, 1977), p. 20.

3. Prepare a set of learning activities that will help bring children new understandings of the relation between past and present in the history of a particular racial or ethnic group, for example, Indians, blacks, or Mexican-Americans.
4. Examine the list of heroines and heroes in Exhibit 7–1. Would you question the inclusion of any of these? Are there others that should be added?
5. Select appropriate literature (poems, stories, biographies) to develop a theme related to freedom and justice. Present your selections to a group of children. What kind of response do you get?
6. What do you think about the sharing of school housekeeping duties among children? What may children be expected to learn? Would you impose any limits on the practice?
7. Examine the problems offered for discussion in the section on "Shared Decision Making." Plan activities in which the full meaning of the three ways to make decisions (authority, consensus, and voting) could be experienced by children in school.
8. This chapter's treatment of law and order focuses on human rights. Use the *Education Index* to locate six recent reports on what is being done to educate children about the law. What other points of concern might be stressed?
9. Does Exhibit 7–2 include all the major areas of human rights? Revise this exhibit to fit your own conception of what is important.
10. How aware are children of current issues with moral-ethical dimensions? To find out, construct a brief test of your own. Administer to a group of children. What do you discover?
11. What do you think is the biggest challenge in developing a program of political education? How would you go about meeting this challenge?

Chapter 8

Social Innovativeness

Very young children take hold of the objects in their environment and try to see what they can do with them. In this way size and shape and weight take on meaning, and children find out how things work in this world. Space, location, and causality — the elements studied by Piaget — come into realization as children explore their surroundings. To act on something is to know it.

Similarly, in the realm of social skills and understandings, children learn by putting their first glimmerings of insight to the test of action. They smile upon those who provide food and comfort, and discover that certain responses are fairly dependable. When playtime comes, they learn to look for a hidden ball and laugh at a funny face. As they begin to play with agemates, children act to find out so many things — the give-and-take of relationships and the comfort of having and being a companion, a playmate, a co-worker.

Chapter 7 reported on what is going on in education for allegiance to the democratic way of life. Finding an arena for action there is not too difficult. Living together in the classroom and school provides a natural action base. But the social education of Americans ought to include learning to question things as they are and have been. Reform is an aspect of self-government that can get lost in the passion to bring children up "right." Earlier, when dealing with everyday living, we paired adjustment or accommodation to things as they are with critical thinking about them. In the arts, we put appreciation and creation together. Here we wish to pair allegiance and reform (or social innovativeness). But defining an action base for what may look to some people like trouble-making is not easy.

WHAT IS NEEDED FOR SOCIAL INNOVATIVENESS

As they grow up, children find themselves in charge of much of their preschool and out-of-school experience. They discover that for the most part they can do what they need and want to do. During their time at school, they continue to develop a sense of social competence. They learn from and with others how to get things done. They learn that they can do many things together that they cannot do alone. Puzzling at first, the bases of social action reveal themselves through much experience.

A Positive Attitude

"It seems to me that I never heard this man say no," reminisced writer Isaac Bashevis Singer about a good man known to him in his youth. "His entire life was one great yes."[1] But where did Reb Asher's yea-saying approach to life come from?

Marcus Aurelius advised that such an attitude develops where there is understanding and love. "Begin the morning by saying to thyself, I shall meet with the busybody, the ungrateful, arrogant,

[1] Isaac Bashevis Singer, *In My Father's Court* (New York: Farrar, Straus, and Giroux, 1966), p. 163. Copyright © 1962, 1963, 1964, 1965, 1966 by Isaac Bashevis Singer.

deceitful, envious, unsocial." But their behavior grows out of ignorance of good and evil, which are known to me. Therefore, I must remain open and accepting: "For we are made for cooperation, like feet, like hands, like eyelids, like the rows of the upper and lower teeth. To act against one another then is contrary to nature; and it is acting against one another to be vexed and to turn away."[2]

Saying yes and uniting with others are both part of learning how to be socially innovative. People's attitudes toward themselves and others have much to do with whether they place a high value on working as hard as they can to make a better world.

Wanting and Willing

"There can be no difference anywhere that doesn't make a difference elsewhere," argued the pragmatist William James; "no difference in abstract truth that doesn't express itself in a difference in concrete facts and in conduct consequent upon that fact, imposed on somebody, somehow, somewhere, and somewhen." But the abstractionist prefers to live in the world of speculation. Such a person "positively prefers the pale and spectral" and given a choice "would always choose the skinny outline rather than the rich thicket of reality."[3] What James is saying, then, is that wanting needs to be accompanied by willing, if something is to get done.

Knowledge of the Facts

Wanting and willing, in turn, must be accompanied by knowing, if efforts at social innovation are to prove worthwhile. One of the primary tasks of any group of would-be problem solvers is to make sure that the problem has been properly understood and that they have an answer that may make a difference. Have they found or

[2] Marcus Aurelius, *Meditations*, ed. James Gutmann, trans. George Long (New York: Washington Square Press, 1964), II, i, 8.

[3] William James, *Pragmatism: A New Name for Some Old Ways of Thinking* (New York: Longman, Green, 1914), pp. 49–50, 68.

created a number of alternatives? Have these been examined for their possible consequences? Finally, are the problem solvers now ready to move from wanting a good answer to being willing to act in behalf of their best judgment?

Awareness of Moral-Ethical Implications

"Yesterday I went to Mr. Alcott's school and heard a conversation upon the Gospel of St. John," noted Ralph Waldo Emerson in his journal for June 16, 1836. Emerson thought "the experiment of engaging young children upon questions of taste and truth successful" and arrived at the conclusion "that to truth [there] is no age or season. It appears, or it does not appear, and when the child perceives it, he is no more a child; age, sex, are nothing: we are all alike before the great whole." A few months later Emerson noted with equal assurance that "The only friend that can persuade the soul to speak is a good and great cause."[4]

The moral force of a new truth or ideal has long been understood as has the nature of resistance to change. "Those who govern, having much business on their hands, do not generally like to take the trouble of considering and carrying into execution new projects," Benjamin Franklin observed. "The best public measures are therefore seldom adopted from previous wisdom, but forced by the occasion."[5]

Tolstoy expressed the conflict between past practice and progress in somewhat different terms:

> What generally takes place is this, that when an idea, which in the past was useful and even indispensable, becomes superfluous, this idea, after a more or less prolonged struggle, gives way to a new idea, which heretofore was an ideal, but now becomes the idea of the present.[6]

Nonetheless, the obsolete may hang on, maintained by those who profit from its survival.

---

[4] *Journals of Ralph Waldo Emerson*, ed. Edward W. Emerson and Waldo E. Forbes (Cambridge, Mass.: Houghton Mifflin Company, 1910), IV, 69, 124.

[5] *The Autobiography of Benjamin Franklin, Poor Richard's Almanac, and Other Papers*, ed. Larzer Ziff (New York: A. L. Burt, n.d.), p. 167.

[6] *The Complete Works of Count Tolstoy*, trans. Leo Wiener (Boston: Dana Estes and Company, 1905), XXIII, 146.

Acceptance of Personal Responsibility

In a series of experimental studies of obedience, psychologist Stanley Milgram set up a situation in which a teacher (the subject) was supposed to see that a learner mastered a list of word pairs. The experimenter (representing authority) would urge the teacher to continue administering electric shocks to the slow learner (a paid actor) even when the latter indicated pain and a desire to stop. And the teacher did what he or she was told. The conclusion: such dreadful actions as those that occurred at My Lai in Vietnam can be understood only as instances of acceptance of authority at the expense of personal responsibility. What is frightening is "the capacity for man to abandon his humanity, indeed, the inevitability that he does so, as he merges his unique personality into larger institutional structures."[7]

The problem of education for personal responsibility is not new. It is central to every moral-ethical system. Only as people realize what it means to speak out against the majority can they begin to appreciate how hard-won freedom always has been — and always must and will be. Liberty begins with a personal statement. "The liberty that is taught in schools has been won at a great cost to individuals, not by the people at large," poet Louis Simpson contends.[8]

Can teachers develop ways to educate children to be social innovators and reformers? If they can, will they be able to implement them in their classrooms? Opening the school day with the Pledge of Allegiance is one thing. But how well will a community or school board accept a noontime picket of the cafeteria — up with tacos, down with sloppy joes? Or an appearance by the fifth grade before the City Council to argue for a traffic light at Elm Street and Avenue J? Or a school assembly culminating a unit study by eight- and nine-year-olds on "American Heroines and Heroes You Never Heard Of," from the fields of woman's suffrage, labor strife, and children's rights?

It is important for children growing up in a democracy to learn how people can change society for the better if they truly wish to. Not all schools accept the necessity of this, but today many schools are doing what they can to recast the curriculum toward sponsoring more chances for children to experience the satisfactions that can

---

[7] Stanley Milgram, *Obedience to Authority: An Experimental View* (New York: Harper and Row, 1974), p. 188.

[8] Louis Simpson, *North of Jamaica* (New York: Harper and Row, 1972), p. 246.

come from bringing about needed changes in the world around them. Let us examine the dimensions of this aspect of values education.

LEARNING HOW CHANGES COME ABOUT

When James Madison called America a "workshop for liberty," he was simply identifying the role it was to play in an "age of experiments." (The latter expression was Benjamin Franklin's.) In the eighteenth century, as the first great planned experiment in self-government, the United States provided an example of how theory looked when put into practice. Americans had "committed themselves to the task of creating a society where human potentiality would at last be realized, where human rights and the dignity of all would seem like self-evident truths, and where practical liberty would be not just a happy accident but the result of enlightened social planning."⁹

The challenge of translating such high-sounding rhetoric into reality remains before Americans. During the past quarter-century, the nation has moved into a new era of social and political activism. Beginning with the civil rights movement that went into high gear after the Supreme Court decision in *Brown* v. *Board of Education of Topeka* (1954), the thrust has extended in many directions. Part of this resurgence has been a call for reconceptualizing many aspects of America's historical heritage. American children can benefit and are benefiting from new insights into what makes a democracy function effectively. Changes don't just happen; they are helped to happen.

Reformers in Action: The Past

In the wake of the sit-ins, marches, riots, and demonstrations of the middle and late sixties has come a new concern for understanding the nature and function of protest in American society. On the pessimistic side, Americans have been described as being violence-prone, and its movements of protest have been viewed as both a response to this violence and a contributing factor. Indians, Mormons, Chinese, blacks, Catholics, and labor leaders — all have been the victims of an

⁹ Donald H. Myers, *The Democratic Enlightenment* (New York: G. P. Putnam's Sons, 1976), pp. vii, 214.

endemic lawlessness that had its worst expression in the vigilante justice of the frontier. And many of the victims have responded with equal lawlessness. Ever since the days of the Stamp Act Riots (1765) and Shays' Rebellion (1786), America has been subject to occasional outbursts of social unrest.[10]

On the more positive side — and this is where we see implications for the education of children — social conflict has been newly perceived as part of the democratic process. Efforts to establish public schools, the abolitionist movement, the woman's suffrage movement, labor's long campaign for recognition — these ought to be properly understood as triumphs of the political process. The history of labor in the United States, as one example, is written in a series of events that may deserve to be better remembered:

1875   Coal miners' Long Strike, Pottsville, Pennsylvania
        (Molly Maguires)
1877   Railroad War, Martinsburg, West Virginia, Chicago,
        Pittsburgh
1886   National strike for eight-hour day — Haymarket bombing,
        Chicago
1892   Homestead steel strike, Pennsylvania
1894   Pullman boycott, American Railway Union, Chicago
1903–4 Miners' strikes, Cripple Creek, Colorado
1910   Clothing workers' strike, Chicago (women leaders)
1919   Steel strike, Pittsburgh and elsewhere
1934   Widespread strikes, many industries
1937   Auto workers' sitdown strike, Flint, Michigan

As one historian notes, the activists of today would do well to "study the principles propounded by radical humanists of other periods."[11] The struggle for human rights is never-ending. Our new concern is that the young be helped to see themselves as heirs of and allies in this struggle.

[10] See Irving J. Sloan, *Our Violent Past: An American Chronicle* (New York: Random House, 1970); and Richard Hofstadter and Michael Wallace, eds., *American Violence: A Documentary History* (New York: Alfred A. Knopf, 1970).
[11] See Sidney Lens, *The Labor Wars: From the Molly Maguires to the Sitdowns* (Garden City, N.Y.: Doubleday and Company, 1973); and Barbara M. Wertheimer, *We Were There: The Story of Working Women in America* (New York: Pantheon Books, 1977).

Children also need to be reminded of the historic role played by third parties in their country's past. When we look at the platform of the People's Party (1892), we find that along with advocating free coinage of silver and gold, pensions for Civil War veterans, and restrictions on "undesirable" immigration, the populists of that period were calling for a secret ballot, a graduated income tax, and government ownership of railroads.[12] More active third-party participation in today's politics, Daniel Mazmanian suggests, could provide "a continual airing of minority views and prodding of the major parties."[13]

Do we need to help children understand more ways in which protest can make itself felt? Attention to the story of leaders like Eugene V. Debs might be in order, or of other reformers listed in Exhibit 7–1. We are proposing not a children's crusade but simply that the young be helped to sense the variety of avenues to action open to an aroused or concerned people. (See Exhibit 8–1.)

Reformers in Action: The Present

Many men and women from every walk of life in this country are devoting energy every day to making this a better world for everyone. We would like to help children get closer to the impulse toward social action that stirs within these individuals.

Martin Luther King, Jr., Rosa Parks (arrested in 1955 for not moving to the back of the bus), Cesar Chavez, Shirley Chisholm, Ralph Nader — these are among the reformers of recent times whose life stories are now available to children.[14] Activist movements of current

[12] "The Omaha Platform of the People's Party," in *Populism: The Critical Issues*, ed. Sheldon Hackney (Boston: Little, Brown and Company, 1971), pp. 1–6.

[13] Daniel A. Mazmanian, *Third Parties in Presidential Elections* (Washington, D.C.: The Brookings Institution, 1974), p. 153.

[14] See Ruth Franchere, *Cesar Chavez* (New York: Thomas Y. Crowell Company, 1970); Susan Brownmiller, *Shirley Chisholm* (Garden City, N.Y.: Doubleday and Company, 1971); Lillie Patterson, *Martin Luther King: Man of Peace* (New York: Dell Publishing Company, 1969); Edward Preston, *Martin Luther King: Fighter for Freedom* (Garden City, N.Y.: Doubleday and Company, 1968); James T. Olsen, *Ralph Nader: Voice of the People* (Mankato, Minn.: Creative Education, 1974); and Eloise Greenfield, *Rosa Parks* (New York: Thomas Y. Crowell Company, 1973).

Exhibit 8-1

Arenas for Action in the Political Process

Educational arena

Membership in activist groups

Association with protest activities of various groups

Search for information: self-education

Political arena

Membership and participation in major party

Membership and participation in third party

Selective voting in elections

Personal arena

Governance of behavior in terms of convictions

Orientation of vocational pursuit toward moral-ethical-political values

Choice of religious affiliation oriented to action

---

interest in the schools would seem likely to include civil rights, women's liberation, children's rights, and consumerism. In some of these, children have already become involved.

Involvement in efforts at integration continues, of course. And today in a good many classrooms children may be partners in several other kinds of social-change enterprises. Ecology continues to be of great concern, as we noted in Chapter 4. In addition, in some classrooms children may be participating in investigations of their study materials for sex bias. Thus, many may be questioning whether their textbooks or other books

Illustrate or describe females engaged in passive activities while illustrating or describing males engaged in action activities?

Use masculine subsuming language to describe the hypothetical person?

Show or describe females as followers or under the direction of males disproportionally to males as followers or under the direction of females?

Have males as the main characters disproportionally in relation to having females as main characters?

Encourage females to be neat, orderly, and punctual while encouraging males to be less organized and more spontaneous?[15]

Awareness of bigotry and bias, unconscious as well as conscious, is a goal of many of today's activist movements. Perhaps June Sochen is right when she contends that sexism, racism, and anti-environmentalism are bound up together.[16]

Some Principles to Think About

Children can become more sensitive to the need for reform through developing a broader base of sensitivity to the needs of others as a foundation for social improvement. Children's literature at its best is

---

[15] Adapted from Kent Boesdorfer et al., *A Guide for Title IX Self-Study* (Kent, Ohio: College of Education, Kent State University, 1975), p. 47.

[16] June Sochen, *Herstory: A Woman's View of American History* (New York: Alfred Publishers, 1974), p. ix.

a great resource here and always has been. In the foreword to one of her regional stories, *Blue Ridge Billy*, Lois Lenski expressed this intention as follows:

> I am trying to say to children that all people are flesh and blood and have feelings like themselves, no matter where they live or how simply they live and how little they have; that man's material comforts should not be the end and object of life.[17]

Love, however it is labeled, is where we start in wanting and willing things to be better for everybody. Can love make a difference? This was Sigmund Freud's "fateful question for the human species": will the instinct of love be able to control the instinct of self-destruction?[18] In the past half-century, there have been many doubts. Nonetheless, much has been learned about the handling of hostility both individually and socially. Children can be made more conscious of where "bad" feelings come from and what they signify. Self-understanding comes first. But dealing with the feelings of others also matters. Again, children's literature, in the so-called "realistic" vein, seems to be providing needed help in this field today.

Respect for others; neighborliness; love; a sense of community; self-understanding and understanding of others; acceptance of the expression of feelings, negative as well as positive; honesty; and human caring — these are some of the bedrock principles out of which may arise a desire to see social changes come about.

Becoming conscious of alternative ways of being and behaving is the first front of value development. If children are to see social innovativeness as offering options for personal commitment, then they need to become acquainted with the stories of reformers, past and present, who knew how to speak for people as well as to people. Growth in sensitivity to the feelings of others must also be a part of it. Finally, children can be helped to identify new occasions for social action, as we shall see in the next section.

[17] From *Blue Ridge Billy* by Lois Lenski, p. xiv. Copyright 1946 by Lois Lenski. Reprinted by permission of J. B. Lippincott Company.
[18] Sigmund Freud, *Civilization and Its Discontents* (New York: W. W. Norton and Company, 1962 [originally published, 1930]), p. 92.

HELPING TO IMPROVE THE WORLD

We need to do more than merely give children information about the political system or about social movements past and present. To the extent that it is possible, they should enter into the political world and "begin to deal with it immediately," as Philip Brenner has proposed.[19] Ideally the school should not be a place apart but an open-access learning center to which young and old can come. The goal of such a newly cooperative society, as envisioned by William Pepper, would be "living in and rebuilding our environment together," with centralized power distributed into thousands of sociopolitical units across the country.[20]

Romance or fantasy? Perhaps. Yet the essence of a dynamic system of self-government is assumption of local responsibility for getting done those things that need to be done. And this involves becoming aware of what needs to — and can — be changed. Here is where it seems to us the school, children, and community can work together. Do things have to be as they are? What alternatives are there? How can or could these be realized?

Children can become involved in a variety of worthwhile projects aimed at improving the community. Participation in these serves a number of purposes. Children may simply learn what it means to be involved, for one thing. It takes time to get something done; sometimes it requires hard work; the benefits always have to be weighed against the costs. Children may also come to understand that a lot of persons have to be brought into a project to make much of anything happen. An idea may originate with one person or a small group. But getting plans completed, persuading others to join in, and carrying the endeavor through are really joint undertakings. And, of course, if social action is to be valued highly as an option for the investment of time and energy, children need to experience the satisfaction that comes from success. They should be given the opportunity to feel that if they try hard enough, they can really change things for the better — and that it's worth all the effort it takes.

[19] Philip Brenner, "Political Knowledge and Experience in Elementary Education," in *Schooling in a Corporate State: The Political Economy of Education in America*, ed. Martin Carnoy (New York: David McKay Company, 1972), p. 225.
[20] William F. Pepper, *The Self-Managed Child: Paths to Cultural Rebirth* (New York: Harper and Row, 1973), p. 204.

Service-Type Projects

Community service projects can develop the kind of practical citizenship that is "the very heart of democratic education," according to Laurence W. Aronstein and Edward G. Olsen. Practical citizenship "must be learned through satisfying personal experiences in community improvement projects during the period of formal schooling as well as afterward. Teachers with foresight and patience can do much to provide functional, realistic, democratic education based partly upon cooperative community service whereby students and community will mutually benefit."[21] In their analysis, Aronstein and Olsen distinguish between volunteer activity, in which students are fitted into existing programs, and service projects in which they have a part to play from the beginning.

Service-type projects encompass clean-up campaigns, safety campaigns, beautification activities, and good-deeds works. (See Exhibit 8–2 for examples of these.) All are relatively simple for schools to organize and are generally well received by the community. In some neighborhoods a few persons may resent alley clean-ups, and some elderly persons may feel they do not need help with shopping or yard work, however kind the intent. For the most part, however, residents of an area are quick to respond when an improvement project promises an immediate return of some kind.

Service-type projects have a place in a program of learning to act to change things, but their value is limited. Most require only that participants budget time and arrange for follow-through or maintenance. And the projects can become exploitative and counterproductive in nature. Should children be enlisted as regular members of the community's trash collection agency? Or should the city council be helped to see the need for better regular service? Why must parks or vacant lots or ponds be allowed to become eyesores in the first place? And if elderly persons need help, aren't there agencies that ought to be contacted?

The missing element in most service-type projects is impact on the power structure. But the long-range hope of proposals for utilizing schools (and their children) as a force in the community has

[21] Laurence W. Aronstein and Edward G. Olsen, *Action Learning: Student Community Service Projects* (Washington, D.C.: Association for Supervision and Curriculum Development, 1974), p. 13.

Exhibit 8-2

Projects for Community Improvement

Type	Examples of projects	Possible partners
Service		
Clean-up	Cleaning up alleys in school neighborhood	Residents, trash collection agency
	Cleaning trash from creek or pond	Parents, older youth
	Cleaning up park	Older youth, park department
	Cutting weeds and clearing off vacant lot	Residents, parents, trash collection agency
Safety	Participating in bicycle safety campaign	Traffic division of police department
	Distributing fire safety leaflets to homes	Fire department
	Conducting home inspections for fire hazards	Fire department
	Mounting parent education program on toy safety	Consumer agency or organization
Beautification	Planting trees in park	Forestry service, park department
	Distributing flower seeds to parents and others in school neighborhood	Garden club
	Planting and caring for roses in traffic island or similar space	Rose growers' club
	Collecting and scattering wildflower seeds (in vacant lots, along lanes and alleyways)	Garden club

Type	Example of projects	Possible partners
Good deeds	Shopping for elderly persons in neighborhood	Parents
	Collecting food and clothing for needy families	Parents
	Soliciting contributions for worthy agencies or organizations	Adult sponsors
	Distributing voter registration information	Public officials, League of Women Voters
Social action		
Campaign for traffic control devices	Counting traffic flow at intersection without light	City planning office
	Checking school neighborhood for poor corner visibility, difficult-to-see stop signs	
	Costing out needed improvements	Traffic division of police department
	Presenting proposals to police department and city council	Police chief, city council members

Exhibit 8-2 (cont.)

Projects for Community Improvement (*cont.*)

Type	Example of projects	Possible partners
Development of new facilities	Laying out baseball diamond or basketball court in neighborhood park	Parents, park and recreation departments
	Turning vacant lot into play area	Property owner, parents, park and recreation departments
	Building play structures in park	Parents, architect-designer, park and recreation departments
	Building shelters at school bus stops	Parents, school officials
Provision of new services	Extending bookmobile service	Parents, library board
	Adding day camp to summer recreation program	Parents, recreation department
	Setting up after-school child care center	Parents
	Developing summer program to teach all children to swim	Parents, recreation department

been that somehow the school would educate the community politically while making use of the community to help educate its
children. As a prime example today, the decentralization of urban
school systems is intended eventually to lead to greater school-
community collaboration in community improvement as well as in
curriculum development, even though results thus far have been less
than promising on either count.[22]

Changes that Make a Difference

I have lived in my neighborhood all my life, many children could
say, and I can tell you all about it — and its needs, too, if you want
to listen. Perhaps this home-grown knowledge and interest are what
we have to build on when we think about trying to go beyond service-
type projects to provide children with active experience in social
innovation and reform.

In our list of projects that schools have sponsored (see Exhibit 8–2
again), we have included and highlighted the campaign for traffic
control devices because it meets most of the criteria for change-
oriented undertakings that are likely to be successful. The need is
quickly determined, the support of the affected area is sure to be
forthcoming, the source of authority is readily identifiable, and
action one way or another is apt to be clearcut. But of course, children
can't work to get stop signs or a traffic light installed every year.
This is meant as an example, not a regular focus of social action.

The two other categories of social action projects in Exhibit 8–2
are obviously catch-alls, but they are meant to be comprehensive.
Development of new facilities can start with construction of a play
area on a vacant lot, yet it need not stop there. A community that
begins to study its own needs and to organize for joint action on them
will find many worthwhile projects in which children can play an
appropriate role. The same claim can be made for the remaining
category, the provision of new services.

"Who runs this town?" is the way the question of power used to

---

[22] See Henry M. Levin, ed., *Community Control of Schools* (Washington, D.C.:
The Brookings Institution, 1970); and Mario Fantini and Marilyn Gittell, *Decentralization: Achieving Reform* (New York: Praeger Publishers, 1973).

be put by community sociologists committed to an elitist view. Nowadays, a pluralist outlook phrases the control question in other terms: "Does anyone run this town?" Decision making has been found to take place at many points with many partners.[23] Citizens young and old need to understand and experience this process at first hand. Changes that make a difference can be brought about by everyone, including children.

ASSESSING SOCIAL PROBLEMS AND ACTIONS

In this chapter we have been trying to report on and evaluate what is going on in the redevelopment of the curriculum to help children experience the satisfactions that can come from social innovations. First, children are being helped to understand how change has come about historically. The teaching of American history is being revised to give more attention to social issues. While this revision first concentrated on a greater cultural pluralism, the racial-ethnic and civil rights base is now being enlarged to include recognition of the social contributions of women, the working class and unions, and a variety of specific social movements. Today activism takes many shapes; society is on the march. The schools are beginning to catch up by helping children understand what is going on around them.

Second, we have described the school-sponsored community improvement projects through which an experience component is being added to the political education of children. Many, perhaps most, of these are service-type projects that may be felt to make a limited even if positive contribution to citizenship education. Some schools, however, are trying to encourage projects of a more demanding nature — campaigns for new traffic controls, new facilities, new services — in which children can learn how the power of decision making functions and is affected by local effort.

Now we would like to propose a third element. We are finding that children can profit from change-oriented study undertakings that

---

[23] See Colin Bell and Howard Newby, *Community Studies: An Introduction to the Sociology of the Local Community* (New York: Praeger Publishers, 1971).

call chiefly for personal commitment rather than for group action. The test of consequences is conducted in part through thinking through what commitment means in a variety of playing-out activities. (See Exhibit 8–3.)

Investigation of Problems

What is meant when people talk about shaping society for the better? Toward what ends — and whose?

Looking at activist movements past and present provides some ends to consider as does working in a variety of community improvement projects. But children on the way to becoming "totally realized individuals — humane, self-renewing, self-directed individuals — who will not only survive in society but will take a conscious role in shaping it for the better"[24] need more than that. In learning to value, consciousness of choices comes first. Some of the choices may be borrowed, but others, at least in the area of social change, must be created by the chooser. If democracy is to survive, surely all that can be done to inspire innovativeness in social problem solving must be undertaken.

Elsewhere, we have proposed that adventuring more extensively into the natural, built, and cultural environments beyond the school be used as a basis for developing life-related concerns among children.[25] If they are to learn something about the problems that face society, children need to have contact with them one way or another. One example of this approach is the experience of a small group of ten- to twelve-year-olds from the Washington Mini School, who visited Congress, walked through a neighborhood with an architect, visited a health center, and talked with a lawyer about consumer needs.[26]

Children must not only become aware of problems, they must have a chance to consider answers to such problems. They need to

[24] *Schools for the 70s and Beyond: A Call to Action* (Washington, D.C.: National Education Association, 1971), p. 20.

[25] Alexander Frazier, *Adventuring, Mastering, Associating* (Washington, D.C.: Association for Supervision and Curriculum Development, 1976), pp. 27–52.

[26] Brenner, in *Schooling*, pp. 224–238.

Exhibit 8-3

Playing Out Consequences of Choice

Type of playing out	Examples in realm of political-social action
Playing games	Win or lose: an election game
	Three strikes and you're out: campaign strategy
	If it please the court: a discrimination suit
Making models	Model town: New City, U. S. A.
	Community center: medical/social/educational facilities
	Park and recreation center
Role playing	Situations where sex bias is evident
	Racial-ethnic viewpoints: housing, school, jobs
	Aged-youth points of conflict
Simulating real-life activities	City council election around key issues
	Campaign for new library
	Organization of third party in state or national election
Imaginative writing	A new world: A.D. 2500
	Where I would like to live
	If children could vote

learn what others have proposed as they prepare to come up with ideas of their own. Naturally, most children who study social problems will not be able to think in broad terms about them. But we need to help children strive for an ever-increasing breadth of perspective.

Discussion and Debate

The first test of a choice of action comes through an exchange of ideas with others. Teachers have not done as much in the past with open discussion and friendly argument as they might have. Too often, as we are all aware, time for talking things over ends up being devoted mainly to recitation. No one would want to minimize the importance of checking to make sure that children have gained and understood needed information. But in helping them develop new ideas, there must be time reserved for another level of intellectual interaction. (See Exhibit 1–2 for the values clarification questions proposed by Louis Raths.)

A person's best thinking often comes directly from efforts to interpret and defend a position. In school and out, people learn by having their statements challenged by others.

Sometimes they gain support, and that can tell something, too. Thus, a class of older children, after studying the issue of law and order, heard a series of work group reports, the first of which dealt with gun control:

We believe that
1. gun control laws are needed
2. police should not wear uniforms or carry guns
3. citizens should be organized to help police
4. lawbreakers should be given help — counseling, education, jobs, better housing
5. prisons should be closed down
6. there should be fewer crime stories on TV

Although other children in the class asked questions and expressed a few doubts, most of the proposals seemed acceptable. The main concern of the class was how to do something to help bring about the needed changes. Would it be a good idea to write a letter to

Congress about gun laws? And to television networks about too many crime programs? Had the committee thought about going to talk with someone at the police department? Clearly, being of one mind does not resolve all the questions that arise from or relate to implementation.

Further Tests of Conclusions

We know that the young can act in behalf of their beliefs. In Crystal City, Texas, students conducted a boycott of classes because they were forbidden to speak Spanish at school.[27] The new street gangs, we are told, sometimes claim true social goals — running off dope peddlers, getting voters to the polls, trying to clean up vacant lots.[28] Sometimes older youth drop out of the majority culture altogether to find a new life in alternative communities of one kind or another.

For most children in most American communities, tests of their commitments in terms such as these will have to come later. Playing out their choices of what needs to be done is about as close as most children will get to the real thing. Games, role-playing situations, and simulated experiences (see Exhibit 8–3) go beyond simply making reports or preparing a display. Even then, values clarification in this realm will still remain more or less verbal.

But imagining new possibilities can be an important part of political education. In truth, it always has been. The impact of utopianism on human behavior has often been underestimated. For example, Charles Fourier's notion of a new kind of self-contained community inspired New Harmony and Brook Farm and fifty other American social experiments in the first half of the nineteenth century. What really counted, of course, was that Fourier spoke to his age of new deeds, new possibilities, and new dreams.[29]

[27] Robert D. Barr, "Confessions of an Itinerant Author," in *Values and Youth*, ed. Robert D. Barr (Washington, D.C.: National Council for the Social Studies, 1971), p. 5.
[28] James Haskins, *Street Gangs: Yesterday and Today* (New York: Hastings House, 1974), p. 138.
[29] See Nicholas V. Riasanovsky, *The Teaching of Charles Fourier* (Berkeley, Calif.: University of California Press, 1969); and Charles J. Erasmus, *In Search of the Common Good: Utopian Experiments Past and Future* (New York: The Free Press, 1977).

SOME ADDITIONAL CONSIDERATIONS

If they are to function as social innovators, children need to become conscious of choices or possibilities; they need to develop some competence in getting done what needs to be done, once they have made their choices; and they need to assess as well as they can the consequences and satisfactions to be gained from proposed actions, something easier to accomplish with community improvement projects than with larger undertakings. Consciousness, choice, action, and assessment are the elements at work in all the many aspects of the new curriculum that is being developed to help children learn to value. In no area can successful valuing be of greater importance than in the renewal of society.

Speaking Up Is Learned

In the past, aggressiveness was usually viewed as something that was picked up indirectly from a variety of circumstances largely beyond the control of the individual. Age played a part, as did gender, race or ethnic group, class, regional origin, and whatever it was that fixed personality more or less permanently on the continuum of inner-outer directedness. (See Exhibit 8–4.)

Now educators are inclined to see speaking up for one's self and one's viewpoint as something that is learned. Effort is needed to frame a point of view or, as we would say here, to examine possibilities and make a choice. The school's responsibility is to set up many occasions for the stating or asserting of commitments and for testing them out. Learning to take a stand and speak one's piece is integral to learning to value.

Americans traditionally have been noted for their individualism, their desire for mobility and change, their fix-it outlook on the problems of the world, and their conviction that the best is yet to come.[30] But today there is a growing concern that too many segments of America's population are willing to sit things out. A study of poor neighborhoods, for example, reveals membership in action groups to be only half of what it is in other parts of the community. In such

---

[30] Wilbur Zelinsky, *The Cultural Geography of the United States* (Englewood Cliffs, N.J.: Prentice-Hall, 1973), p. 40.

Exhibit 8-4

Sources of Differences in Aggressiveness, as Perceived in the Past

Source	Nonaggressive behavior	Aggressive behavior
Age	*Younger*	*Older*
	Bashful, afraid of strangers	Self-possessed, outgoing
Gender role	*Female*	*Male*
	Responsive, accommo-dating, passive	Assertive, proposing, active
Racial-ethnic group	*Minority*	*Majority*
	Hesitant, fearful of affront	Secure, self-confident
Class membership	*Working class, lower middle class*	*Upper class, upper middle class*
	Deferent, embarrassed, fearful of offending	Outspoken, uncon-cerned about reaction of others
Regional origin	*Rural*	*Urban*
	Closemouthed, suspicious	Opinionated, sharp-spoken
Personality	*Quiet type*	*Friendly type*
	Reserved, withdrawn	Excitable, talkative

circumstances, political revitalization becomes an enormously difficult task. The very persons with the most to gain from social action seem the least prepared to act.[31]

This need not be. Social action techniques can and should be learned by everybody. The social skills defined as basic to competence in everyday living in Chapter 3 are the ones we need to build on here.

The Messianic Element

In the aftermath of the social unrest of the late sixties, attacks on the failure of the schools as equalizers of educational opportunity and agents of cultural change were not infrequent. Sometimes the charge was that in America's mass society, the school had allowed itself to become a force for adaptation to things as they were. The need, often expressed, was to "de-mythologize" or expose the school or even to relocate the function of education so that it would serve all the people better.

The present approach, as we have tried to interpret it in this chapter, aims at revitalizing the political-social function of the school. This depends in part on bringing imagination of possibilities back into the picture. To gain a consciousness of choices, children must also experience the creation of new possibilities and sense the possibility of new creation. Here is where critical thinking, creativity, and social reform come together most plainly. And today's children are ready for such experiences. Science fiction, the modern version of utopianism, is a part of their way of life.

Indeed, the messianic element in American thought has taken many curious forms, some of them poetic. "Are you he who would assume a place to teach or be a poet here in the States?" Then you must free yourself of the past. The "great Idea," in the language of Walt Whitman, "the idea of perfect and free individuals,"[32] had yet to be born in the minds of all the people. Or in terms of a concrete image, "the great city" had yet to come into being.

---

[31] Curt Lamb, *Political Power in Poor Neighborhoods* (Cambridge, Mass.: Schenkman Publishers, 1975).

[32] Walt Whitman, "By Blue Ontario's Shore," in *Poems* (New York: Modern Library, 1921), pp. 294–295.

Where no monuments exist to heroes but in the common words and
    deeds . . .
Where the populace rise at once against the never-ending audacity of
    elected persons . . .
Where outside authority enters always after the precedence of inside
    authority,
Where the citizen is always the head and ideal, and President, Mayor,
    Governor and what not, are agents for pay,
Where children are taught to be laws to themselves, and to depend on
    themselves,
Where equanimity is illustrated in affairs,
Where speculations on the soul are encouraged,
Where women walk in public processions in the streets the same as the
    men,
Where they enter the public assembly and take places the same as the
    men . . .
There the great city stands.[33]

Great nations must have great poets, Whitman contended, and great
teachers, too, to keep the vision of perfection before its people.

Social Action in Classroom and School

Our point of view in this chapter has been that principles of democratic action broadly defined should be supported as part of everyday
living everywhere in the school. Participation in planning, a degree
of independence in choice of topics, freedom of inquiry among assorted resources, and many opportunities for intellectual interaction
with other children — these are the elements that belong in any
political education program for children.

The new curriculum seeks to help children to develop a sense of
personal power. It offers more chances for children to learn about
reform movements past and present and to think about the principles
involved. It provides children with opportunities to participate in
practical community improvement projects, both the service type and
the campaign-to-get-something-new type. And it encourages children to study critical human needs and to imagine and test out new
possibilities.

[33] Whitman, "Song of the Broad-Axe," in *Poems*, pp. 162–163.

Obviously, as we have tried to acknowledge, the studies of moral development and the work in values clarification reviewed in Chapter 1 have special reference to what teachers may try to do to help children learn to value more rewardingly in the moral-ethical-political realm. Our own intention has been to highlight the contribution to be made by re-conceptualizing the content of the curriculum to relate it more directly to helping children become aware of, experienced in, and devoted to the satisfactions that come from democratic ways of being and behaving.

In Chapter 7 we specified examples of the kind of content needed for the receptive learning of allegiance to the democratic way of life. In the present chapter, we have dealt with the other end of this values axis — social reformism and innovativeness. There is much content here, too, that is basic to learning to value and enter into socially effective being and behaving.

At this point, we have completed our presentation of what we see to be happening in the development of a new curriculum in support of doing more to help children learn to value. We turn now to our final chapter in which we offer suggestions on implementing the new curriculum in values education.

ACTIVITIES

1. Develop a list of children's rights that might be the basis of study and action by a group of older children.
2. What are some of today's commonly accepted rights and privileges that were once regarded as ideals or impossible dreams? How could the history of how these prevailed be studied by children?
3. Develop a bibliography of biographies and works of fiction for children that are related to one of the reform movements of the past. What problems did you find in locating useful books?
4. Organize an activity to help children develop party platforms. Provide time for presentation and discussion.
5. What current activist concerns are of most interest to children? Prepare a simple questionnaire and collect information from groups of children of different ages in several neighborhoods. What do you find?
6. Select a service-type community improvement project (see Exhibit 8–2) and develop plans for initiating and carrying it through with a class of children. What do you anticipate as your greatest difficulties?
7. Identify other projects that could be added to the categories of development of new facilities and provision of new services (see Exhibit 8–2).

8. Describe the kind of community school you would like to see come into existence. Deal with (1) its use by the community and (2) its service to the community. What role would persons from the community play?
9. Develop plans for a discussion-debate on proposals related to an issue like gun control. Try out your plans with a group of children. What did you learn from the experience?
10. Investigate several assertiveness-training programs for adults. Could some of the ideas or activities you find there be adapted for use with children? What doubts might you have about this approach?

Part III

Values and the
Elementary School

Chapter 9

Implementing the New Curriculum

The point we have made many times in our report on the new curriculum is that there is a revitalized conception of what education should do for children. There is also a revitalized conception of how curriculum should be developed. That is the burden of our concluding chapter. How can schools bring about a truly value-centered curriculum?

The new curriculum, as we have presented it, is committed to value-centered education and to providing the knowledge base needed for valuing. Children need to master the skills and understanding required for effective everyday living, appreciation of the arts, and allegiance to the democratic way of life; otherwise, they will not be really free to choose among the riches that now exist. And beyond these basics, the new curriculum also seeks to help children develop their capacities for critical thinking, creative behavior, and social innovativeness. In this way, children will be able to decide between the best of what is and the best of what — with their help — might come to be.

SCHOOLS AND VALUING

Valuing is as integral to learning as it is to living. Indeed, valuing is a process inherent in learning. And having a chance to learn what it takes to make rewarding choices from an array of truly accessible alternatives is what school is — or ought to be — all about.

Schools can and must make sure that children have a broad base for learning to value. Three elements, as we have emphasized throughout our report, need to be fostered by schools: (1) consciousness of worthwhile options for investment of time and energy, (2) competence to make meaningful choices among these options, and (3) opportunities to test out the consequences or satisfactions of one option as weighed against those of another.

Schools must also strive to do more than they have in the past to reach more students. They must seek to ensure that full access to the great realms of being and behaving and becoming be open to all children by providing a range of experiences that will bring all children into touch with active and successful and exciting learning.

Schools must be more successful in teaching students who have been undertaught — the children of rural America, the children of urban slums, the children of the poor, the children of the working class, bilingual children, the children of some minorities, and many boys.

Schools must provide better for children who have been overtaught. The classrooms hold many children who understand material the first time it is presented to them and thus waste a lot of their precious hours in school waiting for a challenge that seldom comes.

Schools must also work to correct past misteachings, particularly the limitations that may have been imposed on some children through promotion of sex, class, and racial-ethnic stereotypes in educational programs and practices.

Finally, schools must do more to teach entire areas of knowledge that have not been covered in the past. We have long believed that

some children have a much richer and more relevant school experience than others. Here it is not a question of being undertaught, overtaught, or mistaught. Many children are just not taught some things at all.

And perhaps we could even claim that most children in our schools today are not taught some things that they need to be taught.[1]

Any effort to implement the new curriculum, then, must be rooted in a commitment to reaching a higher level of success in meeting the needs of children than has been attained in the past. No longer should children be victimized by unequal teaching. (See Exhibit 9–1.)

FINDING THOSE WHO CAN HELP

New ways cannot come into existence until people accept the fact that they are greatly needed. Fortunately, there is a base of common understandings from which to launch the thrust toward curriculum redevelopment. Moreover, many people have become newly sensitive to the forces in society that make for lethargy and inactivity. Society itself has moved into the arena of values education in a big way in recent years by attacking directly the unexamined attitudes and outlooks that have proved incapacitating to so many Americans — to members of minorities, to women, perhaps to all of us in one way or another. Consciousness raising through confrontation between old ways of being and behaving and new possibilities has become a part of the common experience.

Those of us who wish to develop a value-oriented curriculum for children might well begin by seeking out allies in our society, a society that is in itself in the midst of self-reconstruction. Let us identify some of these prospective allies.

Opponents of Racism and Sexism

Those who oppose racism and sexism share many of the goals and concerns of those who support the new curriculum.

Representatives of racial minorities have already helped open up many options in the school — through human relations programs for both teachers and children, the integration of faculties and student bodies, the provision of a truer picture of the treatment of minorities

[1] Alexander Frazier, *Adventuring, Mastering, Associating* (Washington, D.C.: Association for Supervision and Curriculum Development, 1976), p. 12.

Exhibit 9-1

Children Who Are Victims of Unequal Teaching

Type of inequality	Results of inequality
Children who are undertaught	Fail to learn what they could learn
	Fall behind others and become discouraged
	Develop dislike for school
	May escape from schooling at earliest opportunity
	Find themselves boxed in by lack of education
Children who are overtaught	Waste time in overlearning
	Become bored with school
	May develop distaste for learning
	May fail to find themselves
	Find themselves boxed in by lack of education
Children who are mistaught	Limit interest to subjects thought appropriate to sex role or social status
	May learn to dislike or fear some subjects
	Fail to develop broad base for further learning
	Grow up half educated
	Find themselves boxed in by lack of education

Type of inequality	Results of inequality
Children who are not taught some things at all	Respond less fully to total environment
	May develop prejudices against the arts
	Function at less than best in some aspects of human relationships
	May remain ignorant of important realms of human experience
	Find themselves boxed in by lack of education

Source: Adapted by permission from Exhibit 2 in Alexander Frazier, *Adventuring, Mastering, Associating: New Strategies for Teaching children* (Washington, D.C.: Association for Supervision and Curriculum Development, 1976), p. 14.

and also of their contributions, the introduction of content designed to foster cultural identity and pride, and the use of career education models that look beyond past employment practices.

Opponents of sexism have also been working to increase options in education. Schools have made a start on ridding themselves of the burden of gender stereotyping, but they still have far to go. Sports programs are being re-examined, as we have pointed out. But the lack of involvement of many girls in science and mathematics, and of many boys in reading and the arts, also needs to be looked at with great care. Hopefully, more will be done to eliminate sex bias in career education as well. However, concern for sex bias in the school needs to move beyond examination of apparent inequities. What is required is a vigorous revitalization of the whole program.

Proponents of Social Declassification

For too many years, schools may have functioned as screening agencies for the business-industrial complex.[2] Find the best talent, train it, and let the rest go. But that is not the way it need be any more. Talent is abundant. Getting ahead in the world, we are newly reminded by Christopher Jencks, depends on social status and "personality" — that is, on unique individual learning — and happenstance as much as on grades in school and amount of schooling. And Jencks has urged us to face the truth: income does not have to depend on professional training, it can be a matter of social legislation. The schools, he contends, would do better to mind their own business, that is, to provide an education aimed at personal-social development rather than one geared only to moving up the success ladder.[3]

How far schools should go with this point of view is hard to say. But as more of the population stays in school longer, there seems little doubt of the need to rethink the nature of public education. After the earliest years, schooling at present is still tied very closely to preparation for success in college and career advancement.

[2] See Samuel Bowles and Herbert Gintis, *Schooling in Capitalist America: Educational Reform and the Contradictions of Economic Life* (New York: Basic Books, 1976).

[3] Christopher Jencks, *Inequality: A Reassessment of the Effect of Family and Schooling in America* (New York: Basic Books, 1972).

Critics of class bias in our society form an increasingly vocal element among those seeking to reshape the curriculum. Whose are the 2,000,000 children arrested each year?[4] What happens to the 50,000 children who are in prison?[5] What is the school's role in preserving and protecting the civil rights of children and youth?[6] There are many groups in the larger society who would welcome a chance to help us find answers to such questions as these.

Critics of Commercialism

Exploitation of the consumer takes a variety of forms in our society. Big business curries favor at home by illegal campaign contributions and abroad by bribes. Unless adequately supervised, producers of goods may try to hoodwink consumers by short weights, deceptive packaging, and untested claims. Advertisers sponsor television programs that often seem aimed at the lowest common interest denominator — neurosis and greed in the daytime, violence at night. And on Saturday mornings, children are being induced by jingles and slogans to ask for sugared cereals, overelaborate and self-destructing toys, and special treats from the ubiquitous fast-food franchisers.[7]

Our economy is engineered toward increasingly rapid consumption of resources. That is where the danger lies. Today many people are aware of the impact of unnecessary and prodigal production on the environment. The schools are working to help make children, too, more aware of this. Environmental education is one of the exemplary beyond-the-basics additions that the new curriculum seeks to promote. And the many environmental and consumer groups can provide us with powerful allies in this endeavor.[8]

[4] See Edward Wakin, *Children without Justice* (New York: National Council of Jewish Women, 1975).

[5] See Kenneth Wooden, *Weeping in the Playtime of Others: America's Incarcerated Children* (New York: McGraw-Hill Book Company, 1976).

[6] See David Schimmel and Louis Fischer, *The Civil Rights of Students* (New York: Harper and Row, 1975).

[7] See Arthur A. Berger, *The TV-Guided American* (New York: Walker and Company, 1976).

[8] See James Robertson and John Lewallen, eds., *The Grass Roots Primer* (San Francisco: Sierra Club Books, 1975).

Enemies of Do-Nothing Ignorantism

According to the Oxford English Dictionary, *ignorantism* is "a system which exalts or favors ignorance," a rare but, for our purposes, encompassing term. In both society and the schools, to what extent are people asleep when they should be alert? Barbara Ward, an economist of broad experience and general optimism, asks the question more bluntly: "Is the future possible?" The perils — resource depletion, overpopulation, the uneasy existence of worldwide inequities of many kinds, nuclear pollution, economic collapse, starvation, a war beyond all imagining — are so many and so horrible to contemplate. There must be a "passionate reexamination" of options to action. People must make an effort to discover what it takes to ward off disaster rather than simply succumb to "drift and stupid optimism and no thought for tomorrow."[9]

"Ignorant misery" led to sleepwalking and self-destruction in many past civilizations. But today "another movement is apparent — of mankind reaching out to grasp, intellectually and morally, the meaning of existence and not to conform to the weight of material conditioning but to transfigure and transcend it."[10] The human search for meaning has had a long life. We must awake from our deliberate, self-imposed ignorantism into a new consciousness of human possibilities — and a new resolution to realize them.

All about us we find individuals increasingly concerned about our future as a society and indeed as a planet. One vital aspect of this phenomenon is the revival of initiative in solving local problems. From Jacksonville to Seattle, there have been new grassroots efforts to do the things that need to be done — urban renewal, regional planning, consumer protest. These efforts are indicative of a new release of social energy with which the school must surely ally itself as it works to redevelop its program toward the promotion of personal fulfillment and social effectiveness.[11]

Certainly, then, in our work to bring about a value-oriented curriculum, we will have no difficulty in finding partners among groups and organizations committed to bringing about change. (See Exhibit

[9] *The Home of Man* by Barbara Ward. W. W. Norton & Company, Inc., New York, N.Y., p. 75, copyright © 1976 by the International Institute for Environment and Development.

[10] *Ibid.*, p. 16.

[11] See John Fischer, *Vital Signs, U. S. A.* (New York: Harper and Row, 1975).

9–2). We will find many potential allies in the community from among opponents of racism and sexism, advocates of social declassification, consumer and environmental groups, and a variety of local and national activist groups.

FREEING INNOVATIVE ENERGY

Most schools that are leading the way in recasting the curriculum have built enduring relations with parents and community forces in support of new content and approaches. But these schools have also accomplished something else of great importance. They have found out how to free innovative energy within the school itself.

Curriculum Making in the Past

In the old days, curriculum decisions were made mostly at the top level. Although representative teachers and principals were likely to be involved in the process, teachers by and large were regarded as curriculum implementers rather than curriculum makers. Most of the content to be covered at each grade level was pretty well spelled out for all teachers in a district. The individual teacher might have a degree of latitude within the framework. Persons officially charged with responsibility for curriculum development might be willing to grant that the front-line force working with children ought to be able to make wise decisions about how to present the common content. However, selecting what was to be taught — that remained a task thought to be beyond the competence and indeed the province of the teacher.

More to the point, curriculum making was perceived as an instrument of administrative control. Agreements were made for the district as a whole to make sure that all children in it would receive an equally good education. Spelling out what and when subjects should be taught helped guarantee coverage and continuity. Overlap or repetition could be avoided if some things were designated for eight-year-olds and others reserved for ten-year-olds. Both jump-the-gun enthusiasts and let-it-go laggards, if they existed among teachers in a school, could be brought into line by reference to the course of

Exhibit 9-2

Possible Partners in Curriculum Development

Type of concerned citizens	Examples of interested groups
Opponents of racism and sexism	National Association for the Advancement of Colored People
	Urban League
	National Organization of Women
	Ethnic and racial organizations
	Women's associations of many kinds
	State and federal civil rights agencies
Proponents of social declassification	Labor organizations
	Ethnic associations
	Children's rights advocates
	Groups concerned with unfair housing practices
	Social reform groups in general

Type of concerned citizens	Examples of interested groups
Critics of commercialism	Consumer groups
	Public television: station staffs, advisory boards
	Ministerial associations
	Museum staffs
	Art and music associations
	Environmentalist groups
	Parents and others concerned about television programming for children
Enemies of do-nothing ignorantism	Sierra Club, Wild Life Federation, and other environmentalist groups
	State and federal environmental agencies
	League of Women Voters
	Peace groups
	International relations organizations
	Anti-nuclear power advocates
	Local activist groups in many fields

study issued by the central office. Maintenance rather than improvement was seen as the chief concern of official supervision.[12]

Teachers as Curriculum Makers

These days many school districts take a very different tack. Every effort is made to encourage local schools to participate in curriculum making. This approach was given its first impetus in the years following the Soviets' launch of Sputnik around the earth. Beginning with the science and mathematics projects of the post-Sputnik era, the base of program development began to be broadened. In the late fifties and early sixties, academicians from the universities often found themselves engaged in productive collaborations with teachers of children, which regularly bypassed the supervisory staff. Consequently, teachers sometimes knew more about what was going on than the people in the administration buildings. A new respect as well as a new role for teachers resulted.

The valiant federal effort during the mid and late sixties to encourage more successful programs for "disadvantaged" children and to promote curriculum enrichment in general served to educate a new generation of teachers and administrators in experimental design, data collection, and evaluation. Curriculum making began to be seen as an action-oriented and creative endeavor rather than as something fixed and formal, and as a process that was necessarily collaborative and continuous.[13]

At the same time, changes in public policy also helped to broaden the base for program development. Many urban school districts decentralized operations that were formerly kept under tight control. It was acknowledged that needs differ from one community or area to another and that the curriculum should meet the test of relevance. There was also a growing realization that the demand for more effective teaching is heard most clearly when it is made close to where children are. Thus, teachers might become involved in re-making the curriculum whether they wished to or not.

[12] See Richard L. Derr, *A Taxonomy of Social Purposes of Public Schools* (New York: David McKay Company, 1973).
[13] See John I. Goodlad, *The Dynamics of Educational Change* (New York: McGraw-Hill Company, 1975), pp. 25–50.

From all this emerged the concept of the alternative school. In the old days, new programs that were tried out in a school system survived only if they proved better than the traditional program. Now schools may think in terms of co-existent programs open to parental and student choice. In more than one district, local schools have been encouraged to develop their own programs — and even to maintain two programs at the same time.

Support System for Innovation

When Bertrand Russell in his later years looked back on his experience as a proprietor of a progressive school in the 1920s, he recalled the dreadful necessity of close supervision of his teachers to make sure that things went as he and his wife intended. Some of the staff, "however often and however meticulously our principles were explained to them, could never be brought to act in accordance with them unless one of us was present."[14] This approach ran somewhat counter to Russell's theory of learning. As his daughter described it, her parents "wanted us to do the right thing because we understood its rightness, not because we were compelled to do it."[15] Apparently, this was a principle easier to operate on with children than with adults.

Today educators understand well enough that teachers who are expected to assume responsibility for a program must be involved in developing it. But many persons committed to the professionalization of teaching would go further than that. They believe schools are not getting their money's worth unless teachers are able to test out new knowledge on their own. Certain program agreements no doubt must be made and respected in a district and within a school. But beyond this institutional and hopefully minimal framework, teaching and curriculum making must remain closely allied in the lives of a new generation of innovative teachers.

At the time of this writing, the federal investment in educational research and development has slackened; half of the once heavily

[14] Bertrand Russell, *The Autobiography of Bertrand Russell* (Boston: Little, Brown and Company, 1968), II, 225.
[15] Katherine Tait, *My Father Bertrand Russell* (New York: Harcourt Brace Jovanovich, 1975), p. 73.

Exhibit 9-3

A Support System for Innovation: Conditions and Services Needed by Teachers

---

Conditions

Authority for making decisions about what to teach

Organization for working on curriculum matters as subfaculty or faculty

Subsidized attendance at selected workshops and conferences

Time for study and planning in the school day or week

Services

Professional journals and books

Subject field and other content specialists

Specialists in experimental design and evaluation

Inservice experiences oriented toward change in programs and methods

---

supported regional centers charged with producing new knowledge or coming up with innovative programs have been closed or severely cut back.[16] The permanence of the impact on local programs of the national curriculum projects of the sixties is in doubt. Another look is being taken at how federal funds may best be spent to support education.

Of one thing, however, there can be no doubt: the impact of the national curriculum projects on the outlook toward program development. Curriculum making is now seen by many educators as a creative, continuous, and collaborative process. Moreover, there is greater understanding of what it takes to support innovative behavior in a local school. Authority to make decisions about what is to be taught has to be shared more widely. Organization for decision making must be provided. The search for new knowledge has to be facilitated in a variety of ways. Generation of data about teaching success may also require specialized support.

Teachers need more rather than less help when they are freed to be fully innovative. But the help must be of the right kind. (See Exhibit 9–3 for a specification of some needed conditions and services.)

ASKING HARD QUESTIONS

Developing a new curriculum that focuses more directly on helping children learn to value will be forwarded by seeking partners from among concerned parents and the many groups in society committed to bettering the lot of the individual and the quality of life in general. The process will be forwarded, too, as innovative schools and school systems have discovered, by broadening the base of decision making to provide a more responsible and creative role for teachers.

There still remains the age-old necessity, however, of keeping a keen and critical eye on what happens. Will the proposed changes add up to something worth the required investment of energy, ingenuity, and finances? Evaluation has to be written into currriculum making every step of the way if we want to be sure that curriculum changes really make a difference.

Let us take a look, then, at some of the ways this key question

[16] See Ralph W. Tyler, ed., *Prospects for Research and Development in Education* (San Francisco: McCutchan, 1976).

can be asked. We will inquire first whether the proposed content as we have discussed it is the right content for learning to value. Next we will discuss some topics that might be worth keeping in mind as possible replacements for existing content areas. Finally, we will ask the hardest question of all: what signs of success should educators look for in evaluating curriculum changes?

Is the Proposed Content the Right Content?

In this report, we have identified many emphases or concerns that are causing familiar curriculum content to be reshaped and unfamiliar content to be added for value-oriented study by children. Under the heading of accommodation to everyday living, we have dealt with mastering the skills of book learning, coming into command of the body, and learning to live and work together (Chapter 3). In the companion field of critical thinking, we have chosen to elaborate on helping children understand the environmental crisis, enlarge their sense of the world of work, and become more fully aware of why people differ (Chapter 4).

In a second major area — the cultural heritage — under appreciation or access to the human birthright, we have included entering the wonderland of books, learning to see the varieties of art, and hearing the music of many different drummers (Chapter 5). Pairing creativity or creative behavior with appreciation, we have noted what is going on today to help children do original and imaginative work in the creative arts, perform works both old and new, exercise the arts of invention, and learn how to plan in a variety of directions (Chapter 6).

As we have analyzed it, the third area — the moral-ethical-political realm — yields a number of strands of new content attaching themselves to the building of allegiance to the democratic way of life: finding out about America's historical heritage, developing some understanding of governance, and defining the good society (Chapter 7). With learning to value the best of what exists, we have linked looking ahead to new possibilities. To develop social innovativeness in children, we have proposed that they study how changes come about, engage in efforts to improve the world around them, and learn to assess social problems and proposed solutions (Chapter 8).

So much by way of summary of the content we see developing

for the new curriculum. Now to return to our present question: Is this the right content? Will it work? Will it wear?

Certainly, the major categories we have proposed — everyday living, the cultural heritage, the moral-ethical-political realm — will remain of vital concern. Perhaps we might also predict that much of the content we have described as receptive learning — the basic skills, art appreciation, and education aimed at allegiance to democracy — will remain fairly stable. But we must grant that a good deal of the content selected as relevant to learning to be innovative — and reported in relationship to critical thinking, creative behavior, and social innovativeness — may well be fluid.

Reworking and augmenting of curriculum content always involves some element of the unknown. The new value-oriented curriculum goes even further. Those who wish to implement it must not merely expect new emphases but welcome them. "Possibilities are more important than what already exists," John Dewey noted in an address given when he assumed the honorary presidency of the Progressive Education Association, "and knowledge of the latter counts only in its bearing upon possibilities."[17]

Such knowledge, in this case the knowledge that supports learning to value more rewardingly, must always be subject to criticism and alteration or eventual replacement.

What Else Is New?

Are there other emphases of importance on the curriculum horizon? If curriculum making is to become of continuous concern to teachers — as we believe it must — then more than a welcome needs to be evident in the attitude toward new ideas. They must be actively sought out.

Although it would be going too far to contend that the emergent content areas defined below are sure to survive, we offer them as indicators of the kinds of new intellectual interests and socio-political direction that teachers may wish to be more aware of.

---

[17] John Dewey, "The Science of Education," in *Dewey on Education*, ed. Martin S. Dworkin (New York: Teachers College Press, 1959), p. 119.

International understanding: For many years, the American experience in Korea and Vietnam may have dampened teachers' interest in helping children study about people around the world. But recently there has been a revival of interest in this topic. If a new handbook from the Center for Global Perspectives is any cue,[18] the new thrust is likely to be much more realistic than past presentations. And it may have a base in social biology, despite the criticism that has gone to the social studies program "Man: A Course of Study" on that count.[19] Proposals for teaching foreign languages to elementary school children are also part of this renewed interest in life in other countries.

Extension of human rights: This book has emphasized the importance of alerting children to the many newly defined dimensions of human rights. Yet there may be other aspects of the question that merit consideration in a value-oriented curriculum — for example, rehabilitation of drug addicts and exconvicts,[20] integration in school and society of the mentally retarded and physically handicapped with the nonhandicapped, and concern for the well-being of persons formerly labeled as social-sexual deviates.[21]

Political-cultural geography: Geography was overlooked in the reworking of the social studies during the sixties. But the current concern for land use, particularly in relation to urban decay and the deployment of population to new towns and small cities, could bring it back into the picture as a major field of study.[22]

Economic education: Although interest in straightforward teaching of economic concepts seems to have dwindled, new interest could

---

[18] See David C. King et al., *Education for a World of Change: A Working Handbook for Global Perspectives* (New York: Center for Global Perspectives, 1976).

[19] See M. W. Fox, *Concepts in Ethology: Animal and Human Behavior* (Minneapolis, Minn.: University of Minnesota Press, 1974); and John Napier, *Monkeys without Tails* (New York: Taplinger Publishing Company, 1976); and also Peter B. Dow, "MACOS: Socal Studies in Crisis," *Educational Leadership* 34 (October 1976), 35–39.

[20] See John Heiner, *Drugs and Minority Oppression* (New York: Seabury Press, 1975); and Charles Hampden-Turner, *Sane Asylum: Inside the Delancey Street Foundation* (San Francisco: San Francisco Book Company, 1976).

[21] See publications of the American Civil Liberties Union.

[22] See Sterling Brubaker, *In Command of Tomorrow: Resource and Environmental Strategies for Americans* (Baltimore, Md.: Johns Hopkins University Press, 1975).

arise from public concern about doing more with both consumer education and the world of work.

Human development: Sex education has had a hard time of it, in part perhaps because of uncertainty about its aims. The new focus could extend to low-keyed teaching about the body changes that attend growth and also to the essential elements of social-emotional development that may be thought to transcend gender stereotyping.

Myth and meaning: Childlore, folklore, and fairy tales are all rich in mythic meaning or symbolism, an often neglected aspect of literature and life.[23] Tied to a possible revival of earlier interest in the promise of semantics, a new cluster of content worthy of exploration with children may be identifiable.[24]

Death education: Some persons would maintain that, in our society of small, nuclear families, the need exists for helping the young learn more about death as a natural part of the life cycle.[25]

Family life styles: The family, to the extent that its composition and function is to be studied in school, may need to be redefined realistically to include one-parent households, multiple-family groupings, and other new living arrangements.

"Feeling good": Some approaches to drug education advocate that more attention be given to teaching children life-sustaining ways to reach higher levels of well-being — through physical activity, social interaction, meditation, and aesthetic experience, for example.

Should the school be involved in any or all of these areas? Alertness to new possibilities for content emphasis in the teaching of children must be accompanied, of course, by application of common sense criteria to decide whether a new direction would really be worthwhile. (See Exhibit 9–4.)

[23] See, for example, Mary Knapp and Herbert Knapp, *One Potato, Two Potato: The Secret Education of Children* (New York: W. W. Norton, 1976); and P. L. Travers, *About the Sleeping Beauty* (New York: McGraw-Hill Book Company, 1975).

[24] See F. R. Palmer, *Semantics: A New Outline* (London: Cambridge University Press, 1976).

[25] For a moving photographic record of a child's participation in the care of an aged and dying family member, see Mary Jury and Davy Jury, *Gramps* (New York: Grossman Publishers, 1976).

Exhibit 9-4

**Some Common Sense Criteria for Selection of
Value-Oriented Content**

1. Does the emphasis or area offer understanding or skills that will lead to a higher level of competence?

2. Will exercise of the competence yield satisfactions to the learner?

3. Will the new ways of being or behaving be likely to contribute to personal fulfillment or social effectiveness?

4. Will learning in this field have the support of responsible persons in the wider society?

5. Will the new learning provide a base for further learning of importance?

6. Does the proposed new content have enough weight to deserve inclusion in the curriculum?

7. Is the significance of the new content more than topical or temporary?

WHAT SIGNS OF SUCCESS SHOULD WE LOOK FOR?

Evidence that the new curriculum has made a difference in learning to value must ultimately be sought in the changes people see in the world around them. What are the signs that would indicate that the better schooling of children and youth has resulted in increased individual fulfillment and social effectiveness? In our concluding pages we wish to propose a set of outcomes that are likely to appear if the new curriculum comes up to expectations.

The World of Everyday Living

The content of the new curriculum that deals with everyday living (presented in Chapters 3 and 4) focuses on basic skills broadly defined and on selected problems of critical concern. As a new generation comes through this phase of the program, it will bring with it such changes as these:

A completely literate population, free to seek information and ideas from many sources

A notable increase in formerly underrepresented and undereducated groups in a variety of lines of employment

Better use of neglected and undervalued human resources

Stepped-up consumer protection and consumer action against unfair practices; more informed shopping by consumers

Growth of interest in environmental issues; greater demand for state and federal action in this area

Higher-level physical performance and participation in varied games and sports by both sexes; well-supported private and public facilities for tennis, swimming, team sports, and so on

More campaigns for outdoor recreational facilities for boating, hiking, camping, and the like, to be provided by local communities and states

Lessening of conflicts arising from racial and ethnic differences; strengthening of understanding and relationships between majority and minority group members

These outcomes must be taken as no more than representative of what may be expected to occur as children learn to value what is most satisfying and significant in the world around them.

The Cultural Heritage

New emphases in the arts (as described in Chapters 5 and 6) center on a forthright effort to teach appreciation of literature, the visual arts, and music, and also on a new commitment to provide a larger place in children's lives for learning to behave creatively. As people experience this aspect of the new curriculum, the following results may be expected to occur:

Growth in number of libraries for children; better support for all public libraries

Increased buying of books; more bookstores in all parts of the country

Increased attendance at galleries, art museums, and independent exhibits of the work of local artists

More cooperative workshops and studios available to students and adult artists

More use of sculpture in public places; more attention to landscaping in both private and public sectors

More widely available live performances of music, dance, and drama

More amateur musical, dance, and drama groups aiming at personal satisfaction rather than public performance

Better planning to maintain balanced relationships between natural and built environments

More adult education courses related to the arts — appreciation, performance, other competencies in the creative fields

More pressure on commercial television to improve cultural programming; increased support for public television

Again, any such listing is only a token of what may be anticipated to happen as pursuit of the arts assumes a more important role in individual and community living.

The Moral-Ethical-Political Realm

Much of the content aimed at renewed or augmented attention to the moral-ethical-political aspect of children's learning (presented in Chapters 7 and 8) has to do mainly with what used to be called citizenship education. The need to clarify the elements that make the democratic system of self-government worthy of allegiance is more urgent now than it may have been earlier in the century. Widespread support for including social action projects in the education of children is also evident. If the new curriculum is effective in this area, society should expect results such as these:

Reduction in exploitative treatment of women as sex-subservient (in television advertising, pornography, and so on)

More efforts to protect children, the poor, and the aged from abuse and neglect

More public discussion of moral and ethical issues in general

Increased demand for public debate of critical foreign policy issues: disarmament, nuclear weaponry, aid to developing countries

More recruitment efforts to enroll well-qualified candidates in primary election campaigns

More interest in running independent candidates in local elections

Greater demands on political parties for imaginative proposals having to do with human well-being

Higher voter registration and turnout at the polls

Increase in community improvement projects undertaken by nongovernmental associations of concerned persons

Perhaps the most profound — and desirable — effect of the new curriculum would be a general upgrading of the moral-ethical tone not only in politics and government but in all of society's undertakings.

A FINAL WORD

Our society wants the best for its children. It is demanding that schools offer children more than ever before. Too many children have been boxed in by things as they are because their curriculum has not offered a range of options that would maximize their potential for personal development and forward the full exercise of their talents and intelligence in the improvement of society.

The kind of education that makes for personal fulfillment and social effectiveness involves more than just an awareness of options. If children are to choose wisely among possible ways of behaving, they must know what the options are, they must develop enough competence to be able to make choices among options, and they must have many chances to compare the satisfactions to be derived from behaving in a variety of ways.

The opportunity to try out the options that make for a rich and rewarding human experience and the competence to do so — these are or ought to be the birthright of every child. That is what society is saying to us. Our new understanding of how values develop and how they may be clarified has contributed to our insight into what it takes to respond to the public demand. Old content is being recast and new curriculum emphases are being added to provide more chances for children to learn to value those activities that will be most personally satisfying and most socially beneficial.

"What the best and wisest parent wants for his own child, that must the community want for all its children."[26] John Dewey's proposal is as worthy an ideal today as it was in 1899. But now schools seem to be close to making it come true.

Can the best and broadest possible education be provided to all the children of this nation? We would contend that it can. If the curriculum is reconceived as a context for learning to value and if values, curriculum, and the schooling of children come to be regarded as intrinsic to one another, then the answer to this most critical of all questions will be a resounding and unequivocal yes.

ACTIVITIES

1. School can open windows on the world. Do you recall — or can you locate — accounts of how children growing up in limited surroundings found new horizons when they entered school? Consult biographies as well as novels.

[26] John Dewey, *The School and Society* (Chicago: University of Chicago Press, 1899), p. 1.

2. Examine Exhibit 9–1. Should other groups be included among victims of unequal teaching?
3. Select one of the four groups identified as possible partners in curriculum making. What are the goals sought by this group? Do you think the school can help in realizing some or all of these?
4. What are the attitudes of current books on curriculum development toward teachers as curriculum makers? To what extent do they differ from or agree with the position expressed here?
5. Read several accounts of alternative schools in action. How were their programs developed?
6. Examine the conditions and services proposed in Exhibit 9–3. Are there others that you think should be added?
7. How willing do you think most teachers are to take a chance on new content or content emphases? Check out your thinking by interviewing several teachers.
8. The nine possible new content areas represent a wide range of concerns. Which of these strike you as likely to grow in importance? Which do you view as having no future? Are there others you would add?
9. Do you accept the criteria proposed in Exhibit 9–4? Can you specify instances where you believe the use of the criteria would admit some current concerns but exclude others?
10. Study the outcomes proposed as likely results of the new curriculum. What others might be added? Do you agree that such large-scale changes offer data for evaluation of curriculum innovations?

Selected References

LEARNING TO VALUE

Dubos, René. *Beast or Angel: Choices that Make Us Human.* New York: Charles Scribner's Sons, 1974.

Jelinek, J. J., ed. *Improving the Human Condition: A Curricular Response to Critical Realities.* Washington, D.C.: Association for Supervision and Curriculum Development, 1978.

Kniker, Charles R. *You and Values Education.* Columbus, Ohio: Charles E. Merrill Publishing Company, 1977.

Kohlberg, Lawrence. *Collected Papers on Moral Development and Moral Education.* 2 vols. Rev. ed. Cambridge, Mass.: Moral Education Research Foundation, Harvard University, 1976.

MacDonald, James B., and Esther Zaret, eds. *Schools in Search of Meaning.* Washington, D.C.: Association for Supervision and Curriculum Development, 1975.

Piaget, Jean. *The Moral Judgment of the Child.* Translated by M. Gabain. London: Routledge and Kegan Paul, 1932.

Purpel, David, and Kevin Ryan, eds. *Moral Education: It Comes with the Territory.* Berkeley, Calif.: McCutchan Publishing Corporation, 1976.

Raths, Louis E.; Merrill Harmin; and Sidney B. Simon. *Values and Teaching: Working with Values in the Classroom*. 2nd ed. Columbus, Ohio: Charles E. Merrill Publishing Company, 1977.

Read, Donald A., and Sidney B. Simon, eds. *Humanistic Education Sourcebook*. Englewood Cliffs, N.J.: Prentice-Hall, 1975.

Simon, Sidney B.; Leland W. Howe; and Howard Kirschenbaum. *Values Clarification: A Handbook of Practical Strategies for Teachers and Students*. New York: Hart Publishing Company, 1972.

Toulmin, Stephen. *Knowing and Acting*. New York: Macmillan Publishing Company, 1976.

THE WORLD OF EVERYDAY LIVING

Bailey, J. A., ed. *Readings in Wildlife Conservation*. Washington, D.C.: Wildlife Society, 1975.

Gysbers, Norman C., et al., eds. *Developing Careers in the Elementary School*. Columbus, Ohio: Charles E. Merrill Publishing Company, 1973.

Hardy, John T. *Science, Technology, and the Environment*. Philadelphia: W. B. Saunders Company, 1975.

Harrison, Barbara G. *Unlearning the Lie: Sexism in School*. New York: Liveright, 1973.

Jaggar, Alison, and Paula R. Struhl. *Feminist Frameworks*. New York: McGraw-Hill Book Company, 1978.

Meier, A., and E. Rudwick. *From Plantation to Ghetto*. 3rd ed. New York: Farrar, Straus, and Giroux, 1976.

Sale, Larry L., and E. W. Lee. *Environmental Education in the Elementary School*. New York: Holt, Rinehart, and Winston, 1972.

Sprung, Barbara, ed. *Perspectives on Non-Sexist Early Childhood Education*. New York: Teachers College Press, 1978.

Stapp, W. B., and Mary D. Liston, eds. *Environmental Education: A Guide to Information Sources*. Detroit: Gale, 1975.

Uslander, Arlene, et al. *Their Universe: The Story of a Unique Sex Education Program for Kids*. New York: Delacorte Press, 1973.

Ward, Barbara. *The Home of Man.* New York: W. W. Norton Company, 1976.

THE CULTURAL HERITAGE

Boyle, J. David, ed. *Impact — Interdisciplinary Model, Programs in the Arts for Children and Teachers: A Final Report.* University Park, Pa.: Arts Impact Evaluation Staff, Pennsylvania State University, 1973.

Burgess, Carol, et al. *Understanding Children's Writing.* Baltimore: Penguin Books, 1973.

Chapman, Laura H. *Approaches to Art in Education.* New York: Harcourt Brace Jovanovich, 1978.

Eisner, Elliot W. *The Arts, Human Development, and Education.* Berkeley, Calif.: McCutchan Publishing Corporation, 1976.

Fleming, Gladys Andrews. *Creative Rhythmic Movement: Boys and Girls Dancing.* Englewood Cliffs, N.J.: Prentice-Hall, 1976.

Gaitskell, Charles D., and Al Hurwitz. *Children and Their Art.* 3rd ed. New York: Harcourt Brace Jovanovich, 1975.

Huck, Charlotte. *Children's Literature in the Elementary School.* 3rd ed. New York: Holt, Rinehart, and Winston, 1976.

Human and Anti-Human Values in Children's Books. New York: Council on Interracial Books for Children, 1976.

Hurwitz, Al, ed. *Programs of Promise: Art in the Schools.* New York: Harcourt Brace Jovanovich, 1972.

Kauffman, Draper L. *Teaching the Future: A Guide to Future-Oriented Education.* Palm Springs, Calif.: ETC Publications, 1976.

Lament, Marylee M. *Music in Elementary Education: Enjoy, Experience, and Learn.* New York: Macmillan Publishing Company, 1976.

Schiff, Bennett. *Artists in Schools.* Washington, D.C.: U.S. Government Printing Office, 1973.

Siks, Geraldine B. *Drama with Children.* New York: Harper and Row, 1977.

White, Mary Lou. *Children's Literature: Criticism and Response.* Columbus, Ohio: Charles E. Merrill Publishing Company, 1976.

Yola, Jane. *Children's Literature: An Issues Approach*. Lexington, Mass.: D. C. Heath and Company, 1976.

THE MORAL-ETHICAL-POLITICAL REALM

Blair, Thomas L. *Retreat to the Ghetto: The End of a Dream?* New York: Hill and Wang, 1977.

Butts, R. Freeman, et al. *The School's Role as Moral Authority*. Washington, D.C.: Association for Supervision and Curriculum Development, 1977.

Easton, David, and Jack Dennis. *Children in the Political System*. New York: McGraw-Hill Book Company, 1969.

Georgaskas, Dan. *Red Shadows: The History of Native Americans from 1600 to 1900*. Garden City, N.Y.: Zenith Books, Doubleday and Company, 1973.

Hess, Robert D., and Judith V. Torney. *The Development of Political Attitudes in Children*. Garden City, N.Y.: Anchor Books, Doubleday and Company, 1968.

Kaplan, Sidney. *The Black Presence in the Era of the American Revolution, 1770–1800*. Greenwich, Conn.: New York Graphic Society and the Smithsonian Institution Press, 1973.

Lens, Sidney. *The Labor Wars: From the Molly Maguires to the Sitdowns*. Garden City, N.Y.: Doubleday and Company, 1973.

Morris, David, and Karl Hess. *Neighborhood Power: The New Localism*. Boston: Beacon Press, 1975.

Nies, Judith. *Seven Women: Portraits from the American Radical Tradition*. New York: The Viking Press, 1977.

Papachristou, Judith. *Women Together: A History in Documents of the Women's Movement in the United States*. New York: Alfred A. Knopf, 1976.

Stewart, James B. *The Holy Warriors: The Abolitionists and American Slavery*. New York: Farrar, Straus, and Giroux, 1976.

Ubbelohde, Carl, and Jack R. Fraenkel, eds. *Values of the American Heritage: Challenge, Case Studies, and Teaching Strategies*. Arlington, Va.: National Council for the Social Studies, 1976.

Wertheimer, Barbara M. *We Were There: The Story of Working Women in America*. New York: Pantheon Books, 1977.

IMPLEMENTING THE NEW CURRICULUM

Berman, Louise M., and Jessie A. Roderick, eds. *Feeling, Valuing, and the Art of Growing: Insights into the Affective.* Washington, D.C.: Association for Supervision and Curriculum Development, 1977.

Bloom, Benjamin S. *Human Characteristics and School Learning.* New York: McGraw-Hill Book Company, 1976.

Fantini, Mario, and Marilyn Gittell. *Decentralization: Achieving Reform.* New York: Praeger Publishers, 1973.

Frazier, Alexander. *Adventuring, Mastering, Associating.* Washington, D.C.: Association for Supervision and Curriculum Development, 1976.

Goodlad, John I. *The Dynamics of Educational Change: Toward Responsive Schools.* New York: McGraw-Hill Book Company, 1975.

Gress, James R., and David E. Purpel, eds. *Curriculum: An Introduction to the Field.* Berkeley, Calif.: McCutchan Publishing Corporation, 1978.

Hoover, Kenneth H., and Paul M. Hollingsworth. *Learning and Teaching in the Elementary School.* 2nd ed. Boston: Allyn and Bacon, 1975.

Jones, Daisy M. *Curriculum Targets in the Elementary School.* Englewood Cliffs, N.J.: Prentice-Hall, 1977.

Molnar, Alex, and John A. Zahorik, eds. *Curriculum Theory.* Washington, D.C.: Association for Supervision and Curriculum Development, 1977.

Oliver, Donald W. *Education and Community: A Radical Critique of Innovative Schooling.* Berkeley, Calif.: McCutchan Publishing Corporation, 1976.

Ragan, W. B., and Gene D. Shepherd. *Modern Elementary Curriculum.* 5th ed. New York: Holt, Rinehart, and Winston, 1977.

Rodgers, Frederick A. *Curriculum and Instruction in the Elementary School.* New York: Macmillan Publishing Company, 1975.

Shuster, Albert H., and Milton E. Ploghoft. *The Emerging Elementary Curriculum.* 3rd ed. Columbus, Ohio: Charles E. Merrill Publishing Company, 1977.

Van Til, William. *Curriculum: Quest for Relevance.* 2nd ed. Boston: Houghton Mifflin Company, 1974.

Index

Alternative school, 253
Anti-environmentalism
    through consciousness raising
        activities, 20–21
    arising from countercultures,
        19–20
    as directed against social
        shaping, 18–19
    through personal awareness
        training, 21, 26
    and points of critical concern,
        22–25
Art, appreciation of
    as basis for improving arts
        environment, 117–119
    contributions of artists to, 135–
        137
    ends of, 122, 144–146
    importance of, 21
    through literary study, 124–129
    through musical study, 137–143
    as point of departure, 123
    as receptive end of value axis,
        38
    results of education in, 262
    through study of visual arts,
        129–137
Artist-teachers, 136
Artists-in-the-Schools program,
    136, 138
Arts Impact program, 138
Arts of invention
    activities calling for, 170–171
    exercised in search of new
        answers, 168
    and experimentation in general,
        169
    nature of, 154
    see also Inventiveness,
        teaching of
Arts of planning
    with focus on future, 174, 176
    with focus on learning needs,
        172–173
    nature of, 154
    related to world needs, 175

and study results to be expected,
    262
Arts, visual
    access to treasures of, 131
    bases of appreciation, 130–133
    and environment, 134–135
    inventive activities in, 171
    in popular and school cultures,
        119
    and results of study of, 262
Assertiveness, 25, 41, 238. See also
    Aggressiveness
Authority, 24–25, 105, 185,
    194–195
Awareness training, 25–26, 28

Bacon, Francis, 153
Behavior modification, 65
Berenson, Bernard, 122
Bilingualism, 20, 242
Book learning, skills of, 60–68.
    See also Basic skills
Bruner, Jerome S., 169

Camping experiences, 71–72, 261
Camus, Albert, 151
Carabo-Cone program, 140
Career education, see Work
Caswell, Hollis L., 89–91
Center for Global Perspectives, 258
Center for Vocational and Tech-
    nical Education, 100
Change, study of
    by identifying principles of,
        220–221
    through knowledge of past
        reformers, 216–218
    through knowledge of present
        reform movements, 218–220
    reflected in social changes, 263
    see also Action, social
Charters, W. W., 35, 69
Chavez, Cesar, 190, 218
Child abuse, 185, 199, 263
Child care, 199

Children
exploitation of, 247
as explorers of environment, 211
and need to know, 58, 241
as questioners, 83–85, 233–235
as victims of unequal teaching,
244–245
as victims of value system, 36
Chisholm, Shirley, 218
Choice, see Alternatives
Chomsky, Noam, 56–57, 79, 81,
167
Citizenship Decision-Making
Project, 195
Class
as bias in education, 5, 65, 242,
244
and classism, 104, 190, 196
and declassification, 107–111,
246–247, 261
and differences among people,
107–111, 246–247
as related to vocational choice,
5–6, 98, 103
and social conflict, 79, 191, 217
stereotyping of, 104
and values, 21–24, 234
Clean-up campaigns, 208, 223–224
Coleridge, Samuel T., 119, 130,
145, 150
Commercialism, 23, 198, 205, 247,
250
Community, improvement of
through service projects, 208,
223–225, 227
through social action, 225, 227–
228
Competence
as basic to valuing, 36–37, 56,
78–79
definition of, 41
growth in, 159, 212
as preparation for choice among
alternatives, 60
in relationship to creative behavior, 159

as required for social effectiveness, 184–187, 212–216
as skills mastery, 46, 145, 212
in speaking up, 233–235
in understanding the arts, 129,
137, 141, 145
see also Skills, basic
Comprehensive Career Educational
Model (CCEM), 100
Conformity, 21–24, 84, 86, 106,
149–150, 177, 214, 248. See
also Creative behavior;
Critical thinking
Consciousness raising, 20–21, 27,
104
Conservation, 20–21, 93, 96. See
also Environment, study of
Constraint, 7, 108
Consumer education, 196
Consumer protection, 20–21, 198,
220, 247, 261
Contingency management, 65
Countercultures, 19–20, 22–25
Creative arts
changing outlook on teaching of,
155
and independence as teaching
goal, 159
nature of, 154
need for competence in, 159
and performing arts, 166
purposeful teaching of, 156–157,
159–160
study of reflected in society, 262
time for learning of, 159–160
Creative behavior
and arts of invention, 167–172
and creative arts, 155–159
as innovative end of value axis,
38, 44
as learnable, 177
objectives of, 159, 174
and performing arts, 160–167
and planning arts, 172–176
as reflected by society, 262
teaching, 150–153, 155

Critical thinking
  as active learning, 92
  about environment, 92–97
  as goal, 84
  importance of, 112–113
  as innovative end of value axis,
    38–44
  past efforts to teach, 85–92
  as problem solving, 85
  reflected in society, 261
  about socialization, 104–112
  and teaching methods, 86–87
Cultural heritage
  and appreciation of the arts, 38,
    42, 117–147
  and creative behavior, 38, 42–43,
    149–179
  in terms of popular and school
    cultures, 118–120
  receptive vs. innovative ends of,
    38, 150
  and results of successful teaching
    in, 262
  its scope, 40, 42–43
Curriculum
  and criteria for content selec-
    tion, 260
  impact of national projects on,
    169, 252, 254
  new content in, 253–259
  recasting of, 84, 108, 184, 208,
    260
  relevance of, 252
  and signs of success, 261–263
  value orientation of, 16–18, 248
Curriculum making
  as administrative control, 249,
    252
  characteristics of, 252–253
  evaluation of, 254, 256–263
  federal role in, 169, 253–254
  finding partners for, 243–251
  past practices in, 62, 89–91
  revitalized conception of, 241
  role of teachers in, 252–255
  support system for, 253–255

Curriculum projects, national, 169,
  252, 254

Dalton plan, 63
Dance, 165–166, 262
Death education, 259
Debs, Eugene V., 218
Decentralization of schools, 227,
  252
Declassification, 246–247, 250
Decorum, classroom, 58–59
Democracy
  and authority, 185–186
  developing allegiance to, 183–
    210
  and freedom, 184–185
  and the human struggle, 186–187
  as political process, 186
  what children need to know
    about, 184–187
  see also Self-government, under-
    standing of
Dewey, John, 34, 45, 85, 185, 202,
  207, 257, 264
Differences, cultural
  as contributing to racial-ethnic
    bias, 105
  as gender stereotyping, 106–107
  and need for enabling attributes,
    108–110
  as related to class, 107, 111
  see also Class; Ethnicism; Race;
    Sex
Directive teaching, 65
Disadvantaged, programs for, 20–
  21, 65, 252
Discovery, 57, 153–154, 169
Domains of learning, 61
Drama, 160–164, 166, 262
Dreiser, Theodore, 157–158
Drug education, 259

Economic education, 258
Effectiveness, social
  through acceptance of responsi-
    bility, 215

as acting on self-chosen values, 14
in creating common culture, 6
through critical thinking, 85–91
through innovativeness, 211–237
as major goal, 49, 184
through principled action, 11–12,
220–221
results of teaching for, 261–264
and skill development, 75–78,
222–228
Eisner, Elliot, 169
Elementary and Secondary Education Act, 129
Eliot, T. S., 122, 186
Emerson, Ralph Waldo, 149, 178,
192, 214
Enabling attributes 109–111
Encounter therapy, 25
Environment, study of
through appeal to emotions,
92–93
approaches to, 96
and concern for protection, 199,
220, 247, 261
as ecosystem, 94–95
as influence on values, 18–26
issues in, 93–94
as problem of resource development, 95, 97
Epictetus, 184
Equality
lack of, in teaching, 242, 244–245
as a value, 7, 9, 34, 198–199
see also Democracy
Ethnicism
attributes that transcend,
109–111
and changes in attitudes toward,
261
and conflict, 217
and consciousness raising, 20
differences related to, 104–105,
234
and education of "disadvantaged," 20–21, 65, 252
pride in, 5, 65, 188–189, 210

related to moral reasoning, 11
Evaluation of curriculum
in light of changes in society,
261–263
in terms of needed knowledge,
256–257
related to new concerns, 257–260
in physical education, 73
Everyday living, world of
as accommodation, 38–39, 55–82
and critical thinking, 38–40, 83–
114
and needed knowledge, 55–82
in terms of receptive vs. innovative axis, 38
and results of successful teaching, 261–263
its scope, 38–40

Faculties, innate
nature of, 57, 167
nurture of, 79
see also Chomsky, Noam
Failure to learn, 20, 65
Family life, 4–5, 22, 259
Federal government, 169, 252–254
Feelings, 21–24, 92–93, 221, 259
Fenton, Edwin, 208
Fleming, Gladys Andrews, 166
Fourier, Charles, 232
Franklin, Benjamin, 214, 216
Freedom
acceptance of, 151–152
barriers to, 79
of choice, 33–34, 112–113
nature of, 184–185, 236
theory of, 56, 79
see also Alternatives; Democracy; Self-government
Freud, Sigmund, 221
Friere, Paulo, 107
Fulfillment, individual
achievement of, 6, 49, 144, 177
as enrichment of living, 146
through new options, 56, 102,
121–124

Fulfillment, individual (cont.)
  results of teaching for, 261–264
  and selfhood, 150
  versus social pressures, 21–24,
    109–111
  through successful teaching, 60,
    244–245
  see also Human development,
    full
Fuller, R. Buckminster, 177
Fundamentals, teaching of, 67. See
    also Basic skills
Futurism, 97, 174, 176

Games, 69, 230, 261
Gender roles, 25, 106–107, 234,
  244. See also Sex
Geography, political-cultural, 258
Glasser, William, 76–77
Groups
  growth through experience in,
    75–76
  instruction in, 162–165
  as partners in curriculum
    making, 243, 246–249
  value development through, 9,
    13–18
  see also Teaching, methods of;
    Community, improvement of
Guidelines to behavior
  as values in all aspects of living,
    13–15, 21–24, 38, 41
  as values in moral realm, 7–12
  see also Morals; Values;
    Valuing, process of
Gun control, 231

Heroes and heroines, 189–191,
  210, 215
Historical heritage, study of
  through contributions of ethnic
    groups, 188–189
  through documents of past, 190,
    192–193
  in terms of heroes and heroines,
    189–191

need for, 216–218, 228
  see also Allegiance
Housekeeping duties, 101–102, 210
Howells, William Dean, 122–123
Hughes, Langston, 203
Human development, full
  achievement of, 5–6
  as individuality, 151–153
  part played by values in, 10–12,
    14–15, 18–26
  reflected in society, 261–264
Human relations, 57, 126, 243

Ignorantism, 248–249, 251
Immediacy, 21
Individualization of teaching, 63–
  65, 146, 173
Individually Guided Education,
  64–65
Individually Prescribed Instruction, 64
Innovation
  in the arts, 149–179
  in curriculum making, 249–264
  in everyday living, 83–114
  in moral-ethical-political realm,
    211–238
  see also Creative behavior;
    Critical thinking; Innovative-
    ness, social; Teachers
Innovativeness, social
  and analysis of problems, 228–
    232
  in community projects, 222–228
  and learning about change, 216–
    221
  as reflected in changes, 261–263
  in school and classroom, 236–238
  through speaking out, 233–236
  what is needed for, 212–216
Inservice education, 65, 255
Integration, racial, 198, 243, 261
Interaction
  among children, 9, 183
  as basis of moral development, 12
  as developing social skills, 183

as providing bonds, 75
withdrawal from, 105
see also Groups; Teaching, methods of
Interest, role of, 85, 91, 168
International understanding, 23, 175, 258, 263
Inventiveness, teaching of, 167–171. *See also* Arts of invention
Ives, Charles, 160

James, Henry, 123, 151
James, William, 213
Jencks, Christopher, 246
Justice, 7, 9–10, 24, 34. *See also* Equality; Rights, children's; Rights, human

Kafka, Franz, 202
Kilpatrick, William H., 89
King, Martin Luther, Jr., 191–192, 218
Kodaly method, 140
Kohlberg, Lawrence, 6–7, 15, 18–19, 26–29, 35–36, 45, 202–203
moral reasoning, 10–12

Laban, Rudolph, 70
Labor, organized
and campaign for rights, 217
leaders of, 190–191
and political action, 205
Language arts, *see* Drama; Literature; Reading skills
Language, differences in, 105, 161
Law, 195–196, 198–199, 210
League of Women Voters, 225, 251
Leicestershire schools, 63–64
Lenski, Lois, 221
Library, 59, 262
Literature
accessibility to, 124, 262
for children, 221, 237, 259, 262
classical, 125–126
critical analysis of, 127, 129

in popular and school cultures, 119
as presented by media, 128
as subject field, 124–125
themes in, 126
types of, 127
Lorenz, Konrad, 56, 81

MacDonald, James B., 208–209
Madison, James, 216
Malraux, Andre, 131
"Man: A Course of Study," 258
Marcus Aurelius, 213
Maslow, Abraham, 25–26
Mastery, teaching for, 66, 81
Mathematics, 63–64, 169–170
Mead, George F., 18
Media, mass, 4, 21, 23, 86, 138, 262–263. *See also* Popular culture; Television
Milgram, Stanley, 215
Moral development
and moral conflict, 12
and need for nurture, 9, 12, 28
reflected in society, 263
stages of, 6–12
as studied by Kohlberg, 10–12
as studied by Piaget, 7–10
Moral-ethical-political realm
and allegiance to democratic system, 43, 45, 183–210
receptive vs. innovative ends of, 38, 212
its scope, 43–45
and social innovativeness, 45, 211–237
successful teaching of, as reflected in society, 263
see also Action, social; Change, study of; Democracy; Effectiveness, social; Historical heritage, study of
Moral judgment (Piaget), 7–10
Moral reasoning (Kohlberg), 10–12
Morals
and full range of values, 33

Morals (cont.)
as principles, 12
see also Guidelines to behavior;
Values
Movement
education in, 68–69
in learning music, 140
in dance, 168
Music
attention to elements and forms
of, 139–140
inventive activities in, 171
organized programs for study of,
140
in popular and school cultures,
120
study of, 138–143, 262

Nader, Ralph, 218–219
National Association for the Advancement of Colored People,
250
National Endowment for the Arts,
129
National Institute of Education, 102
National Organization of Women,
250
Needs, 58, 91, 172–174

Obedience, 7, 33, 105, 215
Orff approach, 140
Outdoor education, 21, 71–72, 261

Performing arts
and balance between individual
and group activities, 162–163
complexity of, 160
nature of, 154
study of, 262
types of activities, 163–166
Personal awareness training, 21, 26
Physical education
and changes in society, 261
dance and drama in, 70–71
games and gymnastics in, 69
importance of, 21

inventive activities in, 171
as movement, 68
new programs of, 68–73
outdoor education in, 71–72
scoreboard on, 73
and sexual integration, 69–70
and sports emphasis, 71
Piaget, Jean, 6–12, 15, 26–29, 36,
45, 68, 81, 167, 169
Planning, teaching of, 172–176
Pluralism, cultural, 5, 18, 20, 228
coming to terms with, 26
respect for, 193
see also Class; Ethnicism; Race
Pollution, concern about, 21, 93–
94, 175, 199. See also Environment, study of
Popular culture, 24, 118, 120–121,
128–129. See also Media,
mass; Television
Prizing, 13–14
Problems, assessment of
by means of discussion, 231–232
through investigation, 229
through simulation, 230
Problem-solving, 213–214, 228–232
Program agreements, 253
Project method, 39, 167
Psychomotor domain, 61, 78
Psychotherapy, 25, 33

Questioning, 24, 39–40, 83–86,
103, 168

Race
and differences, 104–105
and educational success, 65
and employment, 103, 261
pride in, 5
and programs for minorities, 20–
21, 65, 252
and racism, 20, 196, 217, 243–246
Radicalism, see Action, social
Randolph, A. Philip, 190–191
Raths, Louis E., 6, 13–14, 27, 29,
36, 45, 202, 231

Subject matter (cont).
    importance of, 39, 92, 113, 145,
        213–214, 241
    integration of, 167, 173
    psychologizing of, 207–208
    specialists in, 255
    value orientation of, 16–18, 41,
        92, 189, 236–237, 243, 256–
        257
    see also Curriculum
Summerhill School, 63
Supervision, 251–255
Support system, 253–255

Taba, Hilda, 76
Teachers
    and attitude toward creative
        behavior, 155
    and concern for democracy, 208
    as curriculum makers, 252–255
    as facilitators of moral reason-
        ing, 11
    and individualization, 63–65
    role of, in valuing, 6, 13–18, 28
    and skills teaching, 59–60, 67
    as sponsors of social innova-
        tiveness, 224–226
    as students of value develop-
        ment, 28
    and teaching problems, 45–49,
        215
    and unequal teaching, 244–245
    see also Curriculum making;
        Teaching, methods of; Values
        education
Teaching, methods of
    in approaching environmental
        problems, 96
    based on small groups, 9
    as community-oriented, 224–225
    for critical thinking, 85–92
    that highlight moral conflict, 12
    importance of, 112–113
    to individualize learning, 63–65
    that lead to unequal learning,
        244–245

in literature and art, 124, 129–
    131, 144–146, 159, 177
problems related to, 45–49
as radical and manipulative, 60,
    68
related to values clarification,
    15–18
and use of role playing and
    simulation, 230
used in emotional re-education,
    20, 25–26
see also Evaluation of curricu-
    lum; Groups; Interaction;
    Interest
Teaching, professionalization of,
    253
Technology, educational, 64
Television, 4, 22, 29, 120, 196, 207,
    247, 262
Testing programs, 66
Time, use of, 172–173
Tolstoy, Leo, 214
Toynbee, Arnold, 194

Unity, cultural, 193
Urban League, 250
Utopianism, 21, 235–236

Validation, 9
Value axes, 38–45, 47–49
Values
    definition of, 41
    private vs. public, 33–34, 219
    selection of, 32–35, 81, 112, 146,
        176, 214, 260
    see also Guidelines to behavior;
        Moral development; Morals
Values clarification
    contribution of, 184
    phases of, 13–14
    questions to be answered in, 14
    scope of, 28
    through subject matter, 16–18
    teaching strategies for, 15–16
    see also Louis E. Raths; Sidney
        B. Simon

Values development
  an aspect of maturation, 6–10
  conditions favorable to, 27
  contributions made by studies
    of, 184
  as growth of moral judgment,
    7–10
  as moral reasoning, 10–12
  stages of, 7–9, 10–11
  see also Kohlberg, Lawrence;
    Piaget, Jean; Values, investi-
    gation of
Values education and re-education
  through consciousness raising,
    20, 25, 28
  as continuous concern, 46
  through countercultures, 19–20,
    22–25
  in terms of cultural heritage,
    117–179
  as curriculum strand, 27
  integrated in subject fields, 15–
    18
  as major curriculum goal, 254–
    264
  through moral conflict stories,
    11–12, 18, 208
  in moral-ethical-political realm,
    183–237
  periodic attention to, 15, 46
  through personal awareness
    training, 25–27
  toward personal fulfillment, 6,
    49, 144, 177
  provision of broader curriculum
    base for, 28
  toward social effectiveness, 11–
    12, 75–78, 211–231
  traditional approaches to, 15
  through values clarification,
    13–18
  in world of everyday living, 55–
    114

Values, investigation of
  by Allport, 21
  by Kohlberg, 10–12
  by Maslow, 21, 26
  by Mead, 18
  through observation, 29
  by Piaget, 7–10
  by Rogers, 21
  by Rokeach, 18–19
Valuing, process of
  curriculum making in support
    of, 241–265
  as integral to learning, 6, 28,
    35–38, 242
  its key terms, 40
  its three phases, 37, 47
  see also Alternatives; Compe-
    tence; Freedom
Victims of unequal teaching, 242–
  245
Violence, 4, 196, 216–217, 231
Vocations, books on, 100, 102

Ward, Barbara, 248
Whitman, Walt, 178, 192, 235–236
Whittier, John Greenleaf, 186–191
Wild Life Federation, 251
Winnetka plan, 63
Work
  in everyday living, 261
  kinds of, 99–100
  and problems or questions, 103
  selection of and preparation for,
    103
  as source of satisfaction, 22,
    100–102
  as specific vocations, 102
  in terms of usefulness, 98–99
  units of, 89–91
Workshops and conferences, 255
Wright, Frank Lloyd, 168–169, 172
Writing, creative, 16–17, 154–157,
  230

Student Response Form

To the student: Will you help us improve the next edition of this book? Your answers to the questions that follow could make a difference. Please return the form to **College Marketing, Houghton Mifflin Company, One Beacon Street, Boston, MA 02107.**

Reaction to Book as a Whole

How would you rate this textbook in each of the following respects?

	Excellent	Good	Adequate	Poor
1. Was it written in a clear and understandable style?	___	___	___	___
2. Was the organization of the book clear and logical?	___	___	___	___
3. How would you rate the exhibits?	___	___	___	___
4. How useful were the examples of classroom and school practice?	___	___	___	___
5. How does this text compare with texts you are using in other education courses?	___	___	___	___

6. Can you cite examples that illustrate any of your above ratings?

_____

_____

_____

7. Which chapters or features of the book did you particularly like or dislike? Why?

_____

_____

_____

8. Were there any topics that were not covered that you believe should have been covered? Were there any topics that deserved fuller treatment?

_____

_____

_____

9. We would appreciate any other comments or reactions you are willing to share with us:

_____

_____

_____

Reaction to Specific Chapters

10. Was the report on moral value development in Chapter 1 useful as background for this book's point of view?

_____

_____

11. Did Chapter 2 serve as a good introduction to the rest of the book?

_____

_____

_____

12. Do Chapters 3 and 4 adequately convey the importance of successful teaching of basic skills and the need to teach children to ask hard questions about things as they are?

_____

_____

_____

13. How well do Chapters 5 and 6 make the case for more attention to art appreciation in school and for more deliberate teaching of the creative arts?

_____

_____

_____

14. Does the viewpoint developed in Chapters 7 and 8 tie in properly with the work on moral development reviewed in Chapter 1? Are the ends of this axis (allegiance/reformism) kept in balance?

_____

_____

_____

15. Are the proposals for curriculum implementation and evaluation in Chapter 9 sufficiently forward looking to suit you?

_____

_____

_____